THE PREP SCH...

A Me......

THE PREP SCHOOL LETTERS

A Memoir

Copyright © 2025 by Rupert Green.

Copyright of all photographs and images reside with the author unless otherwise stated.

All rights reserved.

Book Cover by Rupert Green

Note from the Author

This book is a memoir and work of creative nonfiction. It reflects the author's recollections of experiences over time and the author's interpretation of conversations that took place.

The book is a combination of fact about a period of the author's life and certain embellishments.

To protect the privacy of individuals, some names, characters, events and identifiable characteristics have been changed, invented, altered, compressed or recreated for literary effect.

Events happened in 1972-1976 and therefore circumstances of individuals mentioned could have since changed. The reader should consider this book a work of literature.

The opinion expressed within this book are the author's personal opinions and are merely 'freedom of expression'.

First edition 2025

For my wife, Nicola

Acknowledgements

Father, who I know is proud of me.

Mother, for saving those childhood letters, for whatever reason.

Bev & Jane, for all your help, editing, beers, cheers, listening and holding space for my tears.

Stacey, for believing.

Paul for the times we read outloud our stories and laughed.

Gareth, Rowland, Emilia, Andrew.

SEEN & HEARD
www.seenheard.org.uk

An organisation that supports the wellbeing of past and present pupils of boarding and independent day schools and their families.

Contents

1. New School ... 1
2. Letters Home ... 6
3. Porridge ... 11
4. Education X ... 16
5. The Cut ... 22
6. The Sandwich ... 27
7. The General Synopsis
   Moderate or Poor, Occasionally Good ... 32
8. What's That Word I Keep Hearing? ... 43
9. Snow ... 49
10. No Cricket Cricket ... 55
11. Happy Horror-Days ... 60
12. Bosoms ... 63
13. Dagga-Ragga ... 69
14. Suffering In Suffolk ... 75
15. The Kid With The Slot Machine Eye ... 83
16. V Signs ... 91
17. Ink ... 99

18.	Obstacles	105
19.	The General Synopsis Imminent Becoming Cyclonic	110
20.	Little Boy	114
21.	Au Revoir My Dear Sweet Precious Little Boy	124
22.	Pretty Letters All In A Row	128
23.	The Basement Flat Feelings	134
24.	Tooth Spit Calamity	140
25.	I've Got Some Troubles	146
26.	Rules Of Rugger	154
27.	I Was Hurting, He Was Hurting	158
28.	Laughter In All The Wrong Places	161
29.	When It Comes To Football	168
30.	Kiss Chase	173
31.	Private	177
32.	Pancakes	182
33.	Life On The Front Lawn	188
34.	Ralph Brompton	193
35.	The Last One	196
36.	General Synopsis New Low Expected, High Becoming Rough Later	200
37.	The Last Letter	204
38.	Words, New Found Wisdom	207

39. Prospectus 210

1
New School

BUCKLAND HOUSE SCHOOL is situated in a triangle of villages called Shebbear, Sheepwash and Stibb Cross. In North Devon, a farming County. The southwestern part of England, in a country of the United Kingdom. And politically part of Europe or was about to be in 1972, if only they could make their minds up.

Buckland House
27th May 1972

Dear Mummy and Daddy
Mrs Lancaster is our art and form teacher. I am in Blundell's dormitory the Matron gave me a teddy bear, it is white, and it has a blue jumper. I had a good night, did you? I will get a cricket bat on Tuesday. I have a guardian called Mandrake. The House I am in is called Brownes.
Love Rupert x

New routines, new uniform, white shirt oversized collar, a fawn brown v-neck jumper. A school tie that goes blue then brown, blue then brown. Same old rules and some new rules. No tuck box. New faces, new names, new pencils, exercise books, lots of writing and spelling. New subjects, Latin and Scripture, Science, English and calligraphy.

We are given prep to do, which is like homework only we are not allowed to go home to do it. More's the pity. Prep is long and tedious. I finished ages ago. All this waiting around. I will be nine next Wednesday. This new school has a different smell. Every day there is a new routine to be learnt and a need to be able to tell the time.

11:30 Late morning, we get changed into blue smocks, and we play outside. We all have a number. We need a number so that we can find our towel on the towel rail before we have a shower. And in the changing rooms it is useful to have a number peg to hang your clothes on before getting changed to go outside or play football. Mine is sixty three which is easy for me to remember because that was the year I was born.

13:00 Lunchtime brings new food, no it's the same old, same old. It's a little better. Hold on... Scratch that. No, it is not.

13:40 Rest.
14:30 Free or walk.
16:15 Outside bell for tea.
16:30 Tea.
19:00 Boys lemonade and bun.
19:20 Bedtime for Blundells.

Buckland House
Saturday 3rd June 1972

Dear Mummy and Daddy
Thank you for the watch. I have been sick. On My birthday I had £1 from Brother Number One. Rose gave me a Meccano set. Brother Number Three gave me two pens and four ink cartridges. On Friday coming we are going to see an Army Navy and aircraft display at Kelly College.

My effort marks are: excellent English excellent Maths excellent History good Geography excellent Scripture

Lots and lots of Love Rupert xxx

Receiving birthday presents is a real joy until they are confiscated. My cricket bat wasn't confiscated, probably because it was chosen for me by one of the schoolmasters. I am positive that I do not want to join the Army or Navy, but I wouldn't mind learning to fly.

New cricket bat with a smart red stripe down the back, I must knock it in before I can use it. They said I *must* knock it in. "It'll need a wipe of linseed oil and give it a knock with this old cricket ball." Mr Whitaker said when he handed me the bat after lunch during playtime on Thursday.

"Have you knocked it in properly?" The Headmaster said, looking more and more like, in this instance, a Shoebill Stork.

Menacing.

I wasn't expected to answer.

"I wouldn't use it yet." Mr Beaumont arrived and gave his voice to the conversation. He scratched his head and half closed his eyes, "I think it needs a bit more tap, sunny Jim. More tap-tap. Look, you've hardly touched it. That's it, hit it harder."

Honestly, the way the master's go on, you'd think they didn't want me to have a brand new birthday bat. My first proper cricket bat. I'm excited.

Some of the Masters are the weirdest-weird of weirds.

There are unwritten words I choose not to say. Exit stage left. Maybe I should run after them, catch a few sentences, give voice.

Well, maybe later...

So here I am, the weekend after my birthday, in a strange bed, a room full of beds, I would still rather be at home, our new home Kentisbeare Post Office, in Mid Devon, sleeping in a new home bed, not in this school bed. My train of thought halts and I sit up on my elbows.

"Look!" I said. "It's raining." I pull a sad face. In the bed next to me, Mandrake reads Enid Blyton with his finger. The nose-picking finger. He stops reading, shows me two fingers in the shape of a V, and sinks back into his pillow. The book covers his freckled face.

"Regen." Said Smit. Smit is Dutch. He's all over the place when it comes to speaking English. He doesn't care about rules, he talks when he wants to. Smit smiles a lot, which annoys the hell out of the schoolmasters and he's good at football in the way a nine-year-old is good at most things. I think I like Smit. I am not sure if I like Mandrake. He has a military haircut and he reads a lot. I don't like reading.

Time is slow because it is a Sunday morning, 07:45 and all week the sky has been drainpipe grey. On a Sunday, we get an extra hour to lie in bed and we are advised to read. I pull a teddy bear out from under the covers. Matron gave it to me. It is white and has a blue jumper. I try to twist its head off. I don't read. Who's got time to read a book? I stare at the teddy bear. I don't have much thought about anything. Again, I lose myself out the window. The odd black rook flies past and a cluster of fast starlings. I lean over towards Mandrake "Shut up!" He says before I have even said anything. Smit announces quite loudly to the dormitory.

"I want letters. I want to get..."

Just then, the usually unhurried schoolmaster Mr Whitaker burst through the door, entering the dormitory with a full head of steam. He located and made a B line for Smit, literally drags him by the arm out of bed, pulls down his pyjama bottoms, forces him across his knee and slaps Smit several times. Hold on... Scratch that. More than a slap, more like grown-up high handed wallops.

We are stunned at the ferocity of the assault, this sudden intrusion into our quiet space. Such unnecessary violence on a Sunday morning. We do not know where to turn. Where do we go from here? This display is enough to terrify the best of us. I notice I didn't pipe up and shout "Oi, leave him alone!" But I wanted to.

There is always an internal line to run up to. The line where morality sits and where morality invites you to step over that line but the reins you are wearing tug you back. It's a parachute. Morality offers you a knife to cut the reins. Your better judgment shouts "Leave it!" And so, by this instruction, I continue to fall into helpless passivity. I become a voyeur of violence. Violence metered out as a structured rule, lines not to cross. Vague lines. Spare the rod. Spare me the righteousness. Deliver us from punishment. And so on but a precedent has been set. There is no way back from this – not now. Not now.

Over the other side of the room, Smit is quiet. Not crying just quiet. Nobody talks. Not *now* they don't. They read or just stare at the ceiling and I guess, like me, think of home. An hour can be a long time.

If I remember, I'll tell them all about it in my letter home. I miss being home. I want to go back home. I don't want to be beaten. And so, little by little the 'silence' crept into my life. I wore it like an overcoat and sometime I wore it like a Balaclava.

From now on, at the end of this sentence, I'm not going to talk...

Rupert John Green

2

Letters Home

"LOVE," SAID MR HARRINGTON, "love..." He put his hand to his mouth and coughed. It was a difficult word for him to say. He spoke again, but in no more than a broken whisper.

"The word 'love' would be more appropriate, fitting even... as a farewell remark." He cleared his throat and continued in his normal voice. "An acceptable signing off, more *au revoir* than *goodbye*..."

Mr Harrington was one of the high-ranking schoolmasters at Buckland House School. Against his better judgement, he had agreed to being allocated Form II where he would teach English and Latin. Today he was overseeing our Saturday morning letter writing session. Letters home. But things had gotten out of hand, not much letter writing being done. I should also mention, he was chief hair washer for us boys in the hot and steamy after-games showers. I say that so you understand what page I'm on.

Back in the classroom, he certainly had our attention. It was wise to play along with him. Dissent as to what he might offer up as education was often greeted with a total shutdown of emotion and what followed was the laborious tedium of deconstructing sentences he wrote on the blackboard in latin. And this would continue until the end of the lesson or the end of time depending on which came sooner. Mr Harrington continued.

"... More *au revoir* than *goodbye*. Now, I'm not going to say love is a *nice* word to use, because, apart from being ambiguous, you all know I detest the word *nice*. Sit up, Green! Don't slouch. Boys, sit up at your desks; it is most unbecoming..."

Distracted Mr Harrington strolled over to look out the window. Outside, Sycamore seeds spun and drifted from swaying branches in the early morning wind. As a rule, when Mr Harrington was distracted, handwritten notes would float down the desk rows like paper aeroplanes. Vulgar gestures followed – almost like the thousand-hand Bodhisattva dance.

After a considerable pause Mr Harrington said "Boys, I'd like you to find other words... other words, yes. I admit *love* is the word you should use. But just... find other words, will you?" He swivelled on his heels, as if to catch someone off guard. He looked for and found me, fixed me with a cold stare. "What did you say, Green? Come on, boy – tell us! Speak up!"

I am struck dumb. Sat at the desk solid as a standing stone. A recent memory came flooding back. My hair being lathered up by *you-know-who,* whilst the boys looked on and sniggered at the Mohican sprouting, like a shark fin atop my head – easily procured laughter. Exposed in my nakedness. Where do I put my hands?

"Sir?" I rasped. Across the room, my fear ignited a frenzy of pointing, more sniggering and general boyish derision. Their stifled coughs and whooping laughter slopped across the surface tension in the classroom. It reflected dark and oppressive against the square panes of window glass.

"Mandrake, did or didn't Green say *from*?"

Mandrake gasped and then closed his mouth because no noise came out. Mr Harrington looked to the heavens and asked, "Did he say, did Green say, to end a letter with the word *from*? Did he? Just now..."

Mr Harrington's voice sliced through the silence.

"Mandrake?"

He swiped the blackboard duster several times across the face of the blackboard, now visibly annoyed. Bradley Edwards nudged Mandrake in the back.

"Yes, Sir, he did." Mandrake looked at me, shaking his head. I responded, flicked a V sign, as if playing rock, paper, scissors.

"*FROM,* Green? How about we have some *LOVE* Mandrake?"

Mr Harrington underlined the word *LOVE* as it hung in the air and much like a sparkler, explosive orange and savage raspberry shards could be seen to be shooting off the white trailing letters, only to moments later, they fade to nothingness. The class erupted. Mandrake, looking befuddled and wondering if he was the patsy in the room. He figured he was.

"SHUT UP!" Mr Harrington bellowed. He gestured with a beckoning finger for Mandrake to continue. Mandrake, at a loss, muttered, "Er... Love is better, Sir? Use love to finish a letter, Sir." Mr Harrington smiled and nodded in agreement, *way too much attention.*

Mandrake squinted and wagged a finger at me, pointing out that he now wasn't the patsy in the room, no way. Mr Harrington noticed our play-by-play and looked peeved. He brushed his fringe from his horse-like face, his oversized front teeth, his deep-set brown eyes. Just then a memory of his own school days flashed across his noggin. He snorted, again like a horse, scratched an eyebrow and glanced out the window before continuing to speak. "For heaven's sake Green, I mean... No, put your hand down, boy."

From a thin ledge that ran along the bottom of the blackboard, Mr Harrington picked up and studied a piece of chalk, no bigger than a filter on a cigarette. He rolled it between his thumb and first finger. "Don't let me catch *any* of you using the words *from* or *nice,* in your letters home. Capisci?"

He regarded our blank faces and wheezed, "Oh my Lord, as if any of you understand Italian." He looked to the heavens and slumped like a teenager behind a rather large plinth-like desk. This brought an air of maybe he could have done something better with his life. But not before he scratched and tapped out that ambiguous four-letter word onto the blackboard. We sat in silence waiting for the next instruction. Our fountain pens poised over headed note paper. Not one of us wanted to write that four-letter word that hovered so mysteriously like a hologram in front of the class. We'd long forgotten what the word meant. Besides what use did it have here and how might love be found in such an isolated setting? The next four years could be a loveless experience. Goodbye love... Goodbye.

"Get on with your letters," Mr Harrington took a breath then added with a certain poignancy, "home... You've got ten minutes."

Thereupon, without warning he got up and slung that piece of chalk at me. I ducked wondering if he had been reading my thoughts. The chalk fizzed overhead, hit the back wall and fell onto the floor where it rolled and stopped. When everybody looked back at Mr Harrington, Wilson slid down, stretched out a hand and like a pearl diver scooped up the chalk. Later in the day, Wilson caught up with me placed the chalk in my hand and said, "Look, I believe this was meant for you..."

BUCKLAND HOUSE,
BUCKLAND FILLEIGH,
BEAWORTHY,
N. DEVON.
EX21 5JA

Telephone: Shebbear 222.

Dear Mummy and daddy

I hope you are well. When I played against Mount House U9½'s I scored two goals and won 2·1. On Sunday we are having House Matches. I am in the Colts. I am doing well at School. There are no effort Marks this week. On Sunday we are having two Minute Speaches

love
Rupert.
xx

A prep school letter

> Telephone: Shebbear 222.
>
> BUCKLAND HOUSE,
> BUCKLAND FILLEIGH,
> BEAWORTHY,
> N. DEVON.
> EX21 5JA
>
> Dear Mummy and Dad
>   I hope you are well. I was on dining Hall duty. I Played Football Today and I was left wing and then I was on Centere half and I scored a goal.
>
>   lots
>   of
>   love
>   Rupert xx

Another prep school letter

3

Porridge

DURING WINTER MONTHS, THE cooks would knock the lids off their coffins to rise at first light. Most mornings we ate Sunshine Flakes and for a change, if we'd been really bad, a large pot of black slugs was carried in by two prefects. The pot was ceremoniously placed on the serving table along with a ladle and a stack of white China bowls. Mr Whitaker would then begin to distribute breakfast. We turned our noses up at the thought of eating prune slugs. Until, that is, you found stones, then it was all *rich man, poor man, beggar man, thief.*

In the murky light of the steamed up school kitchen, shadowy figures are dodging hot pots and pans. The gas hob burning blue, orange, peach and apricot orange, flickering blue flames under large pans, where substantial bags of oats are emptied into three industrial sized aluminium saucepans. Followed by three buckets of cold water in each and handfuls of scattered salt. Not much else. A half tuned distorted radio offers news of strikes and general breakdown. The world outside remains distant and unforgiving. We have our world in front of our eyes. That's all that matters to us. The wireless is only seen as a noise to accompany the cooks making our daily breakfast, turning flustered sausages, watching them burn in fat spitting frying pans.

Sinclair shakes large metal trays of fried bread, slams the oven door with a knee, always with an eye on the clock. The dance is over when Sinclair whistles to the boy by the main staircase, who's job is to sound the gong because breakfast is ready.

Hold on... scratch that, before breakfast, before grace, before we sit down. There are four skew-whiff lines in the assembly hall. We are not standing on the hand painted Badminton lines. We boys scratching out the sleepy dust from our eyes. Fingers searching out cabbages in ears and twisting a finger up a nostril. We are scratching our balls and are resigned to another day. Another day means one less to do before half term.

And, um... remembering whilst asleep, wandering the corridors of our minds to find some homely memory to hold on to. A time before boarding school, a time when we were alone at home. Anything will do. It is preferable to these shenanigans.

Then as with all creativity, some bright spark lights up a whisper, throws it into the room. The idea stitches itself like pegs on a washing line.

"P is for porridge pass it on." Whispered Clifton Wentworth deep into Wilson's right ear.

"P is for porridge pass it on." Said an agitated Wilson to Winston Montague.

"It's porridge." Said Winston Montague, as he leant over Hunt.

"Porridge." Barked Hunt. He punched Smit hard above the elbow.

Smit's laugh covered the shooting pain. He looked at Hunt who pointed at me and blasted, "Tell Green porridge."

"Green porridge?" Said Smit all the more confused.

"What?" I said. Hunt hit Smit again and said, "Tell Green, Porridge."

"Oh right, porridge." I said. I looked down my nose at Mandrake. "Porrrrrridge!"

"Yeah, I know," said Mandrake. "I heard everyone." And it stopped there. There was an uneasy shuffle of feet and yawns. Concealed stretches behind backs with both arms. A tap of a shoulder, look the other way. A smile, a gentle knock and a push. The playfulness travelled along the lines.

"Hold your tongues." Said the headmaster as he stepped into the hall, adjusting his wristwatch. Mandrake looked up at me. I stopped holding my tongue and smiled. He shook his head and gazed at his shoes.

Breakfast begins with a duty master and the salutation *for what we are about to receive*. Only then can we sit down. As a collective, we try hard not to talk louder than if we were gathered together in a small-town library - if we did there would be a call for silence. And who wants to sit in silence at the beginning of term? The servers of the ten tables start serving, queueing up, moving along, picking up plates watching them get filled and then the job of serving. Mr Whitaker, Matron and a dining hall duty prefect stand behind a large table dishing out the porridge.

And the line moves on. Lifting off from the table, each server would begin the distribution process. Busy as bees, collecting and returning from flowers with the pollen. There is a general hum in the dining hall.

Heads down like a Fritz Lang movie, we are the workers passing the bowls down the table with metronomic timing. At the head of the table sits the all-powerful, all-knowing master. Each master sits with a funeral face, back to the windows, arms folded and looking for an excuse to spoil the day. They preside over the proceedings with elitist precision and dark foreboding.

School porridge is very complicated. It shouldn't be, but it is. For a start, it didn't ever taste, smell or look like anything one was used to at home. Quite why it had to have a thick skin the colour of an Edinburgh sky, I'll never know. And another thing, porridge should be eaten quietly.

Mr and Mrs Sinclair were the school cooks. Mr Sinclair, standing up close to the cooker, gives the kitchen clock a dirty look. He stirs each pot; the thick porridge takes on a life of its own in the industrial sized pans. Mr Sinclair blinks his grey blue eyes. As a bead of sweat rolls down the side of his face, past his thin dyed moustache. It hangs for a moment from the edge of his chin before it lets go and drops into the porridge. He notices not. He turns the gas burners off to allow the porridge to stagnate.

As a flight of fancy, I often wondered if, Mr Sinclair fancied himself as a classic Hollywood film star. Maybe he would have chosen Clark Gable as his role model. Hence the dyed moustache.

"I reinvent myself!" He would postulate in the bedroom in front of the long mirror before dropping his dressing gown to the floor. This statement often prompted Mrs Sinclair to slam her cup of cocoa onto the bedside table, plump up the pillows, throwback the duvet revealing her siren energy. That through his eyes was pure Marilyn Monroe.

The following morning, sleepy boys from the East Wing dormitories talked of nothing but odd freakish noises. Many tales told of the mysterious noises they heard. The farmer boys explained it was a vixen shrieking for a mate. But could not explain that strange tugboat thudding heard throughout the entire night. Like all night long. Very strange.

"I've no idea." I said.

"Sounds like one of your ghosts," said Mandrake pointing at me. He smiled and nudged Wilson, who looked out the window, not wanting to have anything to do with ghosts.

"Have you actually seen a ghost?"

"Yes, once," I lied. Mandrake grimaced. Wilson decided and said nervously because he still could be wrong.

"I don't believe in ghosts."

Mr Sinclair's wife and cooking partner, whose smile in no way gave you any confidence that she had not just laced the porridge with a few tablespoons of inheritance powder. Easy to add, difficult to prove. Arsenic is the powder of choice because it has no taste and no smell. We would never know as later, we all fell into a big sleep at our wooden desks with obsolete inkwells.

Mrs Sinclair stood. As always, not far from Mr Sinclair's side. She wore a yellow and orange tabard. Number 6 cigarette in hand. Mr Sinclair preferred his Number 6 to be drooping from the side of his mouth.

The service of porridge was down to three choices, which is not always the best thing to have in an all-boys school. It made the delivery mind numbingly slow.
Service options were as follows:
Without milk, without sugar.
With milk, without sugar.
Without milk, with sugar.
With milk, with sugar.
Without milk, without sugar but with a pinch of salt.
Incidentally, you only got the last one if your name started with Mc or Mac. Not that Malcolm McGregor ever wanted porridge without milk, no sugar but with a pinch of pinch of salt.
If it was the 1st of the month, he liked to pinch and punch somebody, preferably a new boy. And in a loud voice he told them that was how he took his porridge concluding his sermon with an emphatic *White Rabbits!*
The best way to have it was with milk and sugar and to be served first. That was the best. The porridge would be warm and sweet and the skin manageable. To be served last, as the nourishment bringers always were, the porridge was vice versa. That's Latin for cold coagulative. And a skin you could use as a replacement soul or better still a replacement sole, for holes rather than holy gym shoes or daps as matron likes to call them.
The thought of cold porridge made the servers bad tempered. They would hurry along, which caused accidents and incorrect orders.
If you unconsciously turned your head because you thought you heard faint, distant laughter, you probably did. It would have been Mr Sinclair watching through the gap in the kitchen service hatchway. Willing, rather manifesting, in his mind's eye boys colliding with platefuls of hot porridge.
"Ah! Now that's perfect."
A broad grin stretched the cheeks on his red face. He took a drag on his cigarette and dropped it in his coffee cup.

"What's that just now?" Said his wife as she untangled a large, smashed mouse from a serrated metal bar of a trap previously set under the double sinks.

After inspecting the rodent, holding it up by its tail before dropping the lifeless creature headfirst into the general waste bin, she coughed and spat. It was the least she could do. What with this being a religious school and her having witnessed the headmaster entering the kitchen. He was after another cup of instant coffee. She crossed herself, muttered an Amen and followed all that with a flick of a V sign.

"Oh no…" Said the Headmaster, "Another rat?" He stirred the powdered milk into his mug of coffee with a Biro. He looked a little distressed. "Don't let my wife see it."

"I'll hide it in the Stew." She smiled a frosty smile. The Headmaster's unsettled smile didn't conceal the growing concern he felt. Mr Sinclair had his back to him so he had no idea if she was joking or not. There was the sound of crockery breaking and a cheer.

"Uh-oh! Dining hall chaos Headmaster. You'd better get back in there." Mr Sinclair poked fun at the headmaster before closing the kitchen service hatchway doors. Before he left the Headmaster put his coffee cup back down on the table before he dropped another sugar lump into his cup. With his daily newspaper now squished under his arm, left the kitchen without a word.

As a side note, it was hilarious. Oh, hang on, try again… It was common knowledge not to disturb the headmaster on a Thursday, when he made himself coffee in the kitchen. Particularly on the first Thursday of the month, because that's when Mrs Sinclair made all the birthday cakes for that month. The headmaster was partial to a late morning slice and would often help himself.

So, it really was hilarious as we all sang happy blah-blah to you, to see the young boy's astonished reaction when presented with the velvety soft Persil white sponge cake, smeared with blue icing and a substantial slice of the cake missing.

That was what life was like in porridge.

4
Education X

During the first lesson, of Mr Whitaker's scripture lesson, the story about the lady who smote a tent peg through the head of a sleeping man was read out. Then another story of how another lady brought the downfall of Samson simply by giving him a haircut. She doesn't love him. I was worried.

"Hold on, when did this happen?"

"Back in the day. Bible-gum, weren't you listening?" Replied Clifton Wentworth holding a glass of milk at first break.

Next lesson. Mrs Lancaster is stood reading from a book. And I'm not listening because I'm still stuck on the last lesson. I am wondering, do I need this monastic life? With all these long periods of silence and following the word, the rules and saying your prayers and walk, don't run in the house. Was prep school setting me up for a fear of women and to live a celibate life? After all, I do have men of the cloth in my lineage. I do keep a bible in my desk. I do sleep in a dormitory and we all say Grace before every meal. Go to church on Sunday… Amen, Amen, Amen, Amen, Amen, Amen.

"Amen!"

"Shh! Don't be silly Rupert."

"Sorry Mrs Lancaster…"

Mrs Lancaster continued. It's Kipling mostly.

The mid-morning sun moved slowly across our desks. Some boys bounce reflected light across the ceiling with plastic rulers whilst others try to blind their neighbour with the metal lids of geometry set cases. Mrs Lancaster's delivery of Kipling weaves a somnolent spell. I couldn't help but yawn in the drowsy, sleepy time moments with the expectation of lunch. The day was moving along nicely and the prospect of more food not too far away.

Just then, with all the subtlety of a brick being thrown through a window, the classroom door kicked open. A small boy swung in, hanging on the brass door knob. Mr Harrington followed. Ceremoniously he wheeled a big television into the classroom. He is followed by the rest the boys from Form II. We pulled faces and flicked V-signs at each other. The classroom door is closed and instructions are fired across the sunlight's beams.

We turn our chairs round, some sit on desks and other go cross-legged on the floor. Most importantly, we are gathered around the wise old television. Mr Harrington, also the projectionist on film nights, went all technical and plugged in the television. Switched it on in. The elder boy's instruction was to blot out the streams of sunlight. They unfolded floor-to-ceiling shutters and locked them halfway with the metal bars, a bit like like a door latch but not. Everyone settled in the semi-darkness. There is a hush of expectation brought on when Mr Harrington casually pushed a button on the television.

"Shut up!" Says Harrington with a wry smile.

We stop talking and asking questions. Therefore we still have absolutely no idea what we are about to watch. Wilson is excused to go to the lavatory. The valves inside the television warm up sufficiently and the picture adjusts from charcoal grey to a pleasant Cornflower blue. In the background on the screen was a clock that had a countdown in progress. Tiny chalk white marks disappeared clockwise in turn with each second. In the centre of the screen was written in capitals PROGRAMMES FOR SCHOOLS AND COLLEGES. Underneath the ever-decreasing seconds on the face of the clock with no numbers, was written one word. Mr Harrington's hand appeared in front of the screen, obscuring the words. He turns up the volume. The room fills with the sweet sounds of light to mediocre jazz, a fanfare suggesting the next twenty minutes will be both groovy and informative. We can't wait. Our expectations continue to mount.

The room's atmosphere almost blown when the classroom door unexpectedly opened and quickly shut. Someone had made a late entrance into the room and it wasn't Wilson. We all naturally looked around puzzled to see who it was. Matron smiled and waved as she ducked down, nestled in next to Mrs Lancaster. Matron stared at Mrs Lancaster for a moment longer than was polite before returning the smile. Mr Harrington coughed as the jazz faded then a clipped, detached female voice made an announcement. It commanded our attention.

"Programmes for schools and colleges. Program One. Copulation."

A nervous laugh spread through the ranks. We looked at each other. Thompson put up his hand and spoke in his deep voice before being invited to speak.

"What does that mean?"

"It means be quiet!" Said Mr Harrington looking at his nails on his left hand. We pull faces, shrug shoulders and then stare at the television with mild curiosity, growing interest and then shock and horror and bewilderment as the informative programme lifts the veil, with mindbogglingly graphic detail, and in colour. We are on the edge of something. Here be dragons! Here be scenes of what to do, what not to do and when to do it and when not to do it – when it comes to copulation. Spoken in an ancient tongue.

A hot air balloon, an over-elaborate overdose, a new direction taken in 1970s sexual education. Everything bar the cigarette.

Amongst a plethora of two people positions, unmentionable acrobatics emerged, with judo-style wrestling, quite interesting to observe. Towards the end, after we witnessed, of all things, a steam train running along parallel tracks, entering a tunnel, the programme told us women give birth to children, while men are better at giving birth to ideas.

"Great!" We spontaneously shout trying to distract ourselves from sitting uncomfortably. Stimulation overload.

"Form I, be quiet!" Scolded Mrs Lancaster. Mr Harrington chimed in with a threat to turn the program off if we didn't have complete silence.

Perverse as the situation was and whilst not wanting to take in the information on the screen but being captivated by compulsive viewing, we kept as quiet as church mice and chewed on handkerchiefs to smother our laughter.

The narrator in the last minutes of the film suggested we all grow up, which was weird because the way she said it made us feel she'd been in the room, listening to our sniggers all along.

"Explain that." I said to Hunt.

"Nah!" He said, "Matron." A dispirited look came over his face. He half put up his hand to ask a question, touched his top lip and only then extended his arm.

"And one plus one makes three." Said Mrs Lancaster as the credits rolled and the mediocre jazz returned. Mrs Lancaster began nudging Matron in the ribs motioning for Matron to maybe say something. Matron closed her mouth and blushed and having seen enough, leant over and whispered to Mrs Lancaster, "I couldn't possibly. I feel perturbed."

Standing up, Matron quietly left under the watchful stare of Mrs Lancaster who at the last moment raised her eyebrows. Wilson barged past Matron as she opened the classroom door. He returned to find his seat taken. He stared at our bemused faces, sees the credits rolling up the TV screen and asks, "What did I miss, what did I miss?"

Whilst others scratched their heads, Mr Harrington beamed from ear to ear and he then treated us to one of his famous blank, oddly strange, disengaged stares, whilst looking directly at Wilson who suddenly felt exposed. Wilson put his hands on his head and sat down.

"Mr Harrington, Sir, what did I miss?" squeaked Wilson.

Mr Harrington put a finger to his lips.

"SIR!" Shouted Thompson, "what is four playing?"

"What's master bashing?" Yelled Hunt falling off his chair. We all laughed.

Clifton Wentworth nudged Wilson and spoke through his fingers, so as not to be heard by Mr Harrington because Mr Harrington was still staring. Wilson listened. "Making babies!" Wilson looked puzzled. Wilson shouted without raising his hand. "Miss!"

"It's Mrs!" said Clifton Wentworth his tone mocking. Hunt pushed Thompson. Bradley Edwards punched Smit on the arm. Smit punched him back. Mandrake dropped his book on the floor. I picked it up and gave it to Hunt. Hunt sat on it. Mandrake put out his hand Hunt shook his head. Wilson looked at the floor. Thompson kicked Clifton Wentworth in the back.

"Hey!" Said Clifton Wentworth turning to see who was kicking him.

"Silence." Said Mr Harrington, "Be quiet!" He added because no one listened.

"Silence." Muttered Mrs Lancaster, she rubbed her brow and smiled wearily.

"But Sir!" said Wilson unable to contain himself any longer. "What did I miss?"

"Right then." Said Mr Harrington ignoring Wilson. "I would like Form II to stand up and follow me. Er... what's your name boy?"

"Clifton Wentworth, Sir." Said Clifton Wentworth, wondering if Mr Harrington had actually heard him through his fingers. He shuddered as if someone had just walked over his grave.

"Just the surname boy." Hissed Mr Harrington. "Now... Wentworth!"

"Sir?"

"What's your name?" He asked gloomily.

Clifton Wentworth looked over to Mrs Lancaster who frowned and said, "Go on Clifton tell Mr Harrington your last name."

"Sir!" Shouted Mandrake. "Hunt wont give my book back!"

"Er... I would ask you not to shout," said Mrs Lancaster to Mandrake. "Go on Clifton..."

"Wentworth but my name is Clifton Wentworth."

"Thank you, Wentworth." Said Mr Harrington, he didn't smile. He continued to talk because he liked the sound of his own voice. The tone was now monotonous. "Not here it isn't. To me you're just Wentworth... Do you understand, Wentworth?"

And in that moment Mr Harrington looked rather unkind. Hard to say but Harrington bristled with a level of annoyance fast approaching angry. It brought about a full stop to the lesson where nothing seemed real, like we were getting the blame for something dreadful that had happened that day in some faraway place called French Polynesia, where fools had been fiddling with 1972 levels of cutting-edge science, *and had* with permission, let off another one of those detestable atmospheric atomic bombs. The scientists were bitterly disappointed, because they had only killed everything within a 300 mile radius of the detonation point. French scientists… but that would be the pot calling the kettle black.

"Yes Sir." Replied Clifton Wentworth when the spell was broken by Mrs Lancaster's loud and sudden protracted sneeze.

"Sir!" Implored Mandrake. Sensing Harrington's mood Mrs Lancaster grabbed hold of Mandrake and encouraged him to sit down. She put her hand out to Hunt who reluctantly placed Mandrake's book in it. "Both of you see me after." Mrs Lancaster looked at Mr Harrington and gestured for him to carry on.

"So, now I know your name Wentworth. Would you be so kind as to open the classroom door so I might be able to leave?"

"Yes Sir." Said Clifton Wentworth the colour returning to his cheeks. He stood up but not before checking in with Mrs Lancaster.

"But Sir…" Protested Thompson, again Mr Harrington put a finger to his lips. Clifton Wentworth went to the door but we could see his head was now full of questions too. He held the door open and gulped back a question. Mr Harrington, ignored Clifton Wentworth as he pushed the television out of the classroom.

"Thank you, Clifton. Well done." Said Mrs Lancaster. "Now come and sit down."

And so it was, without a word of explanation, the television was wheeled out of the room. Form II, as instructed, followed Mr Harrington in a respectful silence. We fidgeted and watched them leave. Some of us waved to our friends, others pulled faces and flicked V signs but only because Mrs Lancaster had her back to us as she opened the window shutters.

"So right. Er… right everyone." Mrs Lancaster said a little nervous tone in her voice. "Alright put your hands down. It is time for a spelling test." We groaned. Mrs Lancaster picked up a writing pad she'd been writing on throughout the film and slammed it down onto the desk.

"I beg your pardon?" Mrs Lancaster said placing her hands on her hips.

"Sorry, Miss!" We said

"Pardon?"

"Sorry MRS Lancaster."

"That's better. I see Thompson has got his spelling book out, good boy. Has everyone got a pencil?" Mrs Lancaster drew a breath in and without looking up from her notes said, "The first spelling is..."

Frustrated and ready to explode Wilson leapt up and bellowed.

"But Miss, what did I miss?"

Buckland House School
Saturday 10th June 1972.

Dear Mummy and Daddy

I hope you are well.

Yesterday night my bed clothes came off. Yesterday we saw a programme about babies being born and a baby takes 9 months and an elephant takes 21 months to develop.

I am looking forward to seeing my birthday cake when I come back home.
Is Noddy okay?
Have the workmen finished yet?
Send my love to Mrs Tancock, please.

Lots Of Love Rupert xxx

My efforts are: 2nd excellent English, 1st excellent Maths, 3rd excellent History, 2nd excellent Geography, 1st excellent Scripture.

5

The Cut

THE OPPOSITION CAPTAIN, SMALL for his age, was in possession of a proper pair of adult ears. They stuck out like wingnuts. He stood at the end of his run-up, a brand-new cricket ball in hand. If I remember from another game, he bowled off the wrong foot and swung both his arms around as if he was about to take off. It was slow stuff. From the boundary they shouted, "Give it a whack!" The bowling was pedestrian because the ball bounced several times before it got down to my end. Therefore, not enough to give it much more than a solid barn door block, followed by a resolute call of "No!"

I was born with a cricket bat in my hand, well not actually born holding a cricket bat, that's not going to work on any level. In the cradle, I was shown by Brother Number Four and encouraged to practice, the various grips for spinning a cricket ball. I was a right-handed batsman and bowler. I could catch the ball nine times out of ten. The times I dropped a catch was when it mattered that I didn't drop it. I could throw straight and with accuracy and when I bowled, I got the ball to turn. I bowled leg breaks.

I was shown in the nets how to play the forward defence by Mr Whitaker. I loved playing the forward defence. For hours I had throwdowns in the nets and then boys bowling at me in the nets. One day a cardboard box arrived in the post for me. It was from Daddy. In it contained a girly pink box, an abdomen protector, a hard cup. It looked like a seashell, a strange shaped thing that covered the private parts when fitted into one's pants.

My father as a boy, had been smashed in the genitals whilst batting at his school, many years ago now. Actually the story goes, he was knocked unconscious by the event and rightly didn't want the same fate to fall unto me, hence the 'gift' - girly pink, too big, (even though it was printed on the side that it was boy's cricket box.) I got a lot of flak for owning that box, even from the headmaster, something ridiculous about being good enough not to need one. I suffered in quiet desperation and didn't wear it.

One day in the nets, I missed a straight delivery from Mr Whitaker, and it hit me fair and square between the legs. I held the forward defensive position and gasped. I couldn't breathe. No air went in. Air went out. I caught my breath. An alarming amount of pain raced around the unmentionables before it made a B-line for my brain. My eyes watered. I fell over, got caught up in the netting.

"You've got your thing on, right?" Shouts one of the bowlers noticing my discomfort. They all laugh.

"Mmm!" I lied. After that day, I always wore my box.

In 1972, I got into the colts cricket team for playing the forward defence. And whatever the delivery was, I played the forward defence. Sometimes I hit the ball just right, sweetly or a bit harder and there was an opportunity to score one run. What a run means, is when you run up to the other end, whilst the other batsman runs down to the end I hit the ball from. Whilst the fielder chased after the ball, picked it up and threw it into the wicketkeeper or bowler, in an attempt to run out either batsman. I wasn't particularly fast and sometimes got run out, which is a form of dismissal, whereby as a batsman, you have to leave the pitch. It's not at all complicated.

So, in the first match I played, over after over this went on. I played forward defence after forward defence. And as the game progressed, the other batsmen came and went, whilst the opposition bowlers gnashed their teeth because they couldn't get me out. Which was a good thing. Until that is, a slower delivery dressed up as a normal delivery arrived. Being in a routine and not watching the ball, I played forward too early, missed it and the ball hit the top of my off stump. I was bowled out but with some measure of distinction and a knowing look of recognition from Mr Whitaker. I can bat. I know where my off stump is.

Mr Whitaker liked the blond-haired boys best. He was our umpire, coach, referee, surrogate father figure, history and scripture teacher, counsellor, driver, mentor, judge, jury, and executioner. And most of all he was an unpleasant person although you will find people who will tell you otherwise.

In the small world of North Devon prep school cricket, I made a name for myself with bat and ball. Worked my way up the batting order to No.1. Now I could potentially bat out every ball of the innings. Forward defence, forward defence, forward defence. It wasn't the only shot I learnt. I was taught how to play the backward defence too. It went a bit like this. Put your bat up, step back, head still, your eyes in line with the ball. Hit the ball so that it falls dead on the ground in front of you. The call to the other batsman is loud and clear and sounds like this 'No!' This meant you're not on any account going to score a run from that delivery. Perfect. I got my game plan down. Forward defence, forward defence, forward defence, backward defence. Over after over, match after match. I would mostly finish an innings 3 not out. I was learning how to bat. Which is why cricket can be seen to be the most boring game in the world. But not if you are playing it. To score fifty runs was the pinnacle of batting in colts and first eleven prep school cricket. I must bat good to achieve this.

Buckland House
Saturday 24th June 72

Dear Mum,
How are you? I won the game against St Petroc's last Wednesday and I scored 27 runs not out and 6 wickets LBW and bowled mostly. We got them all out for 39 runs!! I have had my watched engraved for 35 pence I had R GREEN Engraved on it. Last Thursday A Helicopter flew down and made arrangements for the Royal Marines visit this Thursday coming and you are allowed to come at 2pm. It's been quite sunny laterly. I had a £2 postal order from Grandma and Rose sent me four Hornby railway trucks, which I will give to you to take home Thursday.
Love Rupert x
PS. See you on Thursday.

The umpire said, "Play." Waved an arm and the match started. The captain ran towards me, a determined look on his face. He managed to fling the ball to land outside off stump, ran down after the ball towards my end and stopped. He looked puzzled. The deliveries were half volleys, short and wide just right for the square cut. The trouble is I didn't have the square cut in my armoury. Again the ball left his hand, bounced and went through to the wicketkeeper, who would most times catch the ball. The ball went *thunk!* into his oversized green and blue leather gloves.

Every time this happened, our Umpire, Mr Fairfax would shake his head and under his breath say "For goodness-sake, cut it Green!" Thereafter, he would give an exaggerated look towards the heavens, followed by mutterings and ancient words of derision calling on the Gods for intervention. None came.

The next delivery was too short to drive. If the line of the ball was on stumps, I could have played a backward defense. A shot consistent with the ball dropping to my feet, followed by a firm call of no. Which meant in this delivery, I do not wish to score a run. The wicketkeeper would then have to wade with oversized pads strapped to both his legs up to the stumps. He would then try to gather the ball from the popping crease and throw it to a fielder, so the fielder could return it to the bowler, or throw it to the next fielder in the chain of fielders until a fielder was close enough to throw the ball back to the bowler with a gentle underarm throw.

However, because junior wicket-keeping gloves were overall larger than oven gloves, it was decidedly difficult to throw the ball with any accuracy. Invariably fingers would tip the ball, when thrown, and all 4¾ ounces of hard leather ball would fly over the wicketkeeper's shoulder. The intentions were good. The results were often hilarious, when it would take many attempts as the wicket keeper got further and further away from the fielder, to throw the ball straight.

The St Petroc's umpire took his panama hat, threw it onto the ground, and stamped on it, all the while he screamed at his fielder and wicketkeeper.

"CARTWRIGHT, FOR GOD'S SAKE GO AND TAKE THE BALL FROM HIM. NO BLENKINSOPP, NO. DO NOT THROW THE BALL ANYMORE!! CARTWRIGHT WILL GET IT FROM YOU... LEAVE IT! NO, YOU DON'T NEED TO. DROP IT! LEAVE THE BALL BLENKINSOPP OR BY CRIKEY! I'LL MAKE YOU WALK BACK TO ST PETROC'S..."

And so, it went on and on, over after over.

Buckland House

Dear Mummy

I hope you are well? When we played cricket against St Pelrocs we lost. I got no runs but I got three wickets. The picture is Grump and The hairy Mammoth. Is it all right if Forbes takes me out on Sunday the 25th? Can you come to the fathers Match please?

My effort marcks are: good English excellent Maths good History excellent Geography good Scripture

Love Rupert x

I suppose it did get rather tedious what with, over after over of inherent clumsiness and my leaving or blocking every ball. I say, what a marvellous game cricket is. Good character-building stuff.

After the game and before I could unbuckle my pads, the incensed science-master Mr Fairfax, who had just umpired both innings with a now empty hip flask, grabbed hold of my shirt collar and dragged me up to the cricket nets. Where he demonstrated unto me the most holy of all strokes, the cut shot.

Hold it one moment. I can hear angels sing!

Mr Fairfax illustrated, remonstrated then showed me the cut shot, the late cut but not before the square cut. I picked it up quickly. The now emblazoned Master threw down a thousand balls for me to cut and then it got too dark to see. I thanked him and toddled off.

The next match I was able to instinctively cut the ball sweetly from the middle of the bat for four runs. For this I am ever grateful, I must thank him again, as it became the most satisfying and rewarding of all the strokes to play.

That is until one day I got caught in the gully and then another time caught at point. I connected with the ball either too late or too early. It's all about the eye-hand coordination and timing.

Such a leveller this sideways game is.

6

The Sandwich

From nowhere, a warm salty sea breeze. It blew in with all the force of a cheap hair dryer, across the St Petroc's school cricket field. By the innings break, the wind had reached all parts of the ground and had unfortunately done something to the spam and pickle sandwiches.

Buckland House
July 3rd 72

Dear Mummy
I hope you are well. We have done some exams in Maths I got 91% Thank you for the lovely weekend I enjoyed it at Exmouth with Kev, Michael and the others. Can you send me my sister's address please?
Love Rupert x

Buckland House
7.7.72

Dear Mummy
I hope you are well. On Friday 7th we are playing St. Peters all day match, I will have two innings.
Can you send my Pen Knife please? At Mount House they have a bowling machine, and it can bowl at 90 M.P.H. On Friday Form 6 came in and took us for reading I had Travis
Love Rupert x

Now it was common knowledge, when cricket teams visited St Petroc's, to not touch the sandwiches if the wind blew in from the sea. All the same, I thought as I stood for the first time in the tea interval, mesmerised by the pyramid of double-sided bread triangles with pale pink tongue-like middles stuck together with margarine and brown pickle sauce, I thought, there's always a first time...

I bit into the sandwich and took out the corner. Mmm... I thought, oh wait... what is that vile sea-weedy, rotten egg smell... And what in the name of Belshazzar is that taste? I retched, retched again, wanted to spit, clapped my hand over my mouth. Whatever it was I just swallowed was trying to come back up again and with a vengeance. Alarm bells were going off in my head. *Eject! Run! Eject! Run! Hide! Eject! Run!*

Now I know why I should have listened to the others. I should not have succumbed to the lure of the St Petroc's school cricket tea sandwich. Overcoming my nausea, I gave myself time, I got a grip, stood tall, was polite and concealed the rest of the sandwich in my left hand. And asked a teammate, "Quick, where are the bogs?"

The opposition captain with ears like wing nuts put his head on one side. A cowlick sprung from the front of a head full of straight blond hair. He gave me a look that suggested he liked me, well maybe not. I figured he wanted to watch me eat the entire sandwich. I might have to disappoint him and excuse myself. I dived around the corner from the courtyard where the cricket tea was laid on a table and found a black bog door next to a well-established riot of sickly sweet smelling honeysuckle, it trailed down onto the concrete pathway.

In the semi-darkness, I pulled the chain and watched the sandwich sink through the streams of gushing water bubbles. I spat out everything. A relieved smile broke out on my face as the offending article sank.

Dear Mummy, How are you? At cricket, I drowned a sandwich!

Only the spam and pickle did not want to be drowned. Far from it. For a moment it did nothing but spin round at the bottom of the toilet. Then it surfaced like an emergency surfacing submarine, bobbed about like a frog on the surface. That wasn't in the script. Suffice to say, I wasn't about to lift it out, not now it was alive. With no bog brush available, I couldn't smash it down or hoik it out. I figured there was not much else I could do, so I unbolted the black door and left the cubicle, returning to the bright sunlight and the hair dryer wind.

"Ah! There you are Green, have you had a sandwich?"

"Why? I mean no thank you, Sir." I spoke awkwardly feeling I had been rumbled. I stretched for a piece of sponge cake to hide my embarrassment.

"You should have a sandwich before cake." Said Mr Whitaker, he was doing his best to encourage our boys to eat up the sandwiches and not just the cake. He tilted his head to one side.

"What do you mean? Like, like leg before wicket, Sir?" I asked referring to his *trigger finger* umpiring decisions that brought us to an earlier-than-scheduled tea interval.

"That'll do…" said Mr Whitaker grabbing an extra two sandwiches for his plate, he wandered off to talk to the St Petroc's Matron. And as Matron's go, she was younger than any Matron I had ever known. Matrons, with real blonde hair and a melting gorgonzola face. I judged her prettier than ours, but she might be prettier indoors. I broke out into a cold sweat. I felt nauseous. It was difficult to judge. We'd need a police line-up. Good Lord! That sandwich has made me feel weird. My judgement has gone awry… I'm embarrassed by my thoughts.

"Yes Sir." I said, "Enjoy your sandwich." I smiled and nodded at Mr Whitaker then waved a fly away from my face. I felt dizzy.

I couldn't fail to notice a grumpy-looking opposition captain standing by the tea table, he chirped up and spoke so everybody could hear, his accent plain, clear and with a Devonshire lilt, he barked with a slight hoarseness in his young voice.

"Didn't-nee *like* the san-witch, you?"

He fixed his stare like he was channelling ancestral sea demons. He was starting to scare me. I felt a little faint. I hoped I hadn't gone red.

After a moment's thought, I turned as if to throw the accusation to another boy stood behind me. I looked like a dick. It didn't fool anyone, rather drew more unwanted attention. Those who stood talking around the table either frowned or raised an eyebrow. I walked, scratching away the embarrassment from behind my ear. Mr Whitaker looked on, thankfully he'd been chatting up their Matron and hadn't heard anything, I waved to him and smiled. He didn't smile back and if anything, looked a little confused as to what I wanted. I mimed *What's the time?* pointing to my wrist with over-the-top gestures. *How much time we got, Sir, before the next innings, please?*

Colt's cricket is nothing like Colt's football. In football, you get wet and muddy and have a good chance to fly hack each other or once a game, kick a big old leather ball. After 90 minutes it's all over and you get to have a nice tepid shower with a nice bar of shared soap whilst being watched by a nice schoolmaster. Everyone plays kickball. It's nice and easy.

By comparison, Colt's cricket was littered with the gravestones of boys who tried and failed, only to reject this life-affirming, fantastic outdoor sunshine-only gentleman's sport. I know it is difficult if most of the boys who turn up to play don't do anything all afternoon. It isn't much fun to watch other boys bowl, and bat, run after a very hard ball, and sometimes you'll be expected for unfathomable reasons to catch that very hard cricket ball as it falls like a hot rock from outer space when any sane boy would run and take cover.

If you do get a chance to do something like pad up to go out to bat you're probably going to be scared witless when the fastest bowler in the school is visibly growling as he turns to run in from the boundary, his footsteps thudding as he tears in to bowl, jumps and explodes into a blur of arms and legs delivering the ball of the season that you didn't even see, CRACK! the ball sends your middle stump when hit cartwheeling back out the ground, towards a now excited wicket-keeper who whoops with joy! It sounds like a shotgun and to the delight with ecstatic screams of 'HOWZAT!' from the fielders who rudely point you in the direction back to the bench from where not a few moments ago you had sat for what felt like days shaking hands with fear.

I can see why you'd want to lay for the rest of the afternoon on the parched grass cloudbusting. If this has happened to you, I don't mind if you now want to admit that for these reasons alone you hate cricket!

We won that sunny day. I did well. I checked to see if the sandwich was still floating before I got back into Mr Whitaker's car and it was. And because we won, Mr Whitaker drove back to Buckland House like an aristocrat, albeit with the windows still wound up.

Later, after lights out, I updated the dormitory. Not that it was a great sandwich story more, a tonic for the troops.

The following week I expected to be on vacation, I didn't know to where. Probably a week with my mother and then my father before three weeks with a brother and a week or two with my sister. I counted the days down singing, "Five more days to go, five more days of sorrow, five more days in this old dump, and we'll be home tomorrow!" But it was a hollow song. In my heart, I prepared for the monastic silence to once again accompany my pillar-to-post vacations that kind of came to take my childhood away.

The last day of term arrived, and we all split without as much as a goodbye. Jumped from the frying pan to the fire. A weekend was a brief but welcomed time to be away from school. The post office and village stores were as new a place to explore as any house I have lived in so far in my life. So I guess it was quiet in the post office for a reason. My father was away somewhere, doing something, I wasn't told what. I awoke after a good night of dreamless sleep, I washed, dressed and found my way to the kitchen after walking into the closed shop by mistake. What a lot of sweets.

"Good morning." I sit on the bench at the pine table, the same table and bench from our house in Sussex. Mother still has false teeth. She would crunch her wholemeal toast with excessive noise. I look around the kitchen and out of the new double-glazed window. Nice. I thought, a back garden. Mother calculated her next move. She placed the mug on the table and said.

"Your father and I are getting a divorce."

I started to cry. And whilst I continued to cry she explained where she was going to live and that I would be able to come visit her some of the time. I would now be shared like a baton, in a relay race. *Don't drop the baton.* She handed me a tissue and another.

"What would you like for breakfast?" She said popping the last bit of toast into her mouth.

I sniffed back the tears like a good boy. I felt like it was my fault, but instead of expressing this rage, I swallowed it, like a good boy. No point in being a hooligan. I wanted to go back to school. No I didn't.

"I don't know," I said in answer to her question. The phrase became a mantra. "I don't know."

Weston Super Mare, Somerset
30 AUG 1972

Dear Mummy

I hope you are well. When we went to a safari park, I got an elephant toy with pink fluffy hair. I called him Asif and dad got a koala bear called Ajax and when we played putting, I won the first game and Dad won the second game, is it sunny at Dunkeswell?

It is here I have got Brian Close's autograph and It said To Rupert from Brian Close. We sore the lions, monkeys, Cheetahs, and some elephants and Rhinoceroses. The monkeys jumped on over Peoples cars not ours. It was very Hot in the car.

I have got a cricket-scoring book I am having a good breakfast. Is Michael, Kev and the others all right. I may come back to night to Kentisbeare. Please send my Olympic book to the post office as I am getting lots of cards.

Cheddar caves not as good as Kents Cavern

Love Rupert x

I am a sandwich.

7

The General Synopsis

Moderate or Poor, Occasionally Good

THE HIGH CEILING IN the woodwork shop is halved by a lone dusty fluorescent tube. The light pulses are thrown at a rate of 120 cycles per second. A blanket white light flashes onto a buzz of boys wearing dark blue smocks. No goggles or hearing protection for these lads. They lean against workstations crafting with a concentrated intensity. They invoke Minerva, Goddess of handicrafts, as they hack and splinter planks of pinewood. A sense of satisfaction can be felt once the door is closed to the workshop. I stand at a workbench. I sink my chin beneath the rounded collar of my blue smock and grip tight the hammer. Beating flat round head, silver nails, one after another, into the softwood. It brings a satiated pleasure.

Kentisbeare Post Office
Sunday a.m. 3/9/72

Dear Hilda *[That's my Mother]*

Rupert's dressing Gown seems only o/s item ! We shall meet from time to time I'm sure to discuss Rupert. We both want the best for him. I'm living a day at a time and have <u>not</u> gone back on what I said to you last Thursday a.m. So we must wait and see what the future holds. Meanwhile Rupert is looking forward to seeing you – You have his various "dates" from school so contact me as necessary.

Yours sincerely
Harold *[That's my Father]*

HOBBIES

Christmas Term 1972.

The following activities are available this term - Piano, Violin, Melodica, Recorder, Carpentry, Oil-painting, Scraperboards, Card-loom-weaving, Lampshades, Puppets, Tapestry, Paper Flowers, Lettering, Chess Club, Stamp Club, Riding, Judo, Badminton, Shooting, Putting, Pioneers.

Among the chargeable items, *Rupert* says he would like to take the following, so perhaps you would be good enough to let me know only if this is **not** your wish?

	Piano / ~~Organ~~	(£7.50)
	~~Violin~~	(£7.50)
	Melodica	(up to £2.25)
	Recorder	(up to £2.25)
	~~Riding~~	(£9.00 for the term)
OK X	Carpentry	(£2.10 plus cost of timber used)
	~~Judo~~	(£4.20)
OK X	Shooting	(up to 50p)

17th September, 1972.

Please note :- The Calendar for the term and the Newsletter will be sent with the boys' letters next Sunday.

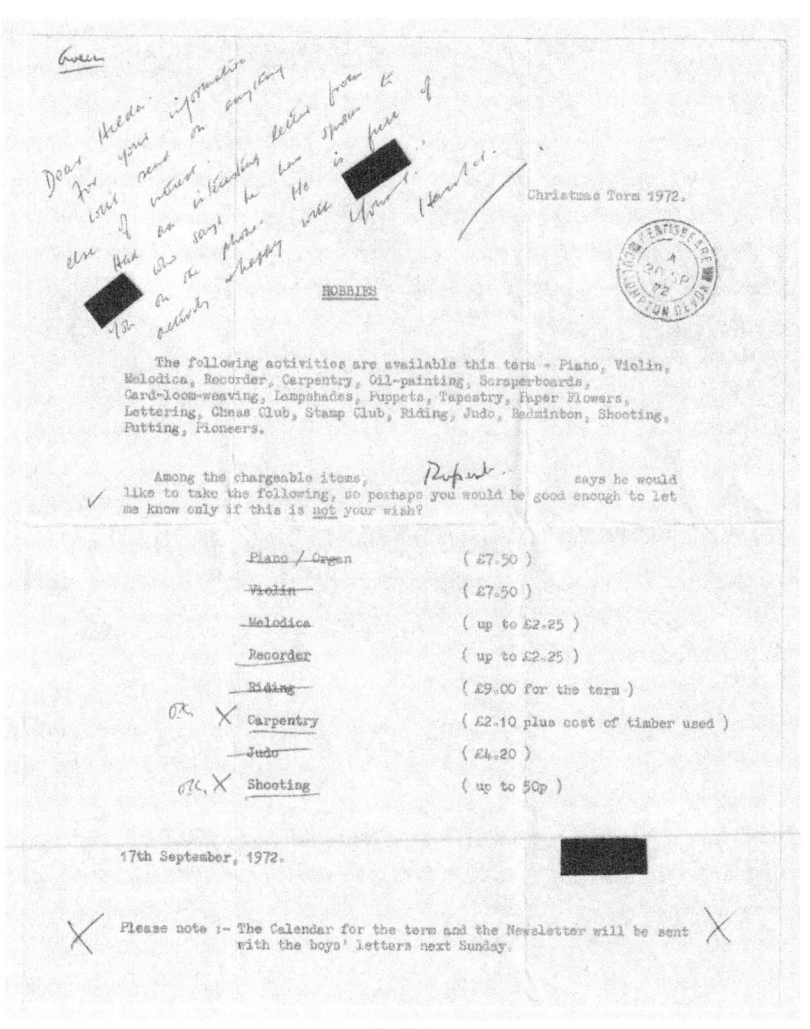

Hobbies

Kentisbeare P.O.
Friday 3 Sept 1972

Dear Mummy

I am looking forward to coming out with you and Kev next Friday. Let Dad know what time you are coming to pick me up. I will send cards to the others from Exmouth to day.

Love Rupert xx

Kentisbeare P.O.
Friday 8. Sept 1972

Dear Mummy
I hope you are well. For my prize I got a book The Misadventures of Dougal. It cost 25p. I am reading it to and they are good stories. Daddy helps if there are any big words but I am getting most of them right. Today it is raining hard but we still might goto Paignton RAF museum. I am send you a photo I did some at Longleat and Exmouth. I hope you like them Noddy is alright. He is wet.
Love Rupert x
PS. Write some letters to me please.

Buckland House
1.10.1972

Dear Daddy
I hope you are well. In shooting I had 12 on the lightest gun. At Football I scored 3 goals in one game. We are collecting some prehistoric animal picture cards in PG Tips have you got any.
Lots of love Rupert x

Buckland House
9th October

Dear Daddy
Thank you for letting me take Ralph Brompton out, I liked it. I enjoy playing with my airport and Scamp is very lively to play with. A boy at school has got mumps.
Lots of love Rupert xx

Buckland House
9th October

Dear mr Green
Thank you for giving me a nice time at Ruperts house and I like his dog very much it has been raining here it was good fun with Rupets soldiers
Love Ralph Brompton

Buckland House
14/10/72

Dear Mummy

Thank you for the letter. The food here is good and I am on table ten and that is outside in the hall. On Saturday we shall be playing a match against St Petroc's I played inside forward

My efforts marks are: Maths Excellent French Excellent English good History good Geography good Scripture good Science good

Love Rupert x

"That's a lot of nails you've put into the table leg there Green!" Said Jesus, the school's carpenter with a chuckle. He stroked his chin with a fat pudgy hand.

"Yes Sir." I said, picking up another nail.

"What are you going to make this term?"

I looked across at the boy leaning in with a chisel. He was poking a block of wood spinning and whirring at terminal velocity at the end of the cold silver-green lathe machine. The nasally *fa-dud-da* whine of sharp metal point against mahogany caused sprouting thin curly shavings to spray out like falling snow. I want to have a go but am far too scared. Too noisy, too much-controlled speed, what if something broke? What if the block of wood fell off, what then?

Buckland House
20.10.72.

Dear Mummy

I have scored 16 goals this term. It is Sunny here now. When I stay with you can I see Skippers Hill please. I hope Rose has a nice wedding I got a plus for Art I am drawing a King with a ruby I will be in the match against Mount House. We have seen a film called The Millon Pound Note it was good.

My effort marks are: Maths Excellent Scripture good English Excellent Science good French ------- History Excellent Geography Excellent

Love Rupert xx

Weirdly enough, because it was the first prep school I went to, Mother took a job as cook at Skippers Hill. It is a strange thing to have done. Maybe there is more to this puzzle than meets my eye... Unfortunately she didn't cook for more than seven whole days before she packed her bags in the night and took flight.

Buckland House
Saturday 21st

Dear Mum

Thank you very much for having me for such a lovely holiday. We are not having a film this week because of Harvest Festival but next week we will. I am in A game playing rugby. I am looking after a new boy called Brian Pike. My hobbies are carpentry, and lettering and chess. What shall I do in carpentry? A bookshelf for your cookery books? How are my lettuces? I got back safely from Brother Number Three's house.
Love Rupert x

Buckland House
28th October

Dear Mummy
Thank you for your letter. What do I do with the wedding invitation. Will I be able to come to it can you tell the Headmaster. I am reading a book called "Five go on a Mystery Moor" I am going to see a film called "Carry on Teacher". On Saturday we play Mount House away. On Friday it is our best day because we get Maths Handwork Art English Science Science
Lots of love Rupert x
Maths good French Excellent English Excellent History Excellent Geography good Scripture good Science good Final Excellent

Jesus the Carpenter smiles and gestures to maybe make a bowl on the lathe.
"No," I said firmly whilst looking at the floor. "I want to make bookcase."
Boys are busy hammering nails and swinging long planks of pinewood about, sanding half-finished bird boxes, tables, and shelves. Many shelves, box cases and spice racks in every shape and size possible are stacked up against an end wall, names marked with a soft pencil scrawl from the hand of Jesus. It smells good in here, vanilla and cinnamon, the varnish is being liberally smeared onto proudly finished pine bird boxes. These creations will outlast humanity and will in some distant future probably be dug up and marvelled at by a future archaeologist species that'll wonder what this one small hole on the side of a box with a sloping lid is and why encase it in a thick caramel varnish like a mosquito suspended in amber?

Buckland House
4th November

Dear Mummy
I hope you are well. Thank you for the letter. The staff had a 'flue injection on Wednesday. I have scored five goals. On John Craven's newsround he said about a

Yeti in the Himalay Mountains. When we played Mount House at football we lost 2-0. Thank you for the book token. Can you send Asif to me please.

Love Rupert xx

my effort marks are: Maths Excellent English good History good Geography good Scripture good Science good

So, it will have four shelves, be *yay* long and almost be too big to fit in the back of a normal car. That's what it turned out like. I spent a freaky age getting to work on the troughs with a chisel after carefully sawing out two lines. It took all term to do and didn't, for some reason, get an obligatory coat of varnish. All carpentry was taken out of the front and left for people to collect when their significant elders arrived. Call it a mix-up and unintentional mistake, you see another boy had made a similar four-shelves bookcase. Mine I have to say was the superior model.

Buckland House
14th Nov.72

Dear Mummy.

I arrived back to school safely. Thank you for the treat at the Dolphins in Brighton, it was a good thing we did not go on the underground train because Mr Cavendish did and the train stopped half way between two stations. I hope you are very well.

Lots and lots of love Rupert .x.x.x.

So, when I was picked up to go home and we loaded up the shelves, imagine my annoyance at seeing another boy's name on the underside of the bottom shelf. He had obviously run off with my creation and now everybody around me said either *Oh dear!* or *Never mind* but it was made apparent that it was tough luck that's how life is so get over it.

Buckland House
18th November

Dear Mummy

I hope you are well. I can do voodoo a kind of witchcraft I did it on Mandrake my guardian I can do it on anyone who has Blue eyes, can you tell me who has got Blue eyes in our family. We had corn fakes, pilchards and fried Bread for Breakfast. We play against Mount House today I hope we win.

Love Rupert x

What is annoying here is the fact that you are brought up on a certain sense of fair play and principles of doing the right thing. To not bully or swear, run in the house, to say please and thank you all the time and of course, say sorry. And when you become a victim to one of these bad unfair things, you are told to shut up.

Buckland House
4th December 1972

Dear Daddy
Thank you for letting me have a nice time. In the exams I came first. I can not wait until Friday to go to see Rose and Nod's wedding. Can you send my slipper to me and my Viking please. I heard an owl hooting last night. My portrait will be on Tuesday, drawn on Tuesday. My examination results are: Maths 4th French 1st English 7th History 1st Geography 3rd Scripture 2nd Nature 4th
lots of love Rupert x

Buckland House
4th December 72

Dear Mummy
I hope you are well. Thank you for the letter, thank you for the telephone nomber, I will send it to daddy. I came first in the exams.
The Headmaster is going to put me on the train and tell the guard to tell me when to get off.
Love Rupert x

9th December 1972 – My sister Rose and Nod get married in St Dunstan's Church, Mayfield, East Sussex. Then it was over the road to the pub on the High Street for food, drink and much merriment. It is a good day. Afterwards Brother Number One drove me back to Hove, talking non stop all the way, wearing his Navy outfit. He gave our sister away because Mother blocked my Father from the pleasure. How that happened I shall never know.

In a brown pastel crayon, the scribbled signature *Hankinson 72* stood out on the bottom right-hand corners of the two portraits of me that had been commissioned by my father. There was a need for two portraits because my parents are now divorced. But I gather you have already worked that out by now. Divorce – it is not unusual around here, but that doesn't mean anything, it still sucks. The more I listen, the more I hear it has infected other lives.

Everybody else gets just one portrait. Well, not the whole school, probably about six of us. Sitting for your portrait meant, in the mornings, time off some horrible lessons. Well, that was good. In the afternoons, time off games. Well, that was an unforeseen bad.

The venue for such a rare artistic adventure was Kelly dormitory, a dark wooden chair placed with purpose on the wooden floor in the centre of the upstairs room. Two south-facing windows would even on this grey day, let enough morning light in for the artist to outline and block colour some of my face in. Kelly College is another public school set on a 20-acre estate in Devon. Their school motto was *Fortiter occupa portum* - Defend your harbours bravely.

I knocked politely and went in. Hankinson was sat behind his easel. He smiled and said the usual pleasantries before a face of concern a look where the bottom lip curls in followed by a long "Hmmm..." a folding of arms and lightly stroking a bearded chin. "Hmm..." He hummed for a bit then whistled a few bars of La Marseillaise or did he intentionally whistle All You Need is Love? I stand on one leg and fidget unsure as to what was supposed to happen. Surely, I will sit here on this chair, and he will draw my picture? Without either of us saying too much, I figure out it is my hair that holds us up. In front of the mirror, with one eye on Hankinson, I brush, and comb and brush and comb do my best to straighten a wayward curly roll of chestnut brown hair. I hate my hair. I give up the struggle, *That'll do*, drop the brush onto the mantelpiece.

In the reflection, I catch Hankinson surgically preparing a selection of autumnal colours. So neatly does he lay out leaf brown and yellow ochre sharpened pencils, placing them on a grey cloth next to the maroon and scarlet pencils, that I feel he might be about to go into surgery. He picks up a teacup and asks me if I want the custard cream lodged against the teaspoon on the saucer. That's a given, I had my eye on it. He told me he noticed. I sit down to self-consciously eat the creamy sweetness and excessively I salivate, rolling the crumbs around and around like a washing machine's end spin and rinse, to make it last, make it last. Content in my victory of scoring a mid-morning snack, I wait, whilst surfing the sugar rush and inevitable onset of boredom, I wait for an instruction.

To generate business and show the rest of the school what was happening, the nearly finished and finished portraits were on display on the streaky grey marble mantelpiece in the hall. On one, unfinished oil painting, the boy's face was a strange emerald green. It didn't look right.

The general conversation and consensus to float about the hall led to the most favourable comment toward my two portraits, *better than the rest*. I cast my eye over the two drawings of me, *no comment*, and the unfinished green oily face reminiscent of *The Green Lady by Vladimir Tretchikoff*, only to roll my eyes heavenward. Guys, it's not a competition and that one's not finished. Still the people will have their say.

First portrait

Mother did not have a say, nor did she choose wisely. She said I was too sad in the first portrait. She took, was given, the second portrait, where I did not directly look out at the world, or more importantly at her.

Second portrait

A holiday-not-holiday letter

8

What's That Word I Keep Hearing?

TODAY DIDN'T START SO well. Not so good. Face to face with a very angry headmaster and only being five days back at school for a new term. He showed displeasure with tightly woven trembling lips whilst looking down his nose at me. Because I am shorter, I am looking up and into his eyes and I have to say, it is dark in there. The feigned look of total innocence has got right up his nose, so to speak and he explained in no uncertain terms what I was about to be caned for. "Tell me boy, from whom did you learn this vulgar word?" His face glowed like a two-bar electric heater. He looked lost for words, he gasped for air. For a start to have released *that* word into the school's atmosphere was more than unforgivable, it was incomprehensible. To have the audacity to let slip such an abhorrent word within earshot of Matron. "Well..." He said, and he grabbed hold of my hair. I half closed my eyes and instinctively turned my head for fear of being slapped. He thought better of it and let go, then bellowed like an ancient water buffalo stuck knee-deep in mud with hyenas approaching. Such was the deafening force of noise discharging from his lungs, the only word I could make out was...

"...ABOMINATION!" and more's the pity, I would have to look up what that word meant.

Matron, for those who don't know, is an angel incarnate. There is our Matron, then three rungs below her on the ladder of saintliness is the Queen Mother. Yes, that's the level of godlike existence I am talking about here. That is what makes this situation so awful. I am in the cooking pot getting boiled alive for a beyond offensive, poor show, gutter language, a flippant remark that she in all her angelic-ness did overhear. It was all eggshells with Matron and I had cracked the egg. This was quite a lecture. And to finish, the headmaster added, I would be expected to go straight from his study up to the sick bay to give Matron a verbal apology followed by a next day written apology, of say, one hundred words with the theme of *Why I will not use that word ever again as long as I have a breath in my body*. Then I was expected to take part in this afternoon's detention, where self-flagellation followed by a cold shower would lead into a call and response of the scriptures, whilst balancing a broomstick on the end of my nose. That's how much of a stinking wretched urchin I was. When he shut up, I was able to breathe again. The air was polluted and smelt like a mixture of Stilton cheese and cigar smoke. I closed my eyes and prepared for whacks.

"Tell me boy, from whom did you learn this vulgar word?" Again, with the questions, his interrogation continued. His left hand, an eagle's talon, clenched hold of my brown school jumper, his nails dug in pinching the skin of my shoulder. I looked up defiantly at him. His top lip began to snarl, and crooked teeth protruded. His hideous freckled face glowed a pillar-box red, errant auburn eyebrows sprouted above black marble eyes. The headmaster was pumped and ready to go. Like a captured old-world vulture he stood in his cage and I am the live prey. I am told to turn round and face the study door, bend over. I place my hands on my knees and didn't know where to look. I sank into the carpet and I listened. The headmaster wrenched open the big old wooden drawer on the bottom of a built-in wardrobe that ran the entire side of the study wall. He stuck his hand into the drawer and rattled the bamboo canes that were sound asleep within. He brought one out and swished it in the air. With a stick in one hand, holding me down with his other, he brought the cane to bear, up against my behind.

Ah! Yes, the mental cruelty metered out. Stomach-churning nausea, a sickness that pulsed through my nine-year-old neck veins, a tinnitus whine within my inner ear. My whole body tingling, the inevitability fuelled by the furnace of my pounding heart, rising adrenaline all fuelling the hot irons of fear that a demon has plunged into my chest. I disengaged the good part of myself and let it run.

So where was the first time I heard this shotgun word? Bent over, I dredged my left brain for an answer, whilst my toes repeatedly jumped inside my sandals. Whilst I counted the strokes... my Skull Cinema screen went from murky glow to full illumination and as I took a seat the episode in question began...

"FUCK!" He said unable to light a cigarette with a match. He stood next to the tractor wheel. He wore green overalls. The John Deere badge over his heart, it stood out in the pale sunshine. It was a cold day. He parked the tractor in the driveway but failed to notice the front wheel had rolled onto next-door's garden, and in doing so, had crushed a gnome and a few daffodils. It wasn't his tractor. He didn't own it. My mother had told me his name, but already I'd forgotten it. He towered over me. I stepped back. What *is* this word I keep on hearing? That word he said. I was having trouble understanding. He coughed and coughed and spat. He thought I was an upper-class boarding school ponce and he would like to demonstrate that fact.

"Are you a virgin? I bet you are." He said finally lighting the cigarette. "With a name like Rupert, what do you expect? Do you smoke, want a drag?" He offered the cigarette. I shook my head, too many questions. I walked backwards to the kitchen door. Let myself in without taking my eyes off Tractor Boy.

Later, after tea, I found out Tractor Boy liked to shout and swear when he was the eldest in the room. Mother and Kev had gone to the pub. Which meant I switched off, disengaged, and fell into silent mode. I listened and observed but avoided eye contact. All six of us are crowded into the box front room, it is getting noisy in here. He barks orders like Kev his father would, at everyone, me included, which was hardly fair. It's got nothing to do with me. I don't even want to be here. I'd far rather be elsewhere. Like back at the post office with my father.

"Fucking tidy up." He shouts. That word again. Mean, easy to say, punchy and there it is again. I figured it out. It is like the next level in profanity, this word is a dirty word. Maybe even the dirtiest of all dirty words. I can't wait to get back to school and tell Mandrake.

"*Fuckyou*Michael!" Shouted the youngest of the younger brothers.

"Then move your fucking toys. I'll throw them out. They're fucking everywhere. I can't fucking sit anywhere." He stepped over a pile of toys only to plant his full weight onto a thick chunk of blue Lego. "OW! Fuck, for fucksake... fucking Lego!"

"*Fuckyou*Michael!" They all shouted like fledglings in a nest.

Now I remember, that's his name. Right there, and what a great name *fuckyou*Michael is. It suits him.

More surprises occurred just then when I noticed as they shouted, that they weren't all brothers. Some of them were sisters. That would explain the girlie names. I thought they were mucking about. Their hair was cut all the same, a hard fringe above their sunken eyes. That neo-gothic lack of sunshine and vitamins pale skin look. It was hard to tell them apart. They all slept nose to tail like vampires in a double bed. Being the eldest, *fuckyou*Michael had his own box bedroom.

In this world, I became aware, of the large family with little to no money, a mother who upped and left, an absent father for hours on end and not much to eat in the house. It is onerous. I am trying not to judge but it is very different and therefore a little difficult not to. I was given *fuckyou*Michael's bed to sleep in. I don't think I will get any sleep. So *fuckyou*Michael would be joining the others in the big bed. He complained bitterly about his predicament and the need to sleep, what with having to go to work in his tractor. Kev, in brackets (father), didn't react too well. He shouted with a broad Devonshire burr in one breath like it was all one-word "*Du-as-yorrr-fffuckin-told.*" Kev raised his right hand as if he was about to knock *fuckyou*Michael into the middle of next week. Mother dissuaded Kev from doing that and suggested they get a drink, drive to the Dunkeswell Arms pub, which they did.

The youngest boy disappeared into the kitchen, and we all, apart from *fuckyou*Michael, had to go and watch the youngest one drink half a bottle of pickling vinegar. They all laughed, as did he. "He likes it!" They shouted at me. "He likes it!" I think he drank the vinegar for my amusement. My not laughing and my look of distress made them laugh even more. "He likes it!" They shouted. "He likes it!" I get it, he likes it. I don't, he does.

Mother had thought it necessary to up sticks and run from the Post Office, around the time, or maybe before the divorce. She left my father for Kev. Seriously? Kev is the father of *fuckyou*Michael and four or five other grunts. The term father is meant in the lightest possible usage of the word, like a soap bubble. Pop! Now can I go back to the post office, please?

I am on holiday from prep school. I have spent time at the post office, the allocated time with my father and now I must do my time with my mother, in her new *Dunkeswell* situation. Her new inherited family. I am plunged into an alternative timeline. And the time is unbelievably slow, it has no purpose. I have no purpose, direction unknown, rubbing shoulders with young feral strangers. With no discernible parameters, the sea is decidedly choppy, I am not sure if it is wise to stand up in this rowing boat. If I stop rowing, how will I make it back to prep school?

Yet Mother was nowhere to be seen because she had driven to the pub or was upstairs in the bedroom, on the bed with Kev. And here spins that word again.

In the front room, *fuckyou*Michael pressed his face right up close to mine. Uncomfortable to say the least. I mean I hardly know the chap. At prep school, it is always arm's length. I say old fruit, could we keep it to an arm's length? There's a good fellow.

He laughed like a Kookaburra and then said with a spoonful of relish. "Rupert, she's having an after-lunch bumpity-bump with Kev. My old man and your mum. An after-lunch tiffin. A fuck Rupert, she's having a fuck! Jesus fucking Christ almighty! Where are you from?"

Once again being the tender age of nine, trying to manage a superiority complex, and having no appreciation of what this word meant, I was having issues as fuse boxes blew and lightbulbs flared to burst in my brain. Intense to say the least. And now the others gathered behind me laughing at my ignorance. They all knew what it meant and I was just sport for these hyenas. I took the metaphorical slaps to the face and considered what if any revenge I might take. I now understand how to say the word, having said that, *fuckyou*Michael tells me it does not compare with the experience. I scratched my head. What experience, is someone now going to show me? I hope not. I'd rather not. It was a most confusing, brutal time. I am not sure I am going to like living here.

The following day, we sat at the kitchen table, like waiting for an ice cream van to never arrive, simply having a dreadful time. But, when I asked, I needed to be here. And so it was after a light lunch of cream crackers and one tin of sardines shared around, watching an inane smile surface on my mother's face as Kev winked and nudged her elbow. We sat quiet and still, apart from *fuckyou*Michael who minutes before had in a massive sulk, stormed out of the kitchen, followed by a cloud of cigarette smoke, gone to sit in his tractor. The rest of us had to watch Mother and Kev climb every step of the creaking wooden staircase. The grinning idiot Kev winked a sheep-like eye at his kids. Kev with his swept-over rusty brown hair and his Noddy Holder sideburns. Quite the looker. A bit of rough. A bit of get it while you can. A bit of Christmas every day. I could only hope the novelty like Father Christmas would soon wear off.

Life's a soap opera and the end credits are about to roll. The theme tune started; it strains through the tiny holes of the pantry window goes under the stairs and out into the kitchen. Slade knock out 'Cum On Feel the Noize' *Fuckyou*Michael blasted it out from the tractor's transistor radio. The others, those younger squabbling siblings, see the end of this episode as some sort of conquest. In triumph, they cheer and clap their hands, they jump around holding the edge of the table making it bang against the kitchen wall and tipping a chair over in the process. They start yelling. They have a new mummy and I have lost mine.

"FUCK!" I said with all that bottled-up holiday-not-holiday rage. I needed to let it out to make an impression.

"That's a bit old hat." Said Mandrake scarcely missing a beat as he nonchalantly turned another page of Three Blind Mice by Agatha Christie.

"No," I said pointing at Mandrake to get back his attention, "No listen, FFFUCK!!" I repeated the word I'd kept on hearing, proclaimed it loud and clear like planting a flag on Mount Everest.

I do like the sound power of my new special word. I picked up the white teddy with the blue jumper and shouted it into his face. That was a big moment for me. Mandrake indicated a warning with a look over my shoulder. That was very generous of him. I turned around and there stood one visibly shaking Matron. She looked like she'd just seen satan himself bite and spit the tail off a white dove and was now sucking out the entrails. A lot of blood. Blood everywhere. I tumbled like a coconut knocked off a holder in a sideshow tent at an Edwardian village fete. I slumped crestfallen onto the dormitory floor. Matron leaned over the end of the bed and snatched the white teddy out of my hand.

"I don't think you'll be needing this anymore, GREEN!" Matron quipped, still visibly trembling. "And another thing. I DO NOT care for that sort of language in my dormitories. The headmaster shall hear of this..." I said nothing and smirked which didn't help the situation. She tucked the white teddy tight under her arm so it couldn't breathe and marched, head held high out of our dormitory, I presumed to go find and tongue-wag the headmaster.

Now if I wore glasses, which I don't, I would have taken them off and rubbed both my eyes before I put them back on, and then I would probably have blown out all the air in my lungs, yawned baboon style and after a moment of resignation, lost to the world, I would accept my fate.

It's God-awful.

> Listen, abomination means like you're a yeti snowman walking about the Himalayas for the rest of your life because you said a rude word and now nobody will talk to you because you've been sent to Coventry which is nowhere near the Himalayas. I don't even know where the fucking Himalayas are.

So don't ask.

9

Snow

I don't remember ordering snow. And yet there it was, delivered to the doorstep. Much, if not all of it, fallen through the night. It looked pretty. And now a lazy morning wind was at play, sculpting snow castles and watchtowers.

Buckland House
15-1-73

Dear Mummy
I hope you are well. Yesterday it started to snow a little, but it has stopped now. I am in Form III and in Eton, a dormitory. Our form teacher is called Mr Cavendish. It is sunny here. I gave the first day Stamps to Mr Fitzwilliam.
Love Rupert x

Our mouths wide open, faces pressed like pickled onions in a jar against dormitory windows. Our eyes wide open, reflecting the smooth white landscapes. Gentle gusts shift the icing sugar snow from gutter to window ledge, ice crystals crisscrossing to add to the coverage of our new pristine playground. It sure looked pretty. The unofficial dawn chorus rang out from the dormitories. "Snow!"

Excitedly, a few of us brave ones descended to the depths of the changing rooms to dress for the great outdoors. We could hardly believe it. Snow on a Sunday with lots and lots of snow, all day to play.

Why this is like Christmas on a Thursday, our hearts a fireside glow. Boxing Day on Friday and we've still got the weekend to go... Oh! Wait... Scratch that. If I am now thinking about being at Brother Number Three's home, which I am, shift work will spoil the season.

Brother Number Three drives off to work. The 2pm to 10pm shift on Christmas Eve, Day and Boxing Day. We are plunged, the rest of us, into a stasis of not doing, in subdued lighting. We are sat around the television because it is glowing. Like the lights on the tree, warming up our eyes, because you can't turn them off, light entertainment, because there wasn't much else to do. And we'd already played our card games. Written out our Christmas cards, I chose a box of Christmas cards with a Robin red breast, perched on a Holly branch with green leaves and cranberry red berries all covered in snow.

The Headmaster wedged himself in the doorway. He stood between us and the snow. "And where do you lot think you're going?"

"Why, outside Sir..." Said Bradley Edwards straightening his smock, popping his collar up thinking it was obvious.

Smit shouted *snow* in Dutch. "Sneeuw!" He slapped his forehead with the palm of his hand and pushed his front teeth out over his bottom lip. It was a bad idea. A wonderful impression of the headmaster but a bad idea. The Headmaster looked suitably unimpressed.

"Not before breakfast you're not." Growled the Headmaster. Smit encouraged by our laughter and not entirely reading the seriousness of the situation, tried but failed to knock the Headmaster out of the way. He took hold of Smit by the throat. He indicated we should hop it with a cursory flick of his chin. We beat a hasty retreat, edging backwards through the inner door, back towards the changing rooms. We withdrew, leaving a somewhat red faced and bewildered, eyes popping Smit behind. His miscalculation was to be our gain.

"He'll probably get two." Said Bradley Edwards, his wrist flicked indicating a swish of a cane.

"Four more like!" Said Hunt.

"What a spanner!" Ellison chipped in. "We're not doing anything wrong."

"Smit is a spanner!" Added Hunt.

Ellison said, "I meant the Headmaster..." We quickened our pace to get to the other outside door.

"Where are you lot going?" Shouted Clifton Wentworth, he skipped towards us.

"Shh! Out." I whispered. We stopped still as we heard a noise like ice cracking in lemonade. It was coming from down the corridor, from the Headmaster's study. We looked at each other, counting, seconds dragged as yet more cracks appeared in the soundscape. They ricocheted down the corridor and up the back stairs. Concerned for our safety, we drifted a few more steps back down the corridor where Thompson emerged from the coats hanging on pegs. He'd been there all the time. "Like several million points for stealth, or what gentlemen?" Said Thompson imitating the Headmaster. No one laughed.

"Shh!!" We collectively hissed at him.

"You Shh!" Replied Thompson. Bradley Edwards and Hunt pushed Thompson against the coats. Bradley Edwards whispered in Thompson's ear. "Shuddup! Smit is getting whacked."

"So?"

Hunt stepped in closer and said. "Well, for a start, we're not supposed to be out of our beds. And if you'd been there, you'd know why, instead you were here hiding like a girl." And for good measure, he knuckle punched Thompson on the top of the head.

"Get off!" Said Thompson pushing Hunt away.

"C'mon let's go..." Whispered Clifton Wentworth, unnerved by the silence.

Outside, the sky was white from horizon to horizon; the tennis court net looked pretty and all was quiet save a lone blackbird perched on low ivy-covered walls, dipping into the greenery for berries. The Blackbird flicked its tail before it took off, broadcasting its characteristic *chink-chink, chink-chink, chink-chink, chink* warning as it left the scene. A gust of wind allowed snow to drop from evergreen branches.

Within moments, a blast of noise. Shouting, followed by the stamping muffled crunch of gumboots running across the ground. And so, we the rabble did appear around the corner of the mansion, us boys yelling, all wrapped up in dark blue smocks, coloured scarves, hand-knitted bobble hats, gloves, cheering and screaming obscenities in sheer delight. Some of us fell, tripped up by others, we gathered up handfuls of the white stuff, threw it in the air. Didn't take long for the group to be smashing and crashing, volleying snowballs through the immediate air, aimed to land in faces and on heads. All the time, the chorus of enthusiastic delight and delirium rang out across the snow blanketed land.

Five pigeons at racing speed flew overhead. They dipped over the conifers that screened St Mary's church from all the wrongdoing within the main house. The outside bell rang and rang. It did not stop until we stopped throwing snow and trudged back in.

The snow stayed for weeks and the day after the next, we were out in it again. So having about an hour's snow, I felt as if I had had enough. Not being able to feel one's hands or feet might have had something to do with it, I don't know, like I said, I had had enough. I left the snow battle, taking hits as I went, yes, I had had enough and wanted to warm up, no big deal.

"Green!" Said the Headmaster. "And where do you think you're going?"

I don't believe it. Not more than three wet steps and I was caught coming back inside, I crept in too.

"Out!" He shouted. What is it with all this shouting?

I complained to the Headmaster about having chilblains, frostbite, gangrene and that I had that no blood feeling in my fingers. You got to believe me, Sir! I had sustained all these things in the last hour. I was colder than I had ever been in my entire life. The wind had turned and an artic power breeze was the cause of my intense misery, Sir! Let me back in...

"Out!"

"But it's not fair..."

Not wishing to incur any more wrath, especially so early in the day, I pushed back out into the Arctic Tundra, the wilderness. Within fifteen minutes, I returned to the back door and this time, I was not going to take any more of this "Out!" nonsense. I needed to get back inside before I became an ice popsicle.

But standing inside the door, the Headmaster once again, protested against me entering, I pushed back and before too long he relinquished control. But only because somewhere he heard a phone ringing. I warmed up and put dry clothes on through crocodile tears. I think I'll put them in my top pocket for another time, I don't mind watching it snow.

Buckland House
20-1-73

Dear Mum

I hope you are well. On Wednesday a boy called Malcolm McGregor fell through the roof of the shooting range. The weather is very wet. The film the week is called "The North West Frontier". Please can you send. Me a Prehistoric Animal Book by Barry Cox published by Hamlyn it is an all colour paperback. In 13 day's time the football colts play Mount House. ~~If you~~ *Could you come at A Quarter past 2. A Buckland House*

Love Rupert x

Malcolm MacGregor did not immediately get up, rather he lay on the floor in a foetus position. I was in the next classroom and when we heard the fall, we all went to have a look at a hole in the ceiling and a body on the floor. Next thing that happened was Mr Whitaker striding through the classrooms, a fixed stare ahead of him. We crowded around and then watched as Malcolm MacGregor was revived, picked up and taken with much haste and fanfare to see Matron. Boys running ahead opening doors and shouting monosyllabic instruction. Other boys came out of the walls to bear witness. Malcolm MacGregor ended up with a bandage wrapped several times around his head. Days later he was told off for stepping outside of the rafters. What a spanner. Obviously his own fault. Sign here, here and here.

Buckland House
27•1•73

Dear Mum
I hope you are well. For Shopping I got A Magnifying Glass. I have had A Letter from Rose and Nod. For French we have A man called Major Templeton. For half term can I bring a boy home Please
Love Rupert x

Major Templeton was no more French than black pudding. I don't think he lasted more than three weeks. About three French lessons.
First: Bonjour!
Second: Comment ça va?
Third: Au revoir!
The masters are slipping through the sieve.
Quick, send reinforcements, send them in the general direction of bucolic Buckland House.
We ran from the classroom out to the front of the mansion where the full moon light bounced off the frozen serpentine lake and fields of snow. It reflected in the tall windows and French doors, where we quickly re-entered the house, running, screaming, stamping up the back wooden staircases and flooding into our dormitories to hide under our beds. All words became whispers.
"And you can *shove off* because we're not coming out!" Shouted Thompson. He liked to break the mold.
"Not until you make us all hot chocolate!" Said Smit. We all cheered and clapped our cold hands.
"You know that's the first sensible thing you've said." Said Bradley Edwards to Smit, he stretched out from under the cover of the metal framed single bed to shake Smit by the hand but instead Bradley Edwards punched Smit on the arm. A friendly punch. At that moment a snowball thudded onto the floorboards, another exploded on the wall, showering several beds with virgin snow. Poking our heads out from under the beds, we all heard the excited laughs of the boys from Kelly dormitory as they skedaddled back along the balcony edge.
"War!" Shouted Smit. He slapped Bradley Edwards on the back of the head and kicked Thompson in the behind as he climbed out from under the bed.

"Right!" Shouted Clinton Wentworth already standing heroically in the middle of the room, "this means war!"

We didn't need anymore encouragement.

10

No Cricket Cricket

WATERLOGGED PITCH. NO CRICKET. Steady drizzle all morning. No cricket. Heavy rain. No cricket. It started to snow. No cricket. An earthquake. No cricket. A tsunami... No cricket.

A volcano erupts in Shebbear. No cricket. A tornado blasts through Sheepwash. No cricket. A meteorite destroys Stibbs Cross. Still. No. Cricket.

Buckland House
May 26th, 1973

Dear Mum
I hope you are well.
The 1st eleven Cricket match on Wednesday had to be cancelled owing to the waterlogged pitch. In Science we are studying worms, we make some irritating liquid for the worms then go outside and make a square and pour the Irritating liquid in the Square and wait for the worms to come up. Then we get a jar and put the worms in the jar with water in it.
My efforts: Latin Excellent Scripture good Maths good Science Excellent French good English good History good Geogarphy good
Love Rupert x

"No! You're it!" I said punching Hunt on the back of his neck. He swung round and gave me a dead leg. It hurt. The evolution of this great game just escalated from a light touch on the shoulder, followed by a chase all over the school, to a poke in the ribs and an argument as to whether we, they or I play *off the ground* rules.

"You spanner! The step is touching the ground." Yelled Clifton Wentworth, obviously he knew everything.

"Yeah, but look, both my feet are off the ground." Said Hunt, he had a point.

It was a ruse to catch your breath. The best game of *it*, for me, was when a projectile was made by scrunching up paper and continuously wrapping sellotape around it until it resembled an oversized snowball, so that when thrown, it would float rather than fly through the air. The projectile ball would not break windows or cause any damage to anyone on the receiving end of a well-directed throw, preferably to the face. Which was a pity since some masters, prefects, boys and friends needed to have the thing smashed into their faces, that was always a satisfying strike.

However, mostly it was good to chase someone and get close enough and with a well aimed throw, to bounce the projectile ball off the top of their head. There would come a point, if you did it too often, that the victim would simply yell. "I'm not playing." And would go and sulk or if they wanted to get me cross, they would calmly sit at their desk and open a book.

When the Sun peeks over the horizon, sending its ivy tendrils of light to dissolve shadows and climb up and over dry stonewalls, to illuminate the woods and forests, to heat the moist dry grass and banish the shadows on the patch of ground where we play colts cricket. That's where I like to be.

The team changed into their whites, and I had requested, being captain, that we be allowed to wear caps, having found out a school secret. The school owned caps. I like caps and felt we should be allowed to wear them. I pleaded with our cricket master, Mr Whitaker, to let us have caps, at least for one match. Mercifully he allowed us but with strict orders to keep the caps straight when on our heads. That was the rule. Nice scarlet and blue harlequin caps, they looked well good. I figured it would say to the opposition *'We look better than you do'*.

Buckland House
June 9th 73

Dear Mum

The Cricket match against St. Petrock's was an exciting draw. They Batted first and declared at 101 for 8, of which 35 runs were byes mostly off our fast bowler. With 30 minutes less batting we scored 83 for 8. Carruthers our captain scored 25. We might have won if some of our team's other batsmen had done better. The weather has allowed swimming every day this week. I am still a non-swimmer. The boys who have tents are camping on the church lawn this weekend. A Party will be plotting the course of the river dart on Dartmoor this Sunday. Looking forward to seeing you at half term.

LATIN Excellent MATHS Excellent FRENCH Good ENGLISH Good HISTORY Average Geography Good Scripture Good Science Excellent

Love Rupert x

Up at the ground, an almost flat field with a gentle slope. One nineteen yard strip of grass was mown tight to the ground, removing all the grass, it had been rolled and rolled. A rectangular box painted with nice straight white lines at each end. A make-do wicket. It looked the part. It was functional and suited our needs. A small basic black scoreboard, had, years ago, been made in the carpentry workshop. It had seven banged-in nails for the numbers. Three nails for the total in top, next, one nail for wickets and on the bottom of the scoreboard, three nails for the first innings score. It had to be dragged up to the pitch, along with the kit bag. Where we stopped was deemed the edge of the boundary. Once there, we would jump about like March hares, kicking our heels up, throwing cricket balls, hitting balls high into the air for catches, practising throwing and hitting a stump, whooping and shouting in sheer delight for the sun up and on our backs. Our white shirts and cream shorts, sleeves rolled up, as we prepared for the match. I stopped, the sweet smell of freshly cut grass, whitener paint on our pads and plimsolls and yes there was some running and skidding too. There is absolutely nothing to be scared of here, no threats or dangerous animals lurking in the bushes, no land mines to accidentally tread on, no snipers up in the trees and nobody was going to get fried in an airstrike. This was an idyllic sleepy backwater where all things were indeed bright and beautiful. How lucky am I, to be here in this moment?

Buckland House
June 23rd 1973

Dear Mum
In athletics, I got a super standard in hundred metres twice and a superstandard in throwing the cricket ball. In Hirdles I came first and got a super standard. In cricket against Mount House I got four wickets and 12 runs we scored 85 for 7. Mount House scored 81.
LATIN Good MATHS Good Scripture Good FRENCH Good Science Good English Good HISTORY Excellent Geogarphy Good
Love Rupert x

Buckland House
June 30th 1973

Dear Mum
Last Saturday the 1st Eleven played St. Michaels. We were beaten by 9 wickets. In a short time, we were all out for 40. St Michaels scored 41 for 1 in 4 overs. Wednesday matches were off owing to heavy rain. It has been delightful to swim

this week. Some boys have had pre-breakfast dips. I am almost a paddler. We have had more sports day practices. Tomorrow there is a Dartmoor trek. Golf Putting and tennis tournaments will be starting soon.

My efforts Latin Good Maths Excellent French Good English Good History Excellent Geogarphy Good Scripture Good Science Good Final Good Points 34
Love Rupert x

Buckland House
July 7th 1973

Dear Mum
I hope you are well. In sports this year I came second in cricket ball throwing. In tennis, I beat Ellison and Smit. I am in the semi-final now. I have to play Bradley Edwards. I cannot win. He is the second-best junior tennis player.
Love Rupert x

My father was a noise in insurance he raised us kids by remote control he said everything is made in China, he quit his job to reclaim his soul. In his infinite wisdom, whilst he ran a small Post Office, my father would like to send me first-day issues of stamps depicting important milestones the royal family had reached. I am a little bit young for this. Mr Fitzwilliam, unlike Mr Cavendish, was interested and took them.

On one occasion, during the summer term, when it got light early and the sky was full of sun, we line up for assembly and the headmaster announces the ruse. My dear father, in all his wisdom, did post with good intention the County Cricket 1873-1973 Test and County Cricket Board Official Medallic First Day Cover. Of course, we weren't privy to what this looked like, but we could only imagine lots of gold lettering and splendidness.

My father suggested holding a Colt's cricket single wicket competition. *Hip, Hip - Hooray!* Everyone, but me shouted. This, my father thought might be more appropriate. On what level of more appropriate I shall never know. Just give the stamps to me. Forgive your parents for they know not what they do. Lord, forgive my father, for verily he is being a spanner. Anyway, the winner would reap the spoils with its certificate of authenticity dated 16th May 1973. A nice book of stamps and a little medal with all the counties that played first-class cricket. I decided I must have it.

"Well..." I said to Thompson the Colts wicketkeeper. "I can't possibly win it or enter even. Can I?"

"Yes, you can." Said Thompson and he ran off to find Clifton Wentworth.

Several days passed and one sunny morning, it was announced that the colts would play for the medallic trophy. I was a little annoyed, having been drawn to play against none other than the scorer. I told everyone I wasn't going to take part or win. However, I simply could not lose that first knock-out match. Letting the scorer beat me, like that's not going to happen.

After lunch, we all traipsed up to the top field. The field I spoke of earlier. The happy field. The rules were agreed upon and off we went. I focused, hit the ball hard and ran and bowled with menace and venom, each scalp only seemed to galvanise my true intention. I must win at all costs. If I left a trail of broken and dejected opponents behind me, then so be it. I was in the business of winning, and before long, I was in the final. Mr Whitaker, acting as umpire, scorer, adjudicator at the coin toss and general spanner watched over the proceedings, with the aloofness afforded by fair play.

A lot was riding on the final match. Things became tricky. I was up against the younger brother of the 1st XI cricket captain. Said captain was a more than good, if not a ruthless, sportsman. I did my thing and was sledged and heckled, by him from first slip, for my trouble. I held my resolve until eventually, as I knew it would, the moment arrived. I hit the ball between two fielders, watched the ball bobble and roll over the uneven ground, to the boundary. Four runs through mid wicket, the winning runs and that was that - cheers for me and lots of tears for younger brother, the loser. On hearing the news of my triumph, the headmaster said, "That's typical!"

The prize was nice if you were like fifty years old. Three postage stamps featuring a cartoon depiction of the master W G Grace playing a forward defensive stroke, the second stamp showed W G Grace standing holding his bat behind him. And finally, W G Grace walked, presumably having been dismissed, back to the pavilion. Next to the stamps was a silver coin with a picture of all the first-class cricket playing counties on one side and a batsman and a wicketkeeper in front of Lords Pavilion on the other. All nicely wrapped in a green plastic wallet.

I won. I won. I won.

11

Happy Horror-Days

ALL SMILES, I TRAVELLED back to a home or something that resembles a home. Where mother lived in Hove, East Sussex.

Brother Number One and wife Geraldine in back garden in Hove, days before they emigrated to Australia

I wake up and make myself some breakfast. Mother is at work. Happy horror-days, the time of my life. Better than being at school. Hold on... Scratch that. I look around the basement flat here in Brighton and Hove and wonder what time my mother will be home from work and whether it was today Rose would come round to visit me. Brother Number One and Geraldine visited with news of a big goodbye. I am sad. Then Brother Number Four with Helena emigrates to Celle, Germany. Where is everybody going? On these days, I am sadder than the saddest sad of sad. Which I don't have to tell you is pretty sad. Sad is never pretty. Sad is being slumped on the couch, detaching one's self, the you that makes you – the real you, from one's body. Not a you who you made up because you watched too much TV. I return only to vacantly stare at the square patterns on the living room carpet. After a while, I get up and switch the TV on.

It's not that I am lonely. It's just that I am alone and with no timetable. No friends to play with. No family to speak of. The shock of the last few years has left me a bit numb at what to do with myself. I feel a bit like one of those pinballs bouncing back and forth, getting sprung by the flipper arms until each night I become a lost ball event, fall into the black hole of sleep. And then fall through the night dreaming soft pink marshmallow dreams. Hold on... scratch that, I lied. I don't have any dreams at all.

One wet and windy morning during the horror-days, a large brown envelope arrived. The old postman had trouble pushing it through the letterbox. He tapped on the door. I opened it and took hold of the letter, it was from Buckland House School. Back in the living room, with the door closed, I cut open the envelope, pulled out the contents. It was a photograph. A black and white photograph. I smiled and remembered the end of term prize-giving event, held outdoors on the lawns above the sunken tennis court. A super posh-looking lady had turned up, said a few words to us boys and then got on with the prize-giving. This years guest of honour to give out prizes for the summer term, the sporting achievements...

The whole school gathered around the table to witness the event. The headmaster and Mr Whitaker aid her. Towards the end of the session, my name is called, along with Ellison for The Sportsman of the Universe Award. *Fnarrr! Fnarrr! Fnarrr!* Because we are both so awesome, *Fnarrr!* We must share the award. *Fnarrr!* No flip of a coin to decide in front of the whole school. *Fnarrr!* We are both so *Fnarrr!* Happy because there is usually a big *Fnarrr!* Prize to take home. *Fnarrr! Fnarrr! Fnarrr!* Like peacocks, we share a look of recognition walking towards the prize giving table to collect our Hockey sticks! Hold on... scratch that...

We are given a hockey stick each. Forget all the *Fnarrr!*

Hockey sticks and some silverware that we are told to hand back immediately and never see again. Wow! Hockey sticks. I have to quickly change the look of disappointment to... *I can hardly contain my excitement! Yeah, out of sight, hockey sticks.*

We don't play hockey at the school anymore and there is nowhere, apart from kicking up the sneeze-ridden dust of the old gym, to sensibly play in. And besides it would only be the two of us hitting a tennis ball back and forth if we did. So great, what a lovely, if a little useless, prize.

But hold on, you ungrateful urchin wretch, isn't it great?

Look hockey sticks! And what an impressive prize, because most of the other boys smiles have turned to envious glowering. Which, I guess is the purpose of these self-esteem crushing events. Sadly for the hockey stick, it didn't last more than one of my Mother's house moves. I am not sure the hockey stick even made it out of the plastic wrapper. Life lessons served to experience invaluable feelings of pointlessness.

In the photo, I can see I am torn between shaking the posh lady's hand or receiving the silver cup the headmaster is waving in front of our noses. Mr Whitaker looks on with his customary, compulsory grin. Mr Whitaker was more than a pair of black national health glasses sitting on his nose. Not the fashionable spectacles Michael Caine or Peter Sellers wore. Just the bog standard spectacles, no fanfare needed. As well as the straight look, Mr Whitaker was tall. We got neck ache to see his face. His head was wider at the top with wispy strands of grey hair that blew like reed grass in the wind. He was predominantly bald. What hair he did have was as a rule, tidy around the edges of his huge ears that stuck out as wide as exterior wing mirrors on classic American cars. When not caning boys or running the tuck shop, he would spend hours in the nets bowling medium pace, a nagging bouncy length, as well as showing boys how to play the forward defensive cricket shot. You never know in life when you might need a forward defence. Like when you are approached by someone with wandering hands.

The whole school is dressed in grey suits with short trousers. With the same blue and brown stripe tie. My hair is a mess. I need a haircut. I do so hate my hair.

I put the photo back inside the envelope and dropped it onto the coffee table. After awhile, I switched the television on.

What else is there to do?

12

Bosoms

Cow milk in stubby glasses set out on a trolley in the muddy boot room, the first-morning break. The stale odour within the room, a mixture of air-dried feet, wet laces where all the rugby and football boots would meet. The cold white creamy milk downed in a gulp painted top lips white. We are the laughing dwarves. Then we read the team sheets. There is joy and disappointment. I scan the team sheets looking for my name, with an insouciant shrug, I head back to the classrooms. I have failed again to make the football team; I am written up as the 12th man touch judge. Touch judge, run up and down the creosote line waving a flag. Touch judge, representing the school and conducting oneself with best positive behaviour and assisting the referee with the offside ruling. Hold on... scratch that, not at this level. No, it'll be more – *I say touch judge, I think you'll find, it is the opposition's throw in.*

Back slouching at my desk, I practise looking sullen, like shoegaze sullen, with thumbs in my pockets. Inwardly, I am a little embarrassed. You see, Father is travelling up, to watch me play in this home game. And he'll get to see me as... touch judge. At lunch, I confess this to Mr Whitaker our coach, our mentor, whilst we sat on Table Number One. Mr Whitaker looks ahead like the sphinx, unmoved.

Buckland House
13/10/73

Dear Mum
Thank you for the conkers and string and skewer. I am going to count them. I am sorry to hear that Nod broke his leg and wrist. I am going to write to him as soon as I can. In Science I have made some crystals. The match against Wolborough Hill was cancelled. We had a fire practice on Wednesday. On Sunday there will be a film called "High Society" it is a musical.
Love Rupert x

my efforts - Latin 5th good Scripture good Maths 11th good Science good French 9th Excellent Final good English 8th good History 10th average Geogarphy 12th average

Is it me or are the Sunday night films getting older and older? *High Society* 1956. Well polished folly! Although Grace Kelly was mystifying in the extreme.

> BUCKLAND HOUSE,
> BUCKLAND FILLEIGH,
> BEAWORTHY,
> N. DEVON.
> EX21 5JA
>
> Telephone: Shebbear 222.
>
> 20th October 1975
>
> Dear Mum,
>   Thankyou for the letter, I am going out with Dad for half term. On the 24th there will be a football match against St. Michaels. The film tomorrow is called "Geordie" it is the film we saw on a night in the Summer holidays & about the Scots man who went to Australia in 1966 and won the hammer throwing. There are No efforts this week. It has been very wet and today's match has been cancelled.
>   love
>   Rupert xxxx

Yet another prep school letter

"Alright." He says after several days deliberation. My name is swapped for another boys and I am now the new centre forward. Everybody! Big shouts out for Mr Whitaker our coach, our mentor, our saviour and my new hero.

On the day, feeling like an emperor, I puff out my chest with pride. I am spurned on as father shouts encouragement from the touchline. One of those fathers shouting is mine. I feel great. The whistle blew and I scored two goals. Nailed it! It never ceases to amaze how well a person can play when somebody you love is watching. Afterwards, we are allowed ten minutes to talk before we are encouraged to say our goodbyes and run along to the showers. We mustn't keep Mr Harrington waiting.

Buckland House
27th October 1973

Dear Mum

Thank you for the letter. Today the 1st XI play against ST Petroc's and colts. On Wednesday when the 1st XV and the colts played against St Michaels, the 1st XV won 13-10 and the colts won 2-0. Wilson and Smit scored. In the exhibition I am putting in another turtle. To morrow night is going to be a lecture and a film about Dr Barbados homes. I am in the choir. I have been moved into a new Dorm called Bryanston.

Love Rupert x

Latin Good, Geography average, Maths Excellent, History good, French Excellent, Scripture____ English good, Science average.

Everybody knows the language of Hymns and Psalms is decrepit. This next hymn we are obliged to sing is the standout. We are the respected nice boys of the school; we must be, or our illustrious music teacher Mrs Sterling would not have personally selected us to be in her church choir.

We are standing for this practice in Form I, a massive classroom next to the main badminton hall. We turn the pages to find the next hymn. A hymn written by Charles Wesley in 1740. He was responsible for *Hark! The Herald Angels Sing*. Mrs Sterling leans in and the old piano responds, we aim to sing the first line with pure castrato tones, loud and clear with good diction until...

Jesu lover of my soul let to me thy bosom fly...

I bury my head into the hymn book and fall about laughing, I don't know who else does. Mrs Sterling is not amused. The C major chord that so beautifully hung in the air broke down into mechanical clanks of rods and rocker pivots. Mrs

Sterling's foot released the sustain pedal, the strings are at once dampened. We shuffle about still giggling awaiting instruction; she pulls a tissue from a sleeve of her black cardigan. She began vigorously rubbing the tip of her long pointy nose. "Let's try again…" She notices who is not ready for the count-in.

Calm returns to the room. We try again and this time we all laugh. Mrs Sterling stops puts her hands on her lap and raises her plucked eyebrows. Her face smooth as a bone China doll, shows no emotion. Her bright eyes sparkle. There is a long pause for *all* the childish laughter to stop. We will wait until there is a complete and respectful silence. Only then do we launch into the hymn and stop. Start again and stop. Again and then again and again we keep stopping until she is satisfied no one has as much as a crinkle on their lips and everybody pronounces the line correctly. For anyone listening on the other side of the door, they must have been creased up, hearing the choir bellowing out *bosom* sixteen times in a row accompanied by a C major chord on the old piano.

The practice ends and two rows of boys facing each other crack open a smile. Ellison collects the hymn books and mouths the word '*bosom*' as he takes hold of the last book, cupping his free hand over his chest. It does not take much to set us off. Mrs Sterling angers, she lifts the piano lid and bangs out the chords, the tempo speeds up from *allegro to presto*. With haste, the hymn books are thrown into the air, caught and ripped open to Hymn 193. We lift up our hearts and we sing.

When you're a juvenile you are amused by juvenile things and for us at 10 years old to even say the word bosom, let alone sing it, would be like watching BB's flying buttresses bounce as she ran down La Grande Dune du Pilat in Bordeaux, France.

O Mercy! I can hear the angels sing!

On a Thursday around 10:15, I have piano. It's not much to remember. A piano lesson with Mrs Sterling. And on this particular Thursday, I have my first one. Mrs Stirling chooses a book from a pile of thin landscape music books atop the piano. She has shoulder-length swept-back Raven black hair and does not smell like she is anyone's Mummy. A smile wouldn't go a miss. She is flat and lean and doll like, not enough sun. I am learning to play the piano because I so loved to play around on the piano at Aunty Florries. It got noticed and now here I am, at Buckland House School. When's lunch?

She slides the book she wants out from under the others and opens it, after writing my name on the top right-hand corner. She has neat handwriting. Would you look at that, my very own music book. Mrs Sterling points at one of the dots on the page. She has long elegant piano fingers. Well manicured fingers you'd expect to find wrapped in fur and on the end of the arms of a Countess, possibly Russian or French. On closer look, she does have well-manicured nails. She has two bunched-up rings on her left hand third finger, a gold band and a diamond ring. We are alone. Alone with an upright piano, two chairs and another one of those ridiculously large windows and beyond another rococo ceiling with a solitary lightbulb. I count 3x5=15 panes of glass, oh look, the grey clouds are back, feels like it might rain. No games again. That's a lot of lines and dots. The title of the piece is Little Ducks. Hang on she's talking to me...

"Every good boy deserves favour. And this note here is middle C." She plays it - ding! Middle C, that's great, I am learning to play the piano. I like missing Maths to play piano. This is easy. Just wait until I show my friends Middle C.

For my birthday, I was gifted a tape recorder. And I use to love recording my self and others talk. I would obsessively hit the rewind button, sending the tape back to the beginning of the reel. So this is what I am going to do now. Hit the rewind button to a time before I was in the choir...

Mrs Sterling is also the organist for the church services on Sundays. She efficiently runs the choir. I want to be in the choir. I am told that I am not going to be in the choir until a place becomes available and that could take years.

In the meantime, to show I am serious about joining I must be seen to join in with every Psalm and Hymn and prayer and look angelic at church next Sunday and the one after and the one after that.

One Sunday morning, I fully commit. In St. Mary's church, there are rows and rows of pews. At the business end, where the choir float perfectly a few inches off the ground in a brightly lit bubble of dressed-up angelic-ness, while the rest of the congregation is squashed in fighting for breath in the stench of nasty schoolboy smells, I stand up and sing and put on a jolly good show. It doesn't go unnoticed that I am the patsy and later on I am known as the punchbag who joins in with everything the choir do. It's all theatre. The choir dresses up in blue cassocks with white frilly surplices and a medal on a long blue ribbon. Boys dressing up. It's either the Bible, the flag or the gun at this school.

The choir process into the church behind the vicar, who in turn is behind a small boy carrying a long crooked stick. That symbol of torture. The Cross. The church floor was a pavement of colour, tiny mosaic tiles of light blue, dark blue and blue. In church, the rule was to shoe gaze and look bored. Listen to the word. Join in if you have to but don't mess about. Unless you wanted to mess about, messing about had its consequences. It was so very boring unless you were a churchwarden or in the choir. I felt I might like the buzz of the choir, so I headed in that direction. Besides you got half day Merit Holidays and the chance to leave school go somewhere different, like the time we were driven to Exeter Cathedral to sing with fifty other boy choirs from the county. In the cathedral we didn't see any bosoms fly.

Mrs Stirling is flat. She has no bosom to speak of but she does have a Grace Kelly elegance about her. Grace Kelly was not flat, she was very lively. The latest Matron has bosoms and smiles. She lets us know too. The Headmaster's wife doesn't smile or have bosoms. Mrs. Lancaster does, Mrs Sinclair, not sure what's going on under that tabard and no one had better ask.

After the sex education incident, seeing all that flesh on TV and probably for the first time since our dear sweet consciousnesses kicked in, witnessing the full realisation and beauty of unshackled bosoms, our interest and notion that size matters grew, not that we would openly talk about it. But we would furtively glance across the room at each other, gesture and laugh.

Brian Pike and I once managed to sneak into the rhododendrons to eat his digestive biscuits whilst playing *follow thy neighbour* with his pin up girls pack of playing cards.

It beats playing conkers.

13

Dagga-Ragga

Hospital corners, light blue blankets, repeat after me.
Hospital corners, light blue blankets, wooden floors, repeat after me.
Hospital corners, light blue blankets, wooden floors, a large circular rococo plasterwork ring on the ceiling in the middle of the room. Repeat after me.
Hospital corners, light blue blankets, wooden floors, a large circular rococo plasterwork ring on the ceiling in the middle of the room, cracked window glass, a rusty fire escape and a multitude of cold draughts. Repeat after me.

Bryanston holds many beds. To reach this dormitory, you must scamper like a mouse runs over hot pipes. Shoot along the balcony edge under the great dome that doubles as a portal to outer space, not heaven. Step over the door threshold and run, dive head first into bed. It is a long way to get back to the facilities. It is a long way to go. There is plenty of room to play inside this bed chamber. Numerous beds line the walls, with two bunk beds at the opposite end to the tall windows and a door that would in the case of a fire be the emergency exit. There is time, if you hear someone shout, 'KV'* - no one is going to creep up on us and be creepy.

*'KV' *Cavere* is Latin, it means Beware! Therefore 'KV' is the shortened version.

I am in bed and I am excited to read the borrowed book about a pride of Lions in Africa, I have waited for an age for my friend Bradley Edwards to finish and hand over this book that I now hold in my hands. My friend in the next bed has told me such wonderful stories about the imagination held within its pages, I gasp as the words begin to chant a spell.

We talk and rest in our beds. The clocks have changed and we are allowed an extra hour in bed. I don't know if it is but it must be Sunday. Up dressed and downstairs, I have a sickness; I am fatigued, run a temperature. Breakfast cornflakes, sweet milk, orange flakes of crunch-crunch-like blotting paper and a china clay taste, milk and magnesia. I stand up, bend over hold my stomach and dash, shivering, sweating. I knock open doors, fled down corridors to get to the outdoor bogs. With hardly a moment to spare dagga-ragga discharges with all the cacophony of a plastic sack of pebbles tipped into a bucket. Groaning in relief, twisting my neck and turning a rose pink, I choke down a mouthful of cornflakes, before coughing the lot up onto the toilet's stone floor, looks like a Van Gogh Sunflower. Gratitude that the main event is now behind me. But I still needed help. I yelp, "Matron! I need Matron." No answer. Losing the power in my legs.

So now officially I am ill in bed with the 'flu. The dagga-ragga is less frequent. I have not eaten. When I do eat, within an hour I get the return of the dagga-ragga and I have to time my run from Bryanston dorm to the bogs. Will there be time to put a dressing gown on, slippers? No. This is day three and I am not on the road to recovery. I feel shivery but I am not cold. The bed is one giant clam. Untucked white sheets and a pale blue blanket. The tiny hairs on my legs are so sensitive and sore to touch. I lie back down. I am bored from counting the tiny white squares in all the cornices. Why do they even bother with that decoration between the wall and the ceiling?

With a headful of self-pity, my hand holding my chin, I fall asleep, my beautiful subconscious punts a rugby ball of suppressed emotions high into the air and when they thump into the mud they bounce into touch. I chase after the ball I have a strong devotion to the team. My team. Before I can reach the ball I slip in the mud and land on my derrière. It is wet in the mud. I get up and run and run. And I run to the bogs but I never quite make it. My dreams are nightmares.

"Argh!" I cry. It is no longer day, it is a dark night and everyone's asleep. "Argh! HELP!! Dagga-ragga in the bed."

"ATTACK OF THE DAGGA-RAGGA!!" They shout and laugh...

"MATRON!"

"Shh! Boys why are you shouting?"

"Matron, Green's dagga-rag-gurd the bed." Shouts Thompson.

"ATTACK OF THE DAGGA-RAGGA!! ATTACK OF THE DAGGA-RAGGA!!" They continue to shout, only now because Matron is here they jump up and down on their beds, monkey laughing.

"Yes alright..." Said Matron. "I said ENOUGH!" The boys fall silent and some semblance of decorum returns to the dormitory.

I am unclean and therefore frog marched and plonked shivering into a warm bath. A bar of soap chucked in and told to get on with it. I wash all the dagga-ragga off my white body and pull the bath plug. Teeth chattering. I am returned dressed in fresh pyjamas, wrapped in my dressing gown and dropped into bed. I soon fall back to sleep. "No, more soiling the bed." Instructs Matron.

The next day begins. The friends and other boys having dressed and left for breakfast, time is tedious. Being ill with nothing to do and not feeling like you want to do anything too. Rain stop play. A day waiting for the next glass of water to be brought to you. Then I hear footsteps along the balcony walk. Matron appears shaking a thermometer in her right hand. "Ahh!" She gestures. I open my mouth. The thermometer goes under my tongue, sticks out my mouth, it wants to wriggle about. It says Matron I want to play. "Hold still." Says Matron. She half smiles and then coming to her senses checks the second hand on her small upside down Timex watch. Awkward silence. Awkward silence. Awkward Matron. Awkward thermometer. Awkward illness. It's all just... well, awkward.

Amo, amas, amat, amamus, amatis, amant. The Latin fills the dead space between my ears. *Amabo, amabis, amabit, amabimus, amabitis, amabunt.* Takes my mind off the breathing silence.

Amo – I love.

"What's my temperature?"

Amas – You love.

"Pardon?" Says Matron. I shake my head, a rare moment of eye contact, my thoughts, *I can't say anything with this stuck in my mouth, can I?*

Matron tore the thermometer from my mouth the glass bulb catching a bottom tooth on its way out. I hate it when that happens it's not natural. Sets my teeth on edge.

"Oh Green, you've still got a temperature. Quite a high temperature." She checks my pulse.

Are you disappointed I'm still alive? She stood up. *I'm listening tell me more. I was expecting to hear more.*

I watched her leave, her metronomic behind struts left, right, left, right across the dormitory's wooden floor.

Er... Matron?

"Those footsteps sound like a sharpening blade. Perhaps you're going to get eaten for dinner? Hello! Feeling any better?" **Blue Monster** turned to look at me. **Blue Monster** with big feet was sat on my legs. A split along the lower side of the head opened up like the beginning of a growl. Revealed tiny rows of sharp little teeth. A deep scarlet red swell with a rolling tongue. It was then that I realised when **Blue Monster** spoke, it was inside my head. Which was weird. Like in two places at once. Outside my head and inside too. What is that... My conscience?

"What do you want?" I said trying not to look too scared or concerned at what I was now talking to. "And get off my legs. Can't you see I am not feeling well?"

"What I want is…" **Blue Monster** hissed but never finished. It closed his deep red mouth hiding all those tiny teeth. "Ssh! Listen. What's that music?" It said. Its claws struck out from the body, four pointed blades pulsed up and down. Hardly moving as if cooling down an orchestra to *pianissimo* before the soloist sings an aria. It looked to be in some kind of distracted bliss.

I wondered if now was the time I should scream. Recall Matron, tell her about this **Blue Monster** sat on my bed. I decide better not, **Blue Monster** dipped its head in agreement to my not calling out and Matron's footsteps diminish like the drip, drip, drip of rainwater. Matron made her exit all the way off to the end of the balcony. A whoosh of silence filled the room. **Blue Monster** says, "What are those footsteps, Marilyn Monroe, Grace Kelly, Greta Garbo, or Rita Haywood?"

"Worth." I interrupted. "Rita Hayworth!"

I close my eyes in the hope of going to sleep, not forever just until next Sunday. I didn't and don't sleep, it's eleven o'clock in the morning hardly night-time. I crouch into a fetal position. Gathering the sheets and blanket around me. I still shiver. I am not cold my knees knock, my teeth chatter, my back aches as do my clenched fists as they tug at the blanket. My head feels as if I am running through a wind tunnel. I close my eyes, I feel as if I am getting smaller. I open them, close them. I rise above the bed and float off, rise higher towards the ceiling. I am slowly turning around and around. I open and close my eyes. This time falling back down and in doing so I crash into my body. I am all in but for one leg that didn't quite make it. I kick out, it snaps and cracks back in. I shiver for a bit longer than is necessary. I close my eyes and this time I fall hopelessly…

"Hey Green, wake up! Matron says you need to get up and make your bed." Said an oversized Hunt standing by the bed. There is little empathy for the sick.

"No, she didn't."

"Yes, Matron said to make sure he doesn't forget hospital corners." Said Duncan Campbell hardly able to contain his excitement.

"And Matron said you were to drink this." Said Thompson offering a red mug for me to hold.

"What is it?"

"Milk!" said Thompson without batting an eyelid.

"Just milk?" Said Duncan Campbell laughing like a hyena.

"Shut up!" They both scolded in unison to Duncan Campbell.

"Alright…" He said shaking his head and trying not to laugh. He took a step back.

"Take it!" said Thompson. "Matron said it'd make you better." I take hold of the mug.

"You have to drink it in one," said Hunt.

"Down in one." Duncan Campbell shouted. I stick my nose into the mug but smell nothing. I look for treachery in their eyes, take a little sip.

"In one!" Thompson chuckled. Duncan Campbell began to burst at the seams.

"What's in it?" I ask. "C'mon tell me..."

"Milk." Replied Thompson, now all smiles "I swear..."

"And something else..." Sniggers Duncan Campbell.

"I was about to drink it. And now I'm not..."

"Shut up, you spanner." Growled Hunt as he swung a fist at Duncan Campbell's nose. Campbell swayed out the way, retreated to a safe distance sits down on a bed. Thompson looked back at me, "Matron said to."

I tip the mug up and pour its contents down my throat. The bit that is not milk drops into my mouth, I swallow it.

"Raw egg! Raw egg!" Duncan Campbell shouts and jumps about. Hunt chases him out of the room. Thompson grabs the mug out of my hand and follows. I hear them shouting, laughing and screaming at each other as they disappear into another time frame. With the palm of my hand I soothe my stomach. **Blue Monster** smiles and winks, it is laying on the bed next to mine. I have stopped breathing and my bottom lip sticks out. My mood darkens.

"I hope..."

"Shut up!"

"I was only going to say, what a nasty trick to play on you..."

"Shut up!"

"And I hope sincerely the raw egg works." I flick a V sign, **Blue Monster** chuckles.

"Yeah, but raw egg!"

"Bog... off!"

And with that **Blue Monster** vanished, I expect it was nicely satiated, therefore mission accomplished. It was feeling my anger and growing stronger by the minute. And I am left fuming. The shivering starts again and my stomach turns somersaults. I grab my dressing gown bail out of bed and run. Can't stop running. Must get to the bathroom. **Blue Monster** appears and flies alongside me singing that most famous of Puccini's arias. It is a classic piece of music and we are in a classic setting running along a balcony for it to be sung. I'm not singing it because I am concentrating on getting to my destination. I am halfway. **Blue Monster** is singing and the words ring out like a church bell across the divide that is the dome that will, if you want it, take you to Heaven. I don't, I want to go sit on the toilet, thank you.

"Dagga-Ragga, Let no one sleep…"

14

Suffering In Suffolk

THROWING A CLENCHED FIST in the air, I spread out my fingers, exploding like a deep space supernova. Sparks spray out of my fingers, falling, bouncing off the street pavement. I swivel my wrist, twist my body around like a clockwork ballerina. I add another pirouette, only to over balance and blunder through white doorways leading to Exeter St David's main platform.

Many times I have stood on platform one but this time I have no idea where I am headed beyond Paddington, because once again Mother has upped sticks to another backwater. Only this time, even further away from Devon. Into obscurity, way off the beaten track. She headed East beyond London, Oh boy! to Suffering Suffolk. It stinks of Mother's mantra: *Somewhere nice you'll like it!*

This time, Mother has a housekeeping job, probably just for the summer, for a farmer and his convalescing wife who had had a hip replacement. Which back then, shouldn't have been the ordeal it was. Being hip was another thing entirely and something I left Rose and Nod to do. Well, one consolation is, I've never heard, been or seen Suffering Suffolk before now. I think they play minor counties cricket and sit and watch the sun go down. Another flat backwater. Losersville.

It was another one of those summer holiday-not-holidays when first I landed, all fake-smiles, my spoon ready for the sunshine flakes, small steps, giant creeps for mankind, upon the flatlands of Suffering Suffolk. The smoke rising from harvested fields, they're double ploughed around the edges to stop the fire jumping but sometimes the fire liked to jump. Great to be travelling again and away, a long way away from the rain at Buckland House School.

Mother's new masters seem friendly enough, for old people. In the farmhouse kitchen, I am subjected to Jimmy Young on BBC Radio 2. What a card he is. Non stop talking. And what is this mulch we are listening to? It is music, but not as I know it. The Carpenters play for the fifth time in a row...

Mr Elwood, the arable farmer, chats without listening to the radio. He nurses instant coffee and crunches on a plateful of broken biscuits. He studies my every move. I don't care for coffee. Mother is being Mother, that means not being anything I recognised since the last time I saw her. When was the last time I gotta see her, where was it, Happy Hove, no. Distressingly defective Dunkeswell, no. I can't think where... I am wary and alert because she is in work mode, playing at housekeeper and the last thing she wants is her offspring moping around spoiling things. The look she just gave me explains fully, with the ink still wet at the bottom of the page, the impeccable behaviour contract I imagine I just signed. Why does everything have to be done by telepathy?

This is 1973. I went, usually alone, from one end of England to the other... So I am rather stuck here and restless, with little to occupy my time. The gulf between school time and home time is like from here to the Moon. What to do. Indeed what to do. Oh! Where are my things, my toys and belongings, my identity?

There is always my love of cricket. The Test Match. The magnificent West Indies are almighty. In this test match, they've scored more runs than I've had hot dinners. I love their style. How they hit the ball and knocked the stumps out of the ground. At least the sun is shining outside. However, I would rather sit inside and keep the score in my little cricket scorebook. Important job.

This job was going well until I was confronted by a cross version of the housekeeper, who used to be my Mother, who suggested I should scramble, and get outside. Get some fresh air. Orders rather than suggestions. Hop to it.

I comply and go find something to do. Where are my toys? I find some drawing paper. I am about to lie down on the grass and draw the little lake by the front lawn, it is all soft greens and browns and the silver birches are speckled, their green leaves sway about casting shadows in the stillness of mid-morning. It is nice and quiet. What was left of the early morning clouds has now moved on and evaporated with the arrival of the yellow Sun. I love the sun. It is climbing and sends its warmth. A breeze drifts by sharing the loveliness of the clear air. A blackbird on a telegraph pole starts jerking its tail feathers. It assesses the scene, takes off from its perch and swoops down onto the grass by the edge of the small lake.

I can draw and with pencil and paper I am about to draw when Mr Elwood steps into my light and casts a shadow over me, his softly spoken voice says, "D'you want to go for a ride?"

At first, I am startled by his presence and unsure exactly what he means. Go for a ride?

"Um... Where?" I ask politely.

"For a ride." He replied shrugging his shoulders.

"Okay."

So I drop the art stuff back onto the farmhouse kitchen table and meet him round the back where he sits waiting in the archetypal Land Rover, with its engine sounding a bit clogged. "No Whiskey, you can't come." Mr Elwood says to the Jack Russell with a brown patch over his left eye. The dog goes back and sits obediently next to the somewhat larger black Labrador called Pip, who lies in the sun by the kitchen door. He's busy on a post-breakfast snooze. It is the Suffering Suffolk way.

The Land Rover lurches forward and so starts the tour of the farm. After several minutes of silence with Mr Elwood looking across at me then back to the old farm road watching the cock and hen pheasants scattering into the undergrowth. "Do you ride a bike?" He asked to break the spell.

"Yes."

"Good, we have one you can borrow..."

"Marvellous," I said feeling like I might finally be able to relax. The journey beings, I look around and see how the Suffering Suffolk countryside unfolds, although predominantly flat, there are hedges and trees. I think that it is a softer, almost straw brown and a lot drier than Devon.

"There's an old airfield from the Second World War to cycle around, miles and miles of flat concrete lines, straight lines." He said taking his right hand off the steering wheel, resting his elbow on the opened window ledge, his fingers began tapping out a tune that had stuck from earlier on. "And loads of bunnies!" He laughed. I acknowledge the several hundred rabbits some ways ahead of the rattling old Land Rover, suddenly they scamper, dash, jump, they all scatter, except the young ones who leave it until we are almost upon them before they dive into the long grass.

I don't know why but we found the last comment more than amusing. We laugh, a genuine laugh for once, laughter with a stranger. Mr Elwood wipes a tear away and continues to talk, all the time he is smiling. I get a feeling he will enjoy some younger company about the place.

"The tracks are mostly concrete. You'll enjoy them. Don't run over any pheasants tho!"

We drive around looking at the corn and the wheat. Pheasants are like rabbits, everywhere.

Cock pheasants emblazoned with two-tone emerald green and purple necks with white flecks, they take life one step at a time, resplendent in soon-to-be autumnal majesty and slaughter. But for now, they attract the young hen pheasants who run ahead of the Land Rover in twos and threes, going every way but out of the way. "I hear you like cricket?"

"Yes," I said.
"Any good?"
"Yes."

Monosyllabic was I but hardly surprising, I hardly knew the guy. I was effectively a guest in his house, like a B&B, not somewhere you could suck on a soda, kick off your shoes and belch the national anthem.

However, I was beginning to feel I could relax a bit more than usual.

My room was decorated for the old. It was normal nice and nothing nice. Not something to write home about. The wallpaper was straight blocks of lines and coloured a shade of green that would drive the blind to alcohol. Already I could tell it was going to be a summer holiday of questions… no answers just questions.

Next to the farmhouse was a church, like at school. It meant it was not just a farmhouse but also a Hall. Some difference but in name only. I guess it raised the status of the place, only to them that give a toss about status, King and country. I would sometimes visit the church in those long passages of time after lunch when you've got nobody but **Blue Monster** to play with and nothing to do. At that time I was able to control this… this other me-not-me. I wasn't of a mind at that point in my short life where I wanted to destroy everything, so the church was more a sanctuary away, away from being given things to do if after lunch I was seen to be moping about.

"Do you want to go for a ride?" Said Mr Elwood. It was becoming a salutation. Mr Elwood had a Suffering Suffolk tradition of keeping a loaded 12-bore shotgun in the corner of the bed-chamber. I worry the only thing he would shoot would be his wife returning to her side of the bed at 03:00 AM having just painfully shown Alice to the chalice, what with the creaking floorboards and squeaky bedroom doors, along with her husky breathing from the pain she was suffering, you know since her hip op. Stood like an intruder in the bedroom doorway. KABOOOOOM! both barrels.

"Rupert!" Snapped mother, "Do you want to go for a ride with Mr Elwood?"

And off we'd go in the Land Rover to inspect the pheasants and the crops. Interestingly enough, Mr Elwood's vitamin C intake was acquired by sucking on a segment of lemon. He sucked on it like I would suck on an ice lolly.

His wife, Mrs Elwood didn't say much. I don't think she liked children. Or it might have been she was in a lot of pain, what with her hip and Mother's flirting.

It was quite annoying really, I was too young to take part in things like driving the Land Rover and not old enough to push off catch a bus into Sudbury and get a haircut or a train to London. Tube it to Heathrow and catch a flight to Tokyo, Japan. I thought about it but didn't have a passport to hand.

So I was kind of trapped and at everybody's beck and call with no one my age for miles around. Not that anyone my age would want anything to do with a strange little boy. The context was off. Who are you, from where?

Having to contend with a developing ménage á trois adult atmosphere. I spent more time outside. Now, Mr Elwood had an old chap come round and do the kitchen garden. Not everyday, I forget his name. He was a sensationally nice old chap. I would spend a while each day in the kitchen garden lost between the rows of runner beans to listen to his broad Suffering Suffolk accent, not understanding what was being said but at the same time glad somebody was actually happy to talk to me and didn't expect anything back. I was most upset when the news came in a letter that he had passed away. "Why does everyone have to die?" I asked through floods of tears. My words bounced back off the end wall. No answers.

Meaning why are people I have strong attachments to, falling off the perch before I am ready to accept them falling off the perch? It was too bloody emotional and all I ever seemed to be doing was standing like a willow tree, head spraying out all this noisy radiation and electronic grit whilst crying my eyes out...

Then one day, the same as every other day something different happened.

We were still losing badly against the West Indies. So it wasn't that that was so different. And mother was not helping by calling their fast bowlers 'wretched' followed by her salutation about how they broke Colin Cowdrey's arm in that Test match 2,000 light years ago when you could still get a double gin and tonic for 1d old money.

After morning coffee, Radio 2 and a biscuit I went out with a stick and Whiskey the Jack Russell Terrier. We walked around the farm, direction unknown. We passed the sweet smelling cathedral sized barns used as grain silos and we passed the tractor and trailers and the gargantuan combine harvesters, Whiskey is piddling on the broad-leaved dock leaves and sniffing around catching up on what creatures passed this way and when. We entered the overgrown tumble-down courtyard, my mind empty and bereft of thought watching the dog go about its business. Like I said another day.

"Whiskey!" I said, the dog snapped, its paw in the air, the dog was pointing, leaning forward its sinews straining, the dog was a loaded rocket and I had just lit the fuse. Two soft brown hens cluck and peck and although wary, took no real notice of us. This must have been what so irritated Whiskey, the lack of respect by a chicken. Jack Russell's think they're more important than chickens. Not sure how the dog ranking system works but they have one and I know this because I am witnessing it now. What I didn't fully realise was, I was the only thing that stood between termination with extreme prejudice and the continuation of what might well turn out to be a rather pleasant day.

As I said, my head was running on empty and the air inside my brain needed a change up, the spiders were asleep having filled the head chamber with a web of pink candyfloss. If the light in my brain was still on, which I believed it was, you could only see it as a faint glow way off in the distance.

The impulse arrived; I twitched, dropped the stick, and grunted. Whiskey began to chunter excitedly and to my surprise, again not really, Whiskey tore across the yard and leapt at the brown hen; it went down like a skittle. Whiskey bit in and started thrashing the hen's neck from side to side. I stared slack-jawed at the frenzied blur, the rattling squeals of excited dog and a cacophony of chicken death. The other bird escaped, took flight. I picked up the stick and shook it at the dog. Delicious feelings surged through my body.

Uh-oh! Here comes the **Blue Monster**.

Fright and alarm, *O God! What did I do? Mr Elwood is going to kill me.*

O God! Mother's going to kill me.

Pleasure, *O God! The dog just tore the bird to bits and on my command, how cool is that? The chicken's body! Is anyone looking, did they hear me shouting?!*

The dog's hot blood cooled enough to heed my jumping up and down, yelling and waving a stick over my head. Whiskey looked at me as if to say *Listen, mate, I was following your orders*. But there it was, staring at me, laughing even, death. I had now seen ugly for what it is.

"Quick say a prayer for the victim." Laughs **Blue Monster**.

"Poor, poor chicken. What is it with bloody dogs? Amen. Amen. Amen." I say, a little paranoid.

I pick up the lifeless body. I need a place to hide it. And then I need a place to hide. Whiskey was under my feet, starting to jump up. All excited again. I had better do this quickly. Where do I put it without the dog getting at it?

The rest of the day I am quiet. To my knowledge nothing ever came of the event, nothing was ever mentioned. I can't believe they didn't miss a chicken.

In the early evening light, Mr Elwood threw down an old tennis ball and I demonstrated my defensive batting technique. After a while, I began to launch the ball over the imaginary boundary beyond where Mother and Mrs Elwood stood not watching, talking. We continued until the bad light stopped play. Mr Elwood over-emphasised to mother his opinion that maybe I should be given a chance at a career in cricket. After all it was something the boy loved.

Mother did her usually tight-lipped thank you, I'll bear it in mind reply and changed the subject. I went off to bed. She had no intention, of course, of me ever, ever, ever pursuing a cricket career, over her dead body . . .

...And to prove it, she spent the next four years asking me what I wanted to do, nothing to do with passion. But then again, I guess that was how she was brought up and the way she was. Victorian attitudes to bringing up six children and an unhappy failed marriage. A dubious morality when it came to other people's affections and an insatiable if strange obsession with most of those cranky old religions. My elder brothers would medicate her with Plymouth Gin. That was the medicine when she was getting too much. "Time for drink ducks?!" Brother Number Three would ask Mother. She was almost likeable after half a bottle of Plymouth Gin. Funny isn't it? What it takes to reveal what or who we really are...

The family history was an unmitigated disaster of my father, who would work all week and at weekends, trot off to prance around a cricket pitch, bringing dirty washing home whilst Mother and four boys and a girl, all under the age of 11, all out of control and he was gone all day on the weekend.

I arrived 11 years after my sister.

"You arrived here for a reason." Mother said to me one night before I went to bed. "I know you've got some brains in that head of yours. But I can't figure out what you're going to do with them."

As with all holidays-not-holidays, the day arrives when you have to say farewell. My mother's reputation was such that I never knew if it was au revoir. Until we meet again or so long goodbye. I hope we never meet again.

I hate the possibilities that a goodbye brings. I hate not knowing what the future holds. The lack of control I have over the next few minutes, let alone years.

Suitcase in the boot and with a final wave I got in and shut the big old Rover door. Trapped my thumb in the door. I was told to open the door then, which I did fully realising as I did the throbbing pain in my thumb. Back into the kitchen, we went for ice and to dry the tears. The radio on the mantelpiece was on, it crackled into life - when I was young I'd sit and grumble about the radio.

Buckland House
22nd-9-73

Dear Mum
I hope Rose's birthday went all right. I had a safe journey back to school. We had a game of rugby football. The blues won 10-6 I was on the blue's side (I did not score any goals) I am in form 4 and I am happy, I am doing toy making and chess. There

is a film on Sunday called "Private's Progress". I am in a dormitory called Kelly. There is a new changing room downstairs where we can hang up our clothes.

Love Rupert x

PS. Give my love to pip whisky and cats and Mr and Mrs Elwood.

15

The Kid With The Slot Machine Eye

> Telephone: Shebbear 222.
>
> BUCKLAND HOUSE,
> BUCKLAND FILLEIGH,
> BEAWORTHY,
> N. DEVON.
> EX21 5JA
>
> 10th November 73
>
> Dear Hurrony,
>
> I hope you are well. Thank you for the letter. In the church today there is going to be a wedding about 12 o'clock. We have a colour television in form I. In football yesterday I scored two goals one off a penalty and one on the Goal kick line. It is cold and wet we may go for a run (BOO!) Tomorrow night there is going to be a film called "The Vanishing Prairie". It is a nature film. Next friday there is going to be flu jabs (BOO!) No efforts this week.
>
> love
> Rupert xxx

At the best of times, we're allowed to be little boys. Other times we strut through Buckland House like illegitimate sons of royalty. We rise and we fall by our actions and our words. We pride ourselves on our ability to cheat, lie, laugh, steal, tell long-winded stories, rub each other up the wrong way and spray our superiority, like writing our names in the snow. We blend in, to fight the good fight or stick out like two little fingers. One thing's for sure, fires at boarding schools burn bright.

Fin put his ear to the door. He looked at the handle and with a light touch, his index finger started tapping it and he began counting fast on inward breaths. After the thirtieth tap, he stood up straight, took a couple of steps back and used his shoulder to barge open the door.

I swivel around, as does Hunt who starts laughing. Fin, a silhouette in the doorway, stands hand on hip, chest puffed out and the other hand stretched wide like a Mexican Matador ready for the fight. Fin gets our full attention. He blows his long, mousy brown hair off his face; it uncovers his slot machine eye. The right eye that all the while had been spinning at an incredible speed on its tiny reel. It shuddered to an abrupt stop *Lucky Number Seven*. Almost out of breath and with a sense of purpose to move forward, Fin forces himself to overbalance, to take a few more steps into the classroom. However, he could only manage to slide his left foot sideways. And that was that. He has us in stitches, I raise an eyebrow at Hunt who does not attempt to hide his derision. We've seen enough of this kid to know he is the weirdest, weird of weirds. And that's saying something. Hunt checks his watch and decides to leave.

"N-No wait!" Fin tightened up, therefore he stuttered. It was fascinating to watch. He fought against aggressive compulsive habits. It appeared he had an overabundance of them. Fin twisted around as if to push away someone or a thing who had pulled the handle on his slot machine eye. The eye started to roll around the socket. Fin blocked the exit, turned and tapped his fingers against the door handle counting out a number with each tap. Again he finished at thirty, stood up straight, turned away, stopped, and turned back, tapped out another twenty. Then calm as you like, Fin walked over to a desk and sat down. Half the top row of his front teeth were false. Fin noticed that we had noticed, so he dropped the denture from his gums and held on to the goofy rabbit teeth with his lips. It was a freakish look. He smiled. He knew something we didn't.

His slot machine eye slowed down and as it did, we could hear a high-pitched, dentist drill-like whirring followed by a decelerating tiny clickety-click, clickety-click, click-click noise. Fin winked his slot machine eye, blinked both eyes and winked again. *JACKPOT* in bright fiery red letters. He pushed his tongue into his cheek, looked away, yawned, swayed forward and back again. Put a thumb up then used it to shove his denture back into place. Hunt and I looked on, amazed, puzzled, indifferent.

"Jackpot!" Fin giggled trying not to stutter.

"So?" I said.

"Are you Green?" Said Fin knowing full well I was.

"No," I said. I am curious to know if he can control his eye, like when it stops. He looked pretty pumped so I thought better of it.

"M-Matron wants to see you. I *have* to take you she said. Come on let's go." Fin stood up.

"Oh!" I said, "That's a shame, I already saw her this morning. So, you're out of luck, so bog off!"

"Goodbye." Said Hunt to us both. "I'm going to bog off too!"

Hunt deliberately elbowed Fin on his way out the door. I picked up all the loose cards Hunt and I had been playing *follow thy neighbour* with and started to shuffle them. Fin ignored Hunt as he left and looked back at me. I dealt the cards and gestured to Fin to come over and play. Fin shrugged his shoulders, blew a raspberry and then to my surprise, threw out a pulse of rotating thought. The wavelength of telepathy smacked me right between the eyes and went in. I picked over the collection of scrambled letters that I could now clearly see in my Skull Cinema. The letters spun like a fruit machine and stopped with a ding! *How would you like your ride - rough or smooth*? The letters read.

It was raining outside, heavy rain of course it was. That's how these things go. Fin was a year older and a foot taller than me. I opened the classroom door and led the way. I wasn't being pushed, but more mentally encouraged to move along by Fin's growing determination to get me to go to the surgery and fast. From the shelter of the dilapidated classroom block, we stepped out into the rain. We ran to the edge of the slippery red brick steps. The drop was steep, I was cautious. I began to notice things were getting a little spooky. It was too quiet.

"What have I missed Fin, tell me, has the zombie apocalypse finally arrived?"

"You'll find out. Keep m-moving."

"Oh! It has then. Don't tell me you're their leader..."

We enter the school's main building by the back door. We sneak past the shower room with rows of boiler suit tops and racks of towels. We press on along dimly lit corridors until we reach the back stairs by the headmaster's office. There are two small light bulbs fixed upon the yellow architrave. The lights had two meanings. Red – *don't*. Green – *come*. I take hold of the stair bannister, swing around and crash onto the first step. The red light comes on. I stamp up the backstairs, one step at a time. I just want the headmaster to know someone's about. Fin had trouble on the stairs. Climbing two steps up, dropping three steps back. I look on, fascinated, then after awhile, with an air of indifference. Four steps up, one step back. Eventually he got to the top.

"C'mon!" Says Fin. He takes hold of my collar. I shake him off. No need for that.

The staircase ends and leads to another staircase that doubles back. I look at Fin. "You want to go first?"

It is here, before I go any further, that I sense an atmosphere of gloom. I don't like what I am sensing. As I climb the steps the landing reveals a long line of boys in white shirts.

No jumpers then?

At this end, at the far end of the queue, the boys were being foolhardy, jeering, egging each other on. Fin prods me to move along past them with a knuckle. And I'm thinking this *is* the Zombie Apocalypse.

The carpet muffles my hesitant footsteps as we step ever closer. The next fifteen boys look shell-shocked as we pass them. After that, I see familiar faces, Ellison, Clifton Wentworth, Mandrake reading Arthur C Clarke, Duncan Campbell, Bradley Edwards and Smit. They are all at the end of the line, not talking, they stand inert as if resigned to their fate. Apart from Mandrake. He continues to read until a prefect confiscates his book.

Reluctantly they start to roll up their shirtsleeves, exposing the left arm. Only their left arm. All this can only mean one thing. The realisation hits me like one of those cartoons. Where the Coyote runs and when he stops, he is off the edge of a cliff, standing in mid-air and when he breaks the fourth wall, looks directly at the camera before holding up a sign that says "UH-OH…" and then he drops, falling with an accompanying whistle to land with a soft bump, in the sand, on the floor of the canyon below. Well, that was me. My legs have frozen and any moment, I might drop. I've got to get out of here.

Fin holds my shoulders down at the surgery's entrance. He rests his chin on my shoulder. "There you go Green, a smooth ride!" His slot machine eye spins and stops on a skull and crossbones on a black eyeball. He shoves me through the door. I half-trip, gather myself and come face to face with Matron whose eyes twinkle as she grins like a Cheshire cat. The headmaster's wife scowled and rubbed a tissue several times on the tip of her aquiline nose. She's always got a cold. The white-haired ancient and slow doctor was hunched over with his back to the room. I can hear a squealing sound from somewhere.

"Ah! At last, we wondered where you'd got to." Said Matron, "Roll up a sleeve too Fin, there's a good boy." Fin looks embarrassed both his feet become rooted to the floor. His slot machine eye rolls around and stops on a yellow lemon. "Gahh!" He mumbles crestfallen, "No prize, no prize..." His hand reaches out to hold the surgery door but instead of holding the handle, he starts tapping counting up to thirty collecting up each considered touch.

"Strange boy." Says Matron as she turns her attention to me. She calculates before action. With one quick movement, she whips my jumper off and grabs my left arm, clicks her fingers, snaps the cuff button and with spider-like fingers rolls up my shirtsleeve. She turns me around and throws my jumper over my head. Like an ostrich with its head in the sand, I stand to attention.

In a loud whisper, the Headmaster's wife says, "This one doesn't like injections!" All knowingly to the doctor. She starts pretending to rub her eyes to signal there might be tears.

"Gut!" Said the white-haired doctor, he glanced over his left shoulder and in no hurry reached for a fresh syringe.

"I know! He still has to have one tho." The Headmaster's wife lets out a shrill laugh and clasps her hands together. I pull the jumper off my head and consider the only reason the headmaster's wife is here is for her own entertainment.

"Ah! Sehr gut!" The doctor slowly returns his attention to the little boy he still holds by the left arm, dangling in mid-air. I am alarmed to see Wilson, his legs kick and wobble as if he is riding an imaginary bike, Wilson lets out a truncated squeal to the delight of his captor. The syringe needle tears out of the boy's arm. The doctor discards Wilson as if tossing a cigarette butt out a car window. Wilson whimpers as he scampers out of the room.

"Well, I never!" The Headmaster's wife croaks. "His mother told me, when they first brought him here, that one day, Wilson her son, was growing up to be Prime Minister of all England!"

"Same family?"Asks Matron. The question makes the Headmaster's wife roar with laughter. Confused Matron picks up her clipboard and bites her top lip.

The Headmaster's wife only gives out boiled sweets to brave boys. She coughs up some phlegm to clear her wattled throat. Pops a sweetie into her mouth. She swings around and points at Matron whilst proclaiming. "He won't get to be Prime Minister if he doesn't take all the sweeties! Will he. No!"

Matron ignores her. The Headmaster's wife throws her head back and laughs until she chokes to death on the boiled sweet that blocks her windpipe.

Oh... what a shame it didn't. Matron swings, karate chops the Headmaster's wife on the back of the neck dislodging the sweet. It flies out her mouth, shatters on the linoleum floor. The Headmaster's wife composes herself, checks the time on her wrist watch against the surgery clock. There are three minutes in it, close enough. Won't be long before the end of long break and the lunch bell. She looks up at the doctor, picks up the paper bag of sweets and wears a smile as if butter wouldn't melt in her mouth. The doctor returns the smile and gestures. The Headmaster's wife shouts, "Matron!" She indicates with a glance at the doctor and glares at Matron *Buckland House doesn't keep the doctor waiting*. "Matron, who's next?"

"Come on Green!" Said Matron looking up from a list of crossed-out names on the clipboard, "You're next."

It's Grand Guignol. Theatrically dark and foreboding, I don't know how to play my part. I didn't think anything could ever be this distasteful. Behind my back, Matron mouths, *this one* whilst pointing an exaggerated finger at the top of my head.

The boys who wait nearest to the surgery door shiver and turn pale. Smit looks in but is careful not to be seen. Those who believe in God, pray. Others drop their heads, and slump over, with tears in their eyes. Way down the corridor, they can hear "You're next," so they fall silent. Older boys put hands in their pockets to hold onto themselves.

"Yes!" cried the Headmaster's wife, "You're next Green. Come on, come on." She bites her fist, and excitedly teeters on the edge of her seat. Her eyes ablaze. The white-haired ancient and slow doctor is peering at me over small round dark rimmed sunglasses, he sucks in a breath of air. He whistles hushed accordion tones. An old Bavarian folk tune '*Spinn, Spinn, Meine Liebe Tochter*'. The tune flows as he hums adding the odd word in German. In a slow deliberate movement, he picks up and shows me a syringe. A sickening smile stretches across his closed mouth. He beckons me to waltz over toward him. I can't stand the sight of needles. Makes me turn somersaults. I must force myself to go on with this charade or I could run. **Blue Monster** drew in a breath and as an aside said, "Run away Rupert."

"Can't run. Legs frozen!"

"Alles klar!" The ceiling light flashes off the doctor's dark glasses. He approaches, one, two, three, one, two, three, dah! dah! di-dah! so pleasant and calm until his top lip noticeably begins to ripple. For a few seconds, his persona fails, betrays his humanity. Now fully possessed, a grotesque demon glares out from the doctor's leathery old face with molten black eyes with reptilian white slits for pupils. They follow my every move. He grows larger as I cower beneath him. He feigns to take hold of my arm. Rather he smacks hard the top of my head.

I throw my arms up for protection. He snatches at my left arm above the elbow and squeezes as if wringing out a dishcloth.

"Hold schtill..." He commands adding a light inaudible. "Dankeschön." With slow deliberate superhuman strength, he squeezes as he lifts my arm until my feet leave the ground, takes his time. At full stretch, the syringe fired at the ceiling abruptly tilts down, I anticipate the needle but it doesn't come. As inevitable as a guillotine the syringe drops, strikes, punctures, stings, scratches. It lacerates the skin on my arm. "Argh! It hurts. . ."

"There, there..." The slow ancient Doctor soothes, he whistles a few more bars from the waltz, reads the strain as it travels up my neck, across my crumpled lips and on up to reflect in my eyes. His nostrils flared, cold watery eyes return, the demon almost gone as sparks of agitation wilt. Everlasting seconds drip from the guttering outside the surgery window. The syringe plunger influenced by whimsy. When he wanted to apply pressure. Make it end. The Doctor breathed out, his breath overwhelming, acrid like a cheese shop on a hot day.

The pain fires through my arm. The hairs on my head turn white and stand up straight like art room pencils thrown into a metal cup. The Doctor lets go. I am released, discarded, allowed to leave. All along I have screamed a duet with **Blue Monster**. I scuttle like a crab across the linoleum floor. I put the brakes on, only to slide into the Headmaster's wife. The hard-boiled cherry drops launch out of the bag. They spray above her head, hold long enough for a fixed semi-circle pattern to form and for the light to glint off the sweets as they reach their zenith. Like a lot of arrows hitting a dart board, they hit the floor. The Headmaster's wife complains but it's too late to say I'm sorry for I am gone. And I'm gone like history. Like so gone, call it archaeology, that was how gone, gone, gone I was.

"So, so...," said the Doctor. He shivers with almost uncontrollable excitement. "Bitte..." He chooses another thin slender clear plastic syringe, holding it up to the light, the needle is almost invisible until brought down to eye level. Shiny weapon of death, controversy, perceived prevention, and cure.

Fin looks on in horror and takes a step back. "Nein!" The Doctor pleads, beckoning for Fin to come forward. Fin takes another step back but only succeeds in falling into Matron's arms. The kid with the slot machine eye hesitates, then begins frantically blinking looking for the correct picture to register in his eye, but all he could muster when the reel eventually stops was a blank, *lose-lose*.

"I want m-my m-mum-ummy." Fin blurted out struggling and grizzling in protest.

"Oh! Fin." Matron's now husky voice was hardly a comfort. She looked like she'd just stormed the party, and everyone was rooting for her to do that impression of that Hollywood film star sex symbol, you know, Mae West. So she did.

"Well Fin, don't tell me you're afraid of a little prick..."

16

V Signs

THE RED HERRING SWAM about the art room. It's alright, Mrs Lancaster had her fishing line in the water. The hook baited. Whilst she continued to ask what colour did black and white make when mixed together. She was well aware of the red herring's intention. So it was hardly a surprise when without hardly moving, she skillfully caught hold of the red herring's head, pulled the line out of the water and addressed its concerns.

Buckland House
17th November 1973

Dear Mum

Thank you for the letter. This morning, I had a letter from Brother Number Three. I would like to go stay with them for a week or two. In shopping, I got a torch. When the flu jabs were on I had to have one. There is the second marathon tomorrow. It was a frosty morning this morning.

Efforts: Latin Good, Scripture Good, Maths average, Science Good, English Good, French Good, History Good, Geogarphy Good.

Love Rupert x

The red herring argument put forward was, what is the origin of the V sign. Whilst half the class sided with Hunt and his entourage, who muted the outrageous notion the V sign originated as far back as 1415 at the battle of Agincourt.

"Ah! Yes I remember it well." I interrupted.

"Shut up!" Said Hunt. With my elbow on the desk, I rested two fingers on my cheek and pointed them towards Hunt. A few boys got it and laughed. Hunt sulked but continued until the other half led by Bradley Edwards insisted it came from a Winston Churchill newspaper cutting that Edwards had seen one breaktime in an Encyclopedia. An encyclopedia he had discovered whilst sat in front of the school library shelf. We all laughed at the thought of Bradley Edwards, or indeed anyone, opening up, let alone reading, an encyclopedia. That was daft. Mrs Lancaster put the two ideas to the vote. Hunt won. His entourage showed everyone their two fingers in defiance.

Mrs Lancaster then elaborated on the theory that the English bowmen would show the French, before battle, that they still had their two fingers because, said Mrs Lancaster, "The French would cut off these two fingers if they captured an English bowmen." That shut everyone up. Especially as she demonstrated throughout, having two fingers, firing an arrow and not having two fingers and not firing an arrow.

"Ah!" Said Wilson finally getting it. "So you can't shoot anymore!"

"Yes!" Replied Mrs Lancaster. "So Winston Montague, any ideas on what colour black added to white makes… anyone?"

We all sat round the art room practising our V signs. Holding them for more than a few seconds somehow diluted them. The trick was to flick a V sign just as you made eye contact with an adversary. It became more pointed somehow. Like an arrow let fly, you might say. It gave the satisfying feeling that the arrow released by the V sign had indeed thudded into a Frenchman's chest.

Mrs Lancaster stood watching everybody as the kettle filled with water. She decided to make a brew because she had lost the battle. As the kettle boiled, she wondered if Winston Montague was called Winston after Winston Churchill. *Good name for a cat*, she thought.

Buckland House
Saturday 1st December 1973

Dear Mum

There is a shortage of fuel, so the hot water has to be turned off sometimes. It is very cold, and it snowed Last night. We have just finished exams, Thank goodness. The last letter from school about ¼ of an hour. Tomorrow evening Mr Beaumont is giving us a lecture about wildlife. On Monday it is choir half holiday. Mr Beaumont's Mother has come back for the rest of term to help Miss Schlüssel and Matron. I am in the finals of billiards. I got a whole plus for tidiness.

Love Rupert x

I liked Mrs Lancaster and Miss Schlüssel. I once called her Mum by mistake. Actually I called them both Mum at different times by mistake. Obviously in a moment of weakness. Very embarrassing. They were both related to each other. Miss Schlüssel was like a Matron not Matron. More of a nurse. She was in charge of buying things for us boys when she went to Bideford. Stuff like sellotape.

Mrs Lancaster's art room had a nice bohemian, relaxed attitude about it. It didn't appear to have any radiators either which is why she always had fingerless gloves on and a mug of tea.

The art room was where one could sharpen pencils with the word *imagination* in gold lettering down one side along with the number 2B. A bit like Will Shakespeare's famous rant. Or not 2B!

I remember, once upon a time, I got some bad news in a handwritten letter from home. I was tearful in an art class and she came to my rescue. But not before her son Stephen Lancaster who was also serving time at Buckland House, kicked open with a choice expletive, the art room door. He was in a right old strop, complaining in Pig Latin to his mum about being bullied by his arch nemesis Mr Whitaker. Mr Whitaker was grey and hardly ever black and white. Mrs Lancaster had had her run ins with Mr Whitaker and found him, as Stephen did, to be most abhorrent.

"Oh my word. A detestable fellow!" She would scream through raucous laughter as she slugged down a *medicinal* whisky chaser before the session really got started in the The Devil's Stone Inn, in Shebbear. When she was asked by a novice schoolmaster to Buckland House to talk about the masters... *and what about the deputy head Mr Whitaker?*

You could explain it away as something to do with unresolved PTSD from the second world war. You could, but then you could also say, if he didn't like you, then he was just a big old bully. He also had authority to dish out the cane. And when the Headmaster was away, the mice did play and Mr Whitaker took on his responsibilities with a certain zeal. Everybody run and hide. Smit didn't and we saw the red lines run down the back of his leg. It wasn't a good look. Smit was learning to fight back, but it cost him. Not as much as it cost the perpetrator in the eyes of Jesus. If we are still playing that game? Yeah, funny that. He never had a Mrs Whitaker either. Hmm... I'm just listening out for the dry notes man... the dry notes of conversation of those jazz musicians playing in the public bar.

Buckland House
Saturday 8th December 1973

Dear Mum

I have won the Junior Billiards Tournament. It is merit half-holiday on Monday. We should have enough oil to last the term. Christmas Dinner is on Tuesday. There is a Carol Service tomorrow evening and another on Thursday at 2.15pm

Love Rupert x

The descants in the carol services hymns delivered angel light into the rafters of the school church. The choir raised the spirit of Christmas to the extent that most boys forgot themselves long enough to say a prayer for the baby Jesus.

Soon after, we ate a candle-lit Christmas dinner on the badminton court under the dome, it was lovely. Everybody's happy, even Stephen Lancaster. It is Christmas and soon we will all be going home. Christmas is the best. And at the end of the meal, two hundred balloons were released from the balcony. A spectacular sight.

Excitement is good. End of term is better. We jump humpback bridges, bump over pheasants on the road kill roads. Jackdaws and Rooks scatter into the air as the minibus swerves avoiding pothole after pothole after pothole.

Tall boys like Fin and Malcolm McGregor hit their heads on the metal roof and laugh. I am sat opposite Hunt at the rear of the minibus. Hunt is using a finger to trace the line of a raindrop on the square shaped rear window.

Now Hunt is flicking V-signs in the general direction of the car following us. Out of character Hunt is mouthing choice obscenities at the young family in the car. The dad driving the car boils over, the shocked mum's chin drops whilst the eyes of a young brother and sister in the back seats stare out at us.

High octane excitement and the end of term. We are all so happy, happy to be going home, inside the minibus we joke and whoop with laughter as our metal box shakes and rattles, rendering the outside to a blur. I shout at Fin "We must be late!" several heads nod in agreement. There's nothing to hold onto so we squash and become squashed. The full mini bus drizzles along the straight bits and splashes around the bends, in the road. We gurgle along at a breathtaking crawl. We shout out the names of the small villages, stirring many brown leaves into a merry dance along the bendy lanes, now behind us, we slide through the countryside on and on towards Exeter St....

"Why have we stopped?" Clifton Wentworth asks Wilson. Wilson pointed at Hunt but didn't say anything. We looked from Hunt to Mr Lewis. From Mr Lewis to Hunt.

Mr Lewis turned off the engine and angrily rattled the gear stick into neutral. He dipped his head, threw a fierce look at Mr Beaumont who gestured *be my guest* in the passenger seat. Mr Lewis wound up his window and waved goodbye to the car that was behind us.

"Why stopped?" Asks Smit.

"COME 'ERE..." Bellowed Mr Lewis now turned facing us. We all jerked a movement as if to get up, realising it wasn't meant for us we sat back down and held onto the wooden plank like seat.

Hunt, visibly rumbled, stood up and edged his way to the front of the minibus. Mr Lewis's bucket left-hand unexpectedly grabbed a handful of Hunt's shirt; Mr Lewis spoke softly, directly and with menace all the time increasing the heat and rage. A jet engine force spewing out of his wide-open mouth. Hunt's skin began to tear away from his face. The hair on the back of his head stuck out straight as his knees knocked together. Hunt had a tough skin but this was a next level rollicking from the hefty frame that was Mr Lewis. It was a squeeze for Mr Lewis to fit in the driving seat, let alone turn round in it. So it didn't take much to set him off. When the bollocking stopped, the imaginary hot air balloon that filled the insides of the minibus deflated. It was a huge relief.

We all kicked Hunt as he stumbled to the back of the mini bus, spurned on by the knowledge Mr Beaumont said that because of Hunt, we'd probably now miss our train and have to spend the holidays at school with Mr Lewis, because everyone else had gone home. So that's why we kicked him so hard, it's what they use to do in the middle ages for punishment and it would not have been proper if we didn't meter out some sort of punishment.

Ah... yes, look at this, Mr Beaumont was lying. We arrive unexpectedly early at the station, first taste of the outside world in three months. The Buckland House School boys in civilian wear, known as *civvies*. With heads held high and resolute cheer, we storm the castle where fire breathing dragons belch out black smoke along parallel rails.

It is a disaster movie. No, it is a moment of freedom. It's a romantic comedy. No, it is more a posh version of Kes, but without the northern accents and bird of prey.

The moment you're no longer at school and your travelling as a train boy. It is the freedom to be yourself because you have yet to meet up with your loved ones, parents or since the divorce, Mother.

Only, which version of Mother I got depended on which housekeeping job she currently held. And if she was sleeping with her boss and so on and so on and so on. I started out life well, my school career started out well but now it slides. This freedom moment was special because you could do you.

"Sir can I go to the toilet?" Clifton Wentworth waved to Mr Beaumont who was explaining the London Underground map to Wilson and Fin.

"No, wait until you get home!" Said Fin.

"Yeah, very funny Fin." Howled Clifton Wentworth. "Seeing as my home is in Nairobi! Sir, I'm bursting." Mr Beaumont smiled and waved Clifton Wentworth on.

"Go on be quick!" Said Fin. Clifton Wentworth flicked a V sign at Fin who returned it without looking.

"Anyone else?" Said Mr Beaumont, having now closed the London Underground map before fully explaining which lines and tickets to buy to get to Kings Cross and Wimbledon. Fin and Wilson simultaneously wore expressions of being peeved and figured to do it themselves when they arrived in Paddington.

After a few moments, Clifton Wentworth returned with a smile on his face. "What have you done?" We asked. He did not say anything, but half pulled out his pocket a small box, taking care to conceal it from Mr Beaumont's eyes. "What's that?" Was the general question batted around the circle now formed around Clifton Wentworth. It wasn't something I had ever seen before and my curiosity waned when he didn't tell, after showing half the face of the strange box. So it was a game, you've got something and we don't know what it is.

"Sir! Mr Beaumont, Sir!" I shouted. For a moment there Clifton Wentworth looked as if he had been rumbled.

"Yes Green, ok, but be quick..."

If I was going to solve this puzzle, I needed to have a look for myself. With purpose, I entered the gentlemen's facilities. Hmm... that smell, a strong piquant of bleach, stale air and strained cabbage. Strange gurgling noises. Water in the central heating system. Water pumped along large overhead pipes. Steam rising out of the cubicles. Strange otherworldly smells of sweat and tobacco smoke. Shiny glossed black toilet seats. Chipped and graffitied toilet doors. Bolts well worn. Bolts with missing screws or not a latch at all. Weird groans and giggles from grills and vents. The wash basins with worn bars of soap. I stopped in front of the frosted window glass and slowly turned my head. On the wall, a slot machine type box for paper towels, boxes and broken. It hangs there empty. Before the invention of hand dryers. The *cleaned once a day* railway station toilets of 1974 England. Devon is a sleepy backwater. Therefore, 1974 equates realistically to 1954. So there's probably still rationing. One toilet roll per day per cubicle.

The Headmaster's voice came gushing back into my head. He told Brian Pike and I that during the war years at his preppy school, boys were issued each morning with two slices of toilet paper. He went on and on and on.

We wanted to ask him if he could drop the whole corporal punishment thing and get us to write out sheets of paper instead, call it sides. Like six sides of paper instead of six strokes of the cane.

"Doing lines. It could work Sir." We had pleaded.

"No." Said the Headmaster. He basically thought it worse to write out sides rather than caning boys.

"It's all over a lot quicker, don't you think?" He said.

I open my eyes and see white tiled graffitied walls. No prophetic saying written on the walls in here. *Millwall FC are the best. Exeter FC are crap. If you suck cock call this number.* I am spooked, I want to leave. Clifton Wentworth stands at the entrance to the facilities.

"C'mon the train's here." He shouts.

"What was that box?" I shout back running after him. No time, the train is here, get on the train. Get on with the holiday-not-holiday, how do you like your freedom now?

On the train, our spirits are up. We chat and eat crisps and ignore Mr Beaumont. We can feel, as surely he does his authority diminish with every minute, every mile we travel up the rails.

"Good book sir?" Hunt is goaded into asking. But only because he's been quiet.

"Yes it is. Alastair Maclean, Ice Station Zebra." We all burst out laughing. I don't know why. Maybe it was the way he said it. "Ok," he says, "I'm going to the buffet car." We laugh again. "Hunt. You're in charge." Mr Beaumont disappears. Hunt sulks some more until he's offered a crisp.

Meanwhile, with Mr Beaumont gone. The subject of small boxes is brought up. Sat opposite me is Clifton Wentworth. He flicks a V sign and leaves his seat, dives into the train's toilet. Engaged. He disappears off to find another toilet all the while holding up a V sign because we saw what happened and are laughing at him.

"Where'd he..." Said Smit.

"Shh.." Said Hunt followed by a 'KV'* as Mr Beaumont returns to his seat.

*'KV' *Cavere* is Latin, it means Beware! Therefore 'KV' is the shortened version.

For some dreadful reason the train made a stop at Trowbridge, of all places. But thankfully we quickly got going again. After a while I said. "A bit over the top, Sir."

"What is?" Said Wilson looking up from a comic. Boys looked at Mr Beaumont.

"I wasn't talking to you Wilson. Sir! A bit over the top, I said. Unscheduled stop at Trowbridge."

"What? Er.. yes taking on water, maybe?" Answered Mr Beaumont. He was enjoying his book somewhat, whilst spilling crumbs down his front...

"Taking on water? What a spanner!" I whispered to anyone who'd listen. "It's not a steam train."

I looked out the window, bored. We left Devon and Somerset behind and press on towards London and unknown futures. I am bored, bored.

Clifton Wentworth returns, he sits down and looks smug. We are offered the chance to see what it was in the box. I stand up and slowly lean over to inspect what it is that everyone is currently laughing, gawking and groaning at. The edge of the table recedes and the sight of his undone trousers and pulled down pants reveals his knob. But not just his knob, no on the end of his knob is a pink plastic thing.

Oh, look! He's covered his knob with a – what's it called?
Oh yeah! One of those things... out that machine in the station bogs.
Yeah! Sure, I know what it is...

I sat back down impressed at the bravado and unimpressed with my innocence, not putting two and two together. And the question I dare not ask...

What's it for?

17

Ink

Turquoise ink from a small glass bottle, a much sought after and prized possession that takes considerable amounts of diplomacy to acquire. The lettering group of boys listen with intent as Mrs Lancaster explains how to put a flourish on a capital letter. I dig the old gothic style of letters and practise again and again, writing out the alphabet. Page after page of patiently applied, capital letters with flicks, tight lines and extended flourishes. As a result, of all this extra study, my handwriting improves and the speed at which I write increases. The connection between brain and hand locks and the fountain pen ink flows.

Red Quink ink is another prized possession. I write *The quick brown fox jumps over the lazy dog* in a stream of distracted consciousness all the way upon every line, to the bottom of the page. The letters still wet are yielding from the nib, soaking into the fibres of the paper. Blotting paper at the ready. The decorative nib cleaned to a shine as the blotting paper absorbs the red ink. It forms neat little semi-circle flowers at the paper's edge. The strange fumes of ink bring ancient scribes to the table. Invite me, to have a drink with them, but I don't. I am more than happy with ink on my fingers, a removable tattoo. Otherwise it was humdrum. Line after line of dedication. I wrote out quotes from a page mounted them on card and waited for Mrs Lancaster to say "Well done!"

Back in class, I was fed on a diet of school issue blue ink. On the odd occasion I was able to smuggle in and fill my fountain pen from the bottle of beetle black ink hidden at the back of the wooden calligraphy cabinet.

Buckland House
January 12th 1974

Dear Mum
I had a safe journey back to school. We have a new master to teach maths. He is called Mr Hall. I am doing Piano, lettering and Chess in Hobbies. There was another storm last night but it is sunny today. There is a film ond on Sunday called

"Two way stretch" It is an a comedy about a prison. There are three new boys none of them are in our form. I am settling down and happy with my friends.
Lots of love Rupert xxx

Buckland House
19th January 1974

Dear Mum
Thank you for the letter. It has been wet all week. We played our first proper games yesterday. I am afraid to say that we are still short of fuel. There is a film on Sunday called "Raising a Riot" In lettering Mrs Lancaster says I am doing well. There are no efforts this week.
Love Rupert xxxxx.

Buckland House
Saturday 26th Jan

Dear Mum
I received the parcel you sent me thank you. The film tomorrow night is called "Please Sir" It is the same on television. Yesterday the colts played against B game. I was in it. The weather is still wet . although we played games yesterday. On Wednesday we had a run I came about last. Half term is only two weeks on Thursday. I had pluses for Piano Latin Geography.
Love Rupert x x x x x

Efforts Latin Excellent 4th maths Excellent 1st Geography Good 11th French average 7th Scripture Good 8th English Good 4th Science Good ----- History Good 10th

Telephone : Shebbear 222.

BUCKLAND HOUSE,
BUCKLAND FILLEIGH,
BEAWORTHY,
N. DEVON.
EX21 5JA

Saturday 2nd February. 74.

Dear mummy,

Thank you for the letter. The Today we had table change. Todays matches have been canelled. Yesterday we did some circuit training, where we climb up wall bars and scramble down and do press ups and running on the spot. The film on Sunday is called "Sammy going South". Half term begins a week on Thursday. Please can you buy me some sellotape. There are no efforts this week.

Love
Rupert
X+++
C.

A prep school letter

Scoop is a magazine where we get to choose and buy books. Books as possessions, to look good on a coffee table, never to read.

Buckland House
9th February 1974

Dear Mum
thank you for the sellotape. Last Saturday we had a run and I came 8= with a boy called Hunt!! In Science we are doing Chemistory and this is what we made. The film tomorrow is called "The Long Duel" it should be very exciting. I got pluses for music, Geography this week. It has been wet all the week and on Wednesday we had snow.
Love Rupert xxxx
efforts Latin average 6th Geography Good 8th Maths Excellent 7th Scripture average 4th= French average 7th Science. Good 5th English average 3rd final average History Good 5th

Buckland House
Saturday 23rd February 1974

Dear Mum
Thank you for the letter. How are you? I had a letter from Mr and Mrs Elliot. The weather is sunnier. Yesterday we played football. On Thursday we had Scoop I got the Ghost Dog of Killicut and the Admada book of cartoons. Next Wednesday form 8 are going to corn well Cornwall to study china clay.
Love Rupert x

Buckland House
Saturday 9th March 74

Dear Mum
Today I got a letter from Brother Number Four. The Colt's match against St Michaels on Wednesday was cancelled and the 1st XI. Today there are two matches against St Michaels and Mount House. The weather is cold. On Monday, Tuesday, and Wednesday, there are Common Entrance Trials, No school exams, thank goodness. The demonstration about Hawaiian guitars last Sunday was very good Minsky sang a song! Tomorrow we may have the final of the Brain of Buckland House. Another master's wife is expecting another baby. We may get a half-holiday.

Please can you buy me the French Waterloo Artillery the small men? I have pluses 1½ for games ½ for music and ½ for tidiness. No efforts this week. The choir half-holiday is on Thursday we have two lessons off.
Love Rupert x

In-school tournaments were never ending. Organised by Mr Whitaker, if you could compete at it, there was a senior and junior tournament for it. The options ranged from Putting, Billiards, Snooker, Draughts, Halma, Dominoes, Snakes and Ladders, Table Tennis, Badminton and Chess. All the results, winners and runners up, meticulously recorded for the newsletter. Who gained a well deserved victory over another. Who was defeated. Who was the defeated reigning champion and who were the losing semi-finalists. I wonder if I will get to be the new singles champion?

Then there were the weekly Easter Term quizzes. A time-consuming activity split between senior, intermediate and junior. Apparently only 8 boys of the 34 entrants stuck it out to complete the 7 papers required, with an overall 175 points available, 162 points was the highest score and merited a first place in the senior category. And then someone thought it a good idea for a competition for music.

Buckland House
16th March 74

Dear Mum
How are you? Last Wednesday there were two matches. The 1st XI won 4-1 and the colts lost 6-0 I was not in the colts because I banged my cheek. We were playing St Petroc's. On Monday the Inter House Music Competition takes place and I will play the piano. On Tuesday there is the merit Half Holiday. On Thursday the Easter Service is at 2.15. I have a plus for music.
Love Rupert x
efforts Latin 7th Good Maths ---- French 5th Good 2nd Excellent Scripture Good English 5th Good History 2nd Good Geography – Good

We are not all in this together and the term comes to an end. I think you really don't get anywhere without love. All this competition is not good. I am returned to Hove wrapped like a brown paper parcel with twine and a couple of first class stamps. I am not the finished article by any means. I am a bit cranky and bent out of shape. My tappets need adjusting. I need a tune up, a bit of a holiday distraction or rest even. I wonder what we are going to do, correction, what I will do with myself this Easter holiday-not-holiday?

Hova Villas, Hove
Wednesday 17th April 1974

Dear Brother Number Four and Helena

I hope you had a nice wedding? Last week Nod made a Vickers Wellington and i made a F111A Jet. And yesterday I made a Stuka, a very small size! Costing 13p. Today Nod is making a Halifax bomber. And painting them. About everyday I play with Lester and Russell, the two boys next door. Yesterday I bought some Tom and Jerry fun doodle transfers.

How is Celle? Is teaching all right? Yesterday afternoon we went to the King Alfred minor swimming pool and it was crowded. I have got some arm bands and almost swimming now!

On Easter Monday we went to The Classic and watched 'The Sword in the Stone' and 'The Incredible Journey'.

Lots of Love
Rupert xxxx

18

Obstacles

FOR GENERATIONS, WELL LUBRICATED Fathers across the land would holler across the dinner table when prompted, "I don't care what obstacles or what it costs. I want my seed to have a proper, decent, education, like I did. Marvellous, pass the port, old thing, will you? Thank you. And another thing, I don't want to have that obstreperous boy living in this house, with me... I mean us. Sorry, darling... oh you agree! Splendid!"

It is with probable intention, that it meant us boys, as obtuse as we were, got a better education than most, a more expensive, better education. A mostly, expensively, betterer education. If we applied ourselves.

A lesser spotted weasel obscured my education. I obfuscate therefore I am.

Obfuscate: To bewilder, mystify and puzzle.

Anyway, I must tell you this...

Everyone was going to have a real good time. God, as always, was watching. His eyes were as blue as they were grey. He lurked in the entrance doorway of the school, like a black cloud, watching the children that bring squabbles and disdain for all things sacred...

07:15 Rising bell. Mr Whitaker enters our dormitory and says, "You may rise."

07:45 Breakfast. A bowl of porridge with milk and sugar, followed by a pilchard on half a piece of fried bread and a cup of tea. Cold toast and Marma-jam, if the Master didn't want it.

08:40 Prayers. I don't have any, besides they don't get answered anyway, because every morning I still wake up here.

The Obstacle Course Race was the highlight of the sports day calendar. And today being summer athletics day, it was heralded as a welcome distraction from a daily diet of no cricket cricket, biff-tennis and pulling the floating face down juniors from the swimming pool water.

Sports Day was another one of those saccharine rituals, where everybody's parents, barring the overseas boys, and mine, showed up to cheer and lavish lots of love upon their little darling ones. They brought siblings along too, for competitive family races, scheduled for the end of the day. Another one of those 'Win at All Costs' events. Which to my mind was tedious in the extreme.

10:15 Milk Break. White moustache competition. Duncan Campbell won. I check the team sheets. They've not changed since last week.

The masters were excused to set up the obstacle course. Mr Beaumont had already roped off the cricket square and now, after a quick coffee, helped the masters set up scaffolding for the dirty black tyre's obstacle. Because of the past week's worth of rain, the Masters had little time to dig a six-foot trench, set the bear traps, relocate the bed of rusty nails, re-light the fire-pit and start the pendulums.

In order to talk, Mr Cavendish would shake his body, his lower jaw jutting out like a defective marionette, he would elevate himself up on tiptoe to stutter each sentence. Mr Beaumont lit a Gauloise, let it hang from his lips, grunted and shrugged his shoulders whenever Mr Cavendish spoke to him. Which was a lot, too much even.

12:00 Long break. Cricket nets and optional swimming. Like every year, word had gone out for strong boys to volunteer and meet at the carpentry workshop at mid-day. The twenty-yard jumbo ladder emerged out of the workshop, carried by volunteer boys, then dragged to the front lawn, before being dropped onto the grass. Mr Whitaker was on hand to position and secure the ladder.

The Ladder, as it was known, was to be the first obstacle in this year's obstacle course race. Long tent peg-like rods were smashed into the ground, to hold the ladder firmly on its side. The end rungs, and some of the middle rungs on the ladder, had been carefully adjusted to capture boys. A Venus flytrap mechanism. Jesus, the school's carpenter, had created The Ladder and it was considered an ingenious invention.

"I like the thought of leaving them trapped in wooden purgatory. I designed it to close around the neck. If a boy starts struggling it closes." He demonstrated with his hands on Wilson's neck, who happened to be passing, in the wrong place at the wrong time. "You see, just the neck, not so much as to restrict breathing, that would be going too far. More to hold the boy, as if in olden day stocks." He smiled and let go. Wilson staggered around and fell over, rolled on his back, shielded the sun from his eyes and got up again. The Ladder was impossible to escape and was therefore both imaginative and clever.

On the tarmac, by the pillars, in the shade, the Headmaster entertained a group of new and prospective parents. "You must have some failures. Otherwise, however, will they learn?" He explained, pointing to the ladder. Parents of trapped boy's would laugh nervously and then, after a confused frown, wholeheartedly agree with the Headmaster's thinking and when asked, would gladly buy another strip of raffle tickets.

The parents weren't allowed to talk to their children during races and being stuck on an obstacle meant that technically, the boys caught, were still racing. Therefore, the parents were encouraged to keep back on the tarmac and to leave quietly at the end of the day, to avoid a scene and any undue stress to the child. After all, the parents could always write a letter when they returned home, to let their son know how ashamed they were of him.

12:50 Outside bell... sports day... The races begin... some boys will miss lunch.

This year was a particularly good year for daisies. Thousands spread out like a deep shagpile carpet of white stars with tiny yellow faces across a galaxy of pear green grass. After the 100 yards foot race won by Ralph Brompton, the starting pistol jammed. A solution was found. Mr Cavendish was tasked with shouting, "On your m-marks, g-get set, g-go!"

If only he could shout. Several false starts meant Mr Whitaker, Mr Beaumont and Mr Harrington at the finish line had to bellow, down wind, "No, go back, go back!" Lots of arm waving. All rather confusing, if comical.

The 70 yards, outsized hurdles race, having been successfully started, after the third time of asking had now finished. Winston Montague coming in third, Hunt second and Fin first. The runners of said race now holding scraped knees, picking out splinters embedded in their legs. They were encouraged to make their way across the sports field to form an orderly queue standing outside the makeshift first aid tent. The front lawn was a battlefield. After some time, a brass megaphone was found and given to Mr Cavendish. A light wind swept in from the south-west and left.

Over the day, as the different races began, some boys chose to run barefoot, I didn't. The eccentrics wore bobble hats. I didn't. Over our hearts, a small, coloured rosette, to identify your house team. I don't remember what colour mine was. It may have been blue. Navy blue. Points were awarded to the winners and the house with the most points won a half-day's holiday. The losers got detention. It's pretty much the same in every other prep school, I would imagine.

When all the junior and intermediate races were run, the parents were invited to drink stewed tea and politely pick at paltry sandwiches and enjoy a slice of Victoria sponge cake. Before the senior races started.

As their boys came over, a chance for praise, the parents to say, "Yes, didn't you do well." To their progeny, when clearly, they hadn't done anything, if the boy in question didn't come first, what was there to talk about?

Sometimes it was hard to see the attraction of private schools, other than it being a centuries old tradition, something the lineage expected, demanded or required.

"I say, didn't the last twelve generations of your bloodline stain the urinals at this prep school?"

"What? No, not this one. I say, didn't all your lot join up, ship out and fall whilst fighting the good fight?"

"What do you mean?"

"You know perfectly well what I mean. Somewhere foreign, somewhere that needed invading, needed saving and degrading, obviously, obviously somewhere to ostracize..."

"Ah! Yes!" And so on, and so on.

Over towards the shade in front of a solitary oak tree, that served as a marker or sightscreen when a cricket pitch was prepared in the middle of the cricket square... not ideal for seeing a dark cricket ball against the oak tree, but like Mr Whitaker said, "We never had a sight screen in my day..."

By the old worn out tyres obstacle, a father and his only son strolled. The father wore a pair of large dark glasses, framed by those still fashionable sideburns, a splash of Brut 33, his arms folded, pink shirt, an old school tie, his Rolex on show, time was always on hand with a twist of his wrist, only moments away. The father and son stood in the shade from the hot afternoon Sun. Their demeanour was classic. Uptight and as out-of-position as a King and pawn on a chessboard. The pawn, his son with straight golden hair, two squares to the side and one square in front much like the intimacy between them. The boy concealed his feelings with hands held tight behind his back. The father didn't move a muscle. They watched, without comment, several batches of boys run past in the intermediate 100-yard relay race. Everyone else was cheering. All this obstinance would soon be over, then they could separate and go their own ways. Return to recognised routines held together nicely, with volumes of unspoken words, self-control and reserve.

In the faraway fields, flocks of sheep grazed, oblivious to it all. Generations turning obstacles into abstinence or quite the opposite.

19

The General Synopsis

Imminent Becoming Cyclonic

WINSTON MONTAGUE, HIS FAMILY and me, went to see *'The Man With The Golden Gun'*. At the village cinema in Totnes, Devon. I must say I was highly aroused by Britt Ekland. She was suitably undressed throughout. It took my curiosity level to: Empire State Building.

Buckland House
20th May 1974

Dear Mum
Thank you for the parcel. When I went out with Winston Montague, we went down to Totnes village and saw Winston's grandma. And we rode back to Winston's House I had Winston's sisters' bike and he had his own. Then we went fishing but we did not catch anything.
Love Rupert x

After the short half term break with Winston Montague, we were returned to school and another master had arrived. He brought an old wife. He was old too. This new old master was called Mr Blackwood, from Costa Rica. He wasn't Costa Rican. Just ran a school there, once. A long time ago. I don't know when.

He was a tall, balding, white haired, almond tanned, leather skinned, multiple moles, kind of man with a chunky gold bracelet chain on his right arm. Gold rings and an ostentatious golden crucifix on a chain around his neck that nestled between the white hairs on his chest. Relaxed, casual and careful. Think Ronnie Biggs 1974.

He appeared one summer's day, during term time and at tea, everybody got treated to a bowl of fresh strawberries. Out of sight! Later on, Hunt stood up in class and claimed, He be called Strawberry-man. The name stuck for a while. After tea, we were sent to our classrooms where, in turn, Strawberry-man visited us and did the big hello, nice to meet you thing.

Now, it was then that I first came aware of my internal radar. It switched on when he kept saying, "I'm really not a nice person." That'll be out in plain sight then.

He didn't last too long; I guess the visible arguments with the headmaster and general smell of the fictional character from a 1970s spy film.

Other less strawberry sweet stories hopped and jumped like frogs from stone to stone across the jungle streams of what, after midnight, *of what* he was really up to. But that was just hear say. I have no proof. Other than spoken words, and the wind picks up spoken words and carries them away.

"Lights out."

Friday 24th May – my 11th birthday. More presents confiscated. My birthday always fell during the summer term time. To have a birthday celebration at home was like holding a Moonstone, very rare. Mr and Mrs Elliot lived in rural Suffolk. Arable farmers they were. Mrs Elliot had had a hip replacement and back then, it took a long time to recover, therefore they needed a housekeeper to help out with everything around the house. Up steps my mother.

The West Indies cricket team were on tour in England. Thousands of beautiful pheasant creatures ran down the concrete roads of a derelict World War Two airfield, the sunlight glinted off their regal plumage. The pheasants were reared for shooting. Those that weren't shot were run over along country roads. The ones that made it through all that, were either torn to shreds by foxes or succumbed to poachers who picked up most of the others. A few did survive the season, but not many.

Buckland House
Saturday 25th May 1974

Dear Mum

Thank you for the small parcel. Dad sent me a mascot of a Scotsman and I call him Scotty! Yesterday Brother Number Four sent me £1 and some space stamps. And Mr and Mrs Elliot sent me a birthday card. I have written to them. Last Wednesday the colts lost against Mount House and the 1st XI won. I got 6 runs and three wickets. Tomorrow the first are playing St Petroc's and I am in it. Today Dad sent me a Geometory set and some toffees. Thank you very much for the felt tips and the Snoopy writing paper and model

efforts Latin Good 6th Maths Good 9th French 10th Good English 11th Good History 2nd Good Geography 2nd Excellent Scripture 4th Good Science 6th Good Final: Good

Lots of Love Rupert x
P.S. Thank Rose for the birthday card.

Buckland House
June 1st 74

Dear Mum, Rose and Nod

The 1st XI played against St Petroc's last Saturday. I was in the match, and I got 4 wickets and caught one. I did not score any runs because I did not bat. We won by 1 run and 1 wicket. On Wednesday the colts and 1st XI won against St Michaels, and I got three wickets and 7 runs for the colts. The colts won by 92 runs we got 114 runs all out and we got them out for 22 runs. And the colts have played St. Petroc's it was a draw and I got 50 runs not out all the runs we got was 111. Winston Montague stuck in with me at 11th batsman and we Declared at tea and dismissed 5 people! Today the 1st XI are going to play Wolborough Hill. I am in the match. Yesterday Mr Lewis said any bowler who gets 8 wickets in a match will get a cricket ball! We have not been in yet. I have made the model you sent me it is small and chubby. I have just received your letter. Hope Rose does well in nursing. How is Rose's boyfriend Nod? Mr Beaumont is having another car Treasure Hunt on Sunday and over 100 people are taking part.

Love Rupert x

Buckland House
8th June 74

Dear Mum

There have been no matches this week, but there is a 1st XI match against Kelly College this afternoon, I am in it. The car treasure hunt was fun, and Mr Thompson came first. Our Matron has been ill, so the Headmaster's wife does surgery. The Common Common Entrance Exams begin on Monday. Thank you for your letter. I have pluses for English and Maths. It is rather cold. The temperature of the swimming pool is only 58°

Love Rupert x

Buckland House
22nd June 1974

Dear Mum

Thank you for the parcel. Brother Number Four sent me a tea shirt of 74 WM. When we played against St Petroc's I got 14 runs and was caught, and I got 5 wickets.

Today there is a match against Wolborough Hill at Buckland. I have made my womble I call him James.

Love Rupert x

Buckland House
29th June 1974

Dear Mum

Last Sunday Bradley Edwards, Winston Montague, Hunt and I went for an all day walk down the woods and Winston Montague got lost. We called him then we decided to go back to school. On the way we found Winston Montague picking strawberries! We have been practising for sports day and I got a standard for Hundred metres. The match on Wednesday was cancelled because of rain. Not much swimming; I have only been in once this term! No efforts. Yes I did get a 50 pence post order from Aunty Florrie.

Love Rupert x

Buckland House
Saturday 13th July 1974

Dear Mum

How are you? The match against St Michaels on Wednesday was cancelled, but we will have it on Saturday. The choir had their half holiday and we went to Bude and Mr Harrington came, our English master. Yesterday there we 2 innings matches against St Peters we drew. I got 16 runs and was caught wicket-keeper and I got 6 wickets.

Love Rupert xx

Buckland House
Friday 27 September 1974

Dear Mum

Thank you for the letter. I wrote to Aunty Florrie, I hope I got the right address. I also had a letter from Brother Number Three. All games of conkers I have played I have lost! It has always been Raining so we have not played games. We went for a run on Friday. The film On Sunday is about 'Dr. Syn' it's about smuggling.

Love Rupert x

20
Little Boy

Prep school letter

Again, I flippin' cry at the end of Old Yeller. I feel so manipulated by that film, sat in pyjamas and a dressing gown, loose slippers. It is too much, so traumatic. The games room door is opened. It is time for bed. We leave, older boys jeer and punch us on the arm.

"Sissy girl..." They say.

"No I'm not." There is nothing like the goodnight punch on the arm to raise your spirits. We long for a goodnight kiss from Mummy and Daddy. The projectionist, Mr Harrington, attends to the projector oblivious to the taunts. He is mesmerised by the workings of the wonder machine. He looks and listens, says to himself over and over, *magic light!* until the reel of film runs out. He's usually the last to leave the room.

We skidded about the grass in the slight to moderate rain. The winter grass was long. It needed a cut. The rugby ball slippery, difficult, like clutching at a bar of soap in the showers. The unpredictable bounce. Just when you think you've got it, it goes another way, a bit like life. Nothing but grey skies and woods, hedges, fields, a solitary crow and another. Everywhere you looked, green grass. I am bored, even the wildlife looked bored. It would explain why so many pheasants jumped in front of passing cars.

Buckland House
26th October 74

Dear Mum

thank you for your letter. I had a bump in rugby! What happened was a boy called Malcolm McGregor had the ball and I ran straight in to him and we bomped heads! (**?!#•≠*?!?) After games I went up to Matron and she put a bandage on my head, now I am all right and if I had been on games yesterday I might have been in the 2nd XV. The film this week is called "Black Beauty" The rugby match is against Mount House.

Love Rupert xxx

We skidded about the grass in the slight to moderate rain. The winter grass was long. It needed a cut. The rugby ball slippery, difficult, like clutching at a bar of soap in the showers. The unpredictable bounce. Just when you think you've got it, it goes another way, a bit like life.

The urge in my nether regions meant I needed to go, so I broke away from the excited shouts, the taunts and teasing and left two track lines across the wet grass. I shuffled and ran, making the noises like a steam train back towards the conveniences. The austere, functional, always cold, rectangular block of an outside toilet stood next to the back entrance to the school, the main house. I shivered as I went about my business as quickly as possible, slightly out of breath and straining. I tried not to breathe in the stench and felt my body heat leave through my blue smock collar. Rainwater dropped back down my neck, hence the shivering and haste.

Buckland House
Saturday 9th November 1974

Dear Mummy
How are you? There was a run yesterday I came 27th= with my friend Hunt. On Wednesday there was a match against Wolborough Hill. We lost 12-0 that is rugby. The film this week is called "Wings of Eagles", it is about World War II. There is a match today. Our Colts play against St Petroc's. Thank you for your letter.

Yes, Rose and Daddy and I got to the zoo. We saw the lions, which were in the film 'Born Free'.

I would like to go to Daddy's until the 21st then go to for Christmas 22nd until the 29th and come up to you for the rest of the hols. Is that all right? Discuss it with Daddy.

Love Rupert x

The school bog roll, like so many other things, was unsatisfactory. I think it was government issue lavatory paper. The sort that is as transparent as tracing paper and as unforgiving as the last nail smote into the cross. When it came down to it, it felt like one was using a Christmas tree branch or sandpaper if you'd rather. Now I know I am going on, but it has to be the most nonabsorbent and uncomfortable bog roll in the world. A far cry from the soft double-ply toilet paper I imagined the rest of England used. But then again this was a 1970s fee-paying preparatory school. A place where boys were funnelled to become soldiers. Supposedly.

Buckland House
Saturday 16th November 1974

Dear Mummy
Thank you for your letter. On Thursday I was sick in the science lesson what happened was I started coughing and I could not stop! And one of my friends Ellison took me to Matron and I was sick! I was put in bed all day.

The lecture this week is about "The Awakening of the Giants" it is about Costa Rica. A master called Blackwood is talking about it. Yesterday we played games, it's about the first time this half of the term: how is Aunty Florrie? I am going to write to her and Aunty Ruth. In maths, we are on book 2 now.

Lots of Love Rupert x

Tuesday 26th November 1974

Whilst still holding my breath, I ran out of the toilet block and collided with Hunt. The call had gone out to find Green. I was the boy with that surname. And now I had been found.

"Found you!" shouted Hunt as if we'd been playing hide and seek, we hadn't.

"What?" I said.

"There you are," Hunt said.

Hunt, friend.

"The Headmaster wants to see you."

The Headmaster was the head of this preparatory boarding school but you know already that.

"What's he want?" I said, a little distracted, and then annoyed, wondering what I had done since breakfast that would warrant the headmaster's attention. I couldn't think. What could it possibly be?

I followed Hunt along dimly lit corridors with flagstone floors. I hung my coat up on my peg. Hunt passed the wrong way through the tall white pillars outside the dining room. He liked breaking the rules. So did I, but I went the right way today for good measure. To balance things out. Once in the Library or the in-between room, much like the assembly room with a hole where the ceiling should be.

The library only had two bookshelves and was more of a room to walk through, although it did house the two long overspill dining room tables. They doubled as table nine and table ten at mealtimes. The library had the main noticeboards on the mantelpiece. I sat on top of table nine which doubled for the Tuck Shop on Saturdays. Again, I must say, several boxes of sweets bought from a local cash and carry, their bulky boxes cut open and the sweets poured out in all their sweetie goodness. I sat and waited.

"Wait there." I watched Hunt go to the staff room door opposite. In the adjoining room to the library, some younger boys with badminton racquets hit shuttlecocks up into the void. The assembly room's massive ceiling went on forever. Whenever I saw badminton being played, I wanted to run in, snatch a racquet and hit a shuttlecock up to touch the dome. A balcony clung close to the assembly room wall, it went round the edge and took you to the largest of the school's dormitories called Bryanston.

Bryanston, another public school set in a 400-acre estate in Dorset. Their school motto was *Et nova et vetera*. Both the new and the old.

Hunt knocked on the dark door, and someone answered and left the door ajar but not so you could see in. The headmaster appeared, he looked coldly at me and continued to talk to Hunt. I saw nothing untoward other than boys who passed by with tight-lipped smiles. Hunt looked over his shoulder at me and glanced back at the headmaster, then his head dropped. Again, the headmaster's eyes surveyed me before he closed the door.

Although I could not read him, I now knew something was up.

Hunt walked over to the table. He looked a little sick and said nothing. The tension no longer trotted, it galloped. I jumped off the table onto the floor and stood up straight. It *was* something. Hunt took a moment. He rolled his eyes looking for the words to say.

"What?" I said.

Finally, Hunt looked over towards the mantlepiece and spoke. "What are you *doing* for the holidays?"

I studied him and replied. "I'm going to be going back home. Why?"

Again he looked away, shook his head, a nervous laugh escaped his throat and he covered it with a cough.

He turned and just looked at me as if trying telepathy. He gave up, slowly shook his head, broke off the stare and returned to the staff room door. Again, he knocked on the dark door only this time before the door opened, he gazed at his shoes.

"*Alright*, I'll do it!" Snapped the Headmaster. "Two minutes. Keep him there."

Hunt returned, somewhat relieved, but still, there was something not being said.

"What is it?" I asked earnestly. A wave of giddy emotion hit me. Hunt shook his head and turned away. Now I began to worry. I don't understand what I have done wrong.

I sat down on the bench by the edge of the table, I started to count the nail holes in the floorboards.

Waiting for the Headmaster was like waiting for the dentist, both unpleasant experiences. Eventually, the headmaster opened the staff room door. A flick of his chin indicated I should follow.

O crap! I am going to get caned but what for?

However, I was surprised. For the first time, I was shown into the inner sanctum of the school, an old antique room. A chamber where, over the centuries, one might entertain errant Devonian nobility. A sheltered place where they might take an after-Church aperitif. A before-lunch tipple. A slug of the hard stuff to promote conversation. The driest English Sherry carefully poured into a crystal schooner, for instance. The chestnut brown liquid sipped with a canopy of pheasant. The colour of the sherry matched the wooden panels that adorned the room and three narrow musty lead-lined diamond glass windows held back the daylight nicely. The chamber was thick with an atmosphere of stale olden times. It felt old too, complete with faded curtains, stained furniture and silver cobwebs hanging around the off-white cornices.

I am invited to sit on an old beaten-up leather couch. The Headmaster sat on my left-hand side. He placed a hand on my right shoulder. He spoke as if underwater. It sounded hollow.

It was the ignition.

Then the realisation hit. Within an instant, I am torn apart by anguish and confusion, I am utterly destroyed. The top of my head lifts off and travels skyward to mushroom like that Little Boy atomic bomb. And now the mushroom is billowing smoke high up into the ceiling. My body is held to the floor by the headmaster's hand. I shrug it off but the sudden gash of pain that jumped out of my chest snapped back in. I shudder and sob uncontrollably. The headmaster's words replay, this time the words landed and when they did, they smashed my brain to smithereens.

"I am very sorry to have to tell you Rupert, but your father died last night... Is there anything you wish to say?"

As far as I was concerned, The Taj Mahal just exploded. The Great Wall of China did nothing at all because I have nothing to say, I have nothing prepared.

There is no right thing, at the age of eleven, to say to catastrophic news. I am still processing what just happened, I mean before, outside, in the library, outside the staff room. And what was that with Hunt? What was that? I swallowed down a pineapple-sized lump now lodged in my throat. It made it easier to speak. "What will happen to my father's car?" I say this out of a sense of duty because the headmaster asked if there was anything I wished to say. It's an awful business and quite frankly it would be better if this sort of thing only happened in the holidays.

The heat of the shockwave burns.

Within an instant, I am transported back through time. A young me sat on my father's lap, holding the steering wheel as we drive along, that's right I can't see the road, although I can see the sky and trees. I am happy, I feel his lovely warm energy and quiet reassuring voice, and I can ignore everything else for a split second until my mother's voice shatters the illusion with caustic remarks. I lose the connection with my father. He is gone. I have lost him and now I must navigate this world alone. No more chess. No more going to watch cricket. I feel devastated. I hold my stomach because it feels like a hole just appeared in it. I miss him so much. I remember the last talk we had had. One of the last times I went home for a long weekend was late October, or was it early November? I sat on his bed in my pyjamas. He talked about *the grown-up stuff*. Confusion. I don't want a girlfriend. I don't want to learn to drive. I don't want no public school. Get off of my Cloud.

The blast impact hit me squarely in the chest.

I miss him. It is so hard. I have nobody to talk to. A bell rings and I am encouraged by the headmaster to go off to class. I am met by Hunt. We are sad together. He was there for me. He was sorry. He knew my father from a long weekend spent at my father's last home, Brixham, Devon.

Nowhere to hide, I can only sink deep within. I don't see anything. The classroom has desks and us boys sit quietly at them. I am not there. I rubbed my numb face with the wet handkerchief. Choking on tears.

"Sir, why is Green crying?" Said Thompson, he put his hand up and repeated the question.

I stared up at the blackboard, bit my thumb and fell into the blackboard's void, who is it who dragged me back into the room?

"SIR! GREEN IS CRYING!" Shouted Wilson.

"Er... No need to shout. Oh, ignore him. He's had some bad news." Said Mr Harrington like the bad news was my fault. Mr Harrington held a piece of chalk in the air. He is standing beside the blackboard. Is he going to throw it or write something? Time stands still. I find a knot in the wooden desktop to stick a pencil into and snap off the lead. I wished for everything to go away. My father is dead. O, let me weep. My father is dead. Dead I tell you.

I shall sit here a while longer. I wish I had a candle to remember his light, for the feeling goes and returns from deep within and nobody can reckon to the magnitude of its force. I am shipwrecked and with this rising tide, cannot be prepared enough for yet another wave. And again, it smashes into my heart but like a shower of hard rain. It soon blows out and the sunlight returns. It is no doubt a process in which I have to avoid drowning in and I dwell grasping at fortunate days and fond memories until the pumice stone is worn down with sufficient tears as to no longer cause me to limp along this forgotten road, where you and I, myself will one day bid everlasting return and face the warm fires of my house in what the state sponsored people call *Heaven*. Words can help to express the melancholy sorrows that death brings as it callously reaps friends and loved ones, who once stood tall and waving on a loop in the St David's rail station car park inside the skull cinema of my mind.

And then comes the fallout.

In the evening, car headlights were reported and the knowledge passed down the line. Seen way off in the distance, heading towards the school. Shortly after, Brother Number Three switched off the car engine, glanced at Buckland House through the windscreen and turned to Jo his wife. Without a word, they got out the car. I have been summoned. It is both good and upsetting to see friendly, worried with love faces again. But again, it is hard. After twenty minutes of silent, raw, jangled, burning on the inside screaming, paralysed terror, our eyes stand out like florid glass marbles. Daring not to hug beyond an arm in the hallway, faltering to show these confused feelings of love-spiked-grief-anger. Compassion, even for the situation. I am disorientated, standing between the two phosphorescent pillars on the ground floor. And behind me, the out-of-bounds switchback, sweeping wide red carpet stairway. I am now at my lowest point.

In what seems like no time at all, Brother Number Three and Jo are ushered out by the Headmaster. Encouraged to leave through the main double doors. I am left behind. I am unbalanced, standing on one leg, biting my hand, awkward. I am at full stretch like a pirouetting ballet dancer. I am ordered to go back to prep. But all I want to do is go back home with my brother and his wife, leave this hell. I falter as my instinct leans towards running and yelling after their departing car. My programming insists I be a good boy and do as I am told. I can't fight it anymore.

The Headmaster said it was in my interest to detain me. Only my mother had the authority to take me out of school that night. It didn't count for anything. She was miles away and nowhere to be seen. Not even a phone call. I feel hard done by. I feel angry, I feel hopeless, I feel useless, and deep within the motionless flame of my spirit dims. I can't fight it anymore. I suffer in a sickness of desperation until I don't feel anything at all. I have run aground on the black sands of despair. Marooned by this savage cruelty. I am informed that I will be permitted to leave at the weekend. And at that moment, the weekend felt as far away as that shuttlecock, the one I hit to reach the assembly room's high vaulted dome ceiling. The impossible has happened.

The world changed in one sentence. And I didn't like it.

The days go by, and Saturday arrives. A car pulled up. It's Mother.

I am bundled into the car, no-nonsense, and driven an hour and a half back to Brother Number Three's council house in Uffculme, Mid Devon. Once there, I am reunited with my elder, wiser, all grieving siblings, apart from Brothers Number One and Two who were in Perth, Western Australia. Brother Number Four, having driven 13 hours alone, all the way back from Celle, Germany. Nobody was talking which made it all a bit difficult. The Funeral is the following week on Monday 2nd December and apparently, I am not allowed to attend. Later, my father was to be cremated in Torquay.

It is upsetting because I am not allowed to attend. It is disastrous that I am not allowed to attend. Why can't I go? Nobody tells me anything.

On Sunday evening, having had one night away, I am drop-kicked back through the school gates and that was that. Get on with it. I am numb but as I recover, another wave knocks into me, the delayed destructive effects of grief.

"I usually find that boys get over their father's death within three days." The Headmaster said. "Goodbye Mrs Green, see you at Christmas?"

I watched the two small red lights disappear at the end of the drive as Mother's car rejoined the road. And in that moment, I never felt so alone. I looked up into the sky, the stars sprinkled their light onto me. I took a lungful of air. I swivelled round to face the school's entrance. I swear I could hear someone laughing, talking, calling my name. I wiped a tear from my cheek, leaned against the cumbersome double door entrance and sunk back into the school's bubble. From around the corner sprung Hunt.

"HEY!" Shouted Hunt, "You're back!"

"It appears so..."

For a split second, we locked eyes. He recoiled, not wanting to engage with the exploding shrapnel of emotion coming off me. Eventually, he thought of something, Hunt lunged forward, and with two fingers, tapped me on the shoulder, mouthed, "YOU'RE IT!!" And before I could react, he turned tail and skipped merrily down the dimly lit corridor like a demented cartoon duck, knocking coats off their hooks as he went.

Apollo 17 Moon Mission is launched. The crew takes the photograph known as The Blue Marble as they leave the Earth. It's a Thursday...

Buckland House
Thursday 7th Décembre 1974

Dear Mum
How are you? Please can you get me Subuteo rugby for Christmas? If not something else will do!! Our last match was against Wolborough Hill we lost 4-28. I was not in it. That's why we lost! On Thursday it was the choir half-holiday. Also on that day I found an angel fish had got caught in a test tube, so I rushed down to the church and got Darwin, he is the boy in charge of the fish and he came and looked at it, it was dead so I disposed off it! The Christmas Dinner is on Tuesday and after that there is a film called "Young Bess". It is about Queen Elizabeth. On Monday there was a badminton match. I was in it we won every game. In exams I came 12th which I think is two positions up! Love Rupert xxxx Rupert!

Exeter St David's railway station in Devon, was where we train boys would be shuffled and collected. At the beginning of each term, or deposited at the end. There was always a strange air of freedom and inevitability about the place. A strip of land that will always be packed with emotions of separation and adventure. Always coming or going, never still and quiet. I never had the time to reflect until now.

They stood outside this old railway station. I am sat inside the school minibus looking out through the two small back windows. My family standing in a line. Goodbye to Father, Rose, Nod, Brother Number Three and Jo.

We are waving, then we are not waving anymore.
Is that the moment?
Is this where I have to let him go?
Be a big boy. A long pause, then the minibus turns and I turn away from the moment. Did I know, at the back of a minibus, holding it all together knowing it would be the last time I would see him?

That secretive whisper behind my right ear. The voice you hear but you don't hear.

The knowing not knowing. How did I not know? The hope that he is not dead and one day I will see him on the street. But he won't recognise me because he is living another life. Perhaps the moment you die, you are born in a different country.

I don't want him to be dead.

21

Au Revoir

My Dear Sweet Precious Little Boy

SMOKE CLOUDS. LEAVE IT a minute. Platform four through thirteen, diesel engines smoke clouds. They stand. They are the British Rail Class 52 diesel-hydraulic locomotives. More smoke clouds. It rolls out, alack, alack, inky blackness octopus squirts. Spews and spiral skirts lifting off the engine's roof, enfolding plumes of smoke into the evaporating vastness of empty roof overhang.

Deep growling, throbbing, sobbing noises. Every step is covered in unfiltered sound. Onward the hustle, onward the hassle. Onward the consultation between elite members of the train travel club, everyday jerks, workers and bezerkers. They've all come down to town. They stand as a crowd as one, desperately divided. Magnetised adventure hand in hand, to stand and deliver if only they could find which platform they needed to be on. Collected thought sways as one, like high tide seaweed, the way it clings to the edges of mollusc-driven seawalls. I wait for the tide to fall before stepping into that light. We left them staring at information boards.

All my senses are locked onto the captured split-second, short-time moments. In overdrive, they captured passing fragrances, hardened deodorant, exhausted fumes, slicks of pungent hot oil fast food, wet bleach disinfectant and no I don't want fish and chips. I want chips. Everyone's going somewhere, me included. Buy me some chips. I've got some spare change.

A distant distorted voice blurts out the last arrivals, late departures and the trains that will be delayed. The inevitable cancellations echo about the space. Numbers and letters rattle as they inevitably have to change. The dark blue boards like a cricket scoreboard they stretch the information across the station front and the white letters jumble, tumble and jump down to the penultimate destination. They are linked to the sway of the crowd's impetuousness. People break away from the mass funnel and run towards a gate.

When the yellow-faced diesel train growls, it releases a shout of compressed air. Like *"All aboard!"* Except this is not Disney, this is a reality all stark, dark and enough to make a hound dog bark. It sounds like a howl. That's the bubble inside railway stations like a multitude of blue-sheened flies that throng around horse dung. Intoxicated nourishment the dung brings life. In slow motion, the people flee from and to waiting trains as the seconds tick, recorded by a suited and booted guard as yet unseen.

Most insistent, the snorts of vehicle horns. They're snaking, a low rider, winding a way through the melee. They pull coupled trolleys twenty containers long. They're all loaded with professional trunks, suitcases, precious cargo. Along the station stretch, stand station staff. They shout orders and give individual warnings to the public as they trample along the existing concrete. It is a departure. Events are marked. A timeline, heavy footfall avoiding death by the narrowest of margins, a fag paper between a balanced knock to the edge and dead on the rails.

I try to keep up and follow along, I skip, trip and stumble but with childlike innocence, I trail behind Mother who weaves through the people. At a steady pace, I sing *Onward Christian Soldiers*. I don't know why. It is the rhythm of the long-distance runner. I reach out but fail to take hold of Mother's hand. My feet fall into step therefore hinting at a transition, my rôle from traveller to passenger. "I want sweets, not chocolate, Everton mints."

"It's too late." Shouts Mother, she points to the wall clock. "We have no time."

I need to talk, a day's worth of chatter in what time remains. "How high do you think Brunel's brutalist arches travel..." I point in the general direction when she looks around and I add, "...and that bend such elegance. I can not describe." I don't get a reply. I trace Brunel's lines past a snapshot of pigeons on the wing dropping below the skyline to platform level.

"Oh God! I am back here again." I shout. Paddington station, once again seeking the West Country train. I wonder if Brunel had a loving mother. I still want sweets.

The nightmarish thing of the lonely is to see inanimate objects come to life, like Disney but not Disney more Dali, but not Francis Bacon, more like a mix of the two, make way for Hieronymus Bosch. That'll do.

See here the Roman numeral clock face high up fixed against the station wall, see it look down scornfully at us, its hands covering its eyes as the multitudes scramble, push and shove each other pressing towards unrealistic expectation. We are late and I am ushered lifted, call it what you will, but most definitely head first passed through the window to gain passage on the West Country train. Mother hopes it is the right one. It should be. "Get in!" Urges Mother. "Get in!" My turn to scramble, I look at the other passengers, but there is nobody to ask. The carriage door slams shut, as do our hearts. Once again closed, shut, locked, stinging nettles weave around the small wooden box I keep my heart in. Where was the warmth of an embrace?

Au Revoir my dear sweet precious little boy.

Kisses have no meaning. I have run out of patience for an affectionate goodbye. I will see you in three months.

Mother through the window, as the platform moved. I watched Mother turn and weep covering her face. Now I feel bad and start to burn from the inside. This is why I need some sweets.

For the last forty miles of this ordeal, tired boys are squashed into the back of the minibus and driven at speed. Along dark bendy roads. Back inside the minibus we are fighting centrifugal forces and barbed jibes as to what we did and considered best about being on holiday not holiday. Slipstreaming to a faraway place for another dose of imperialist isolation. And I can't say how funny it is that I can't wait to get there.

Buckland House
Saturday 11th January 1975

Dear Mum

Thank you for your lovely Christmas present. I am in form 5 (whitch) witch is one form up from last term. I am still in Bryanston and (sleepling) sleeping in the bed I was in when I first went in Bryanston! Can you send me a birthday card for Uncle Arthur's birthday on the 16th. Our head boy George is ill! I'm settling in well. I had a good joyney back to school I was (all) almost sick in the school-bus. Nearly everyone is back. We have two new boys I have forgot there names! In hobbies I'm doing Chess, Soft Toys, Piano and Carpentry I will ask Jesus the school's carpenter if I can make a trolly if not a coffee table alright?

Love Rupert x

P.S. I asked my friend Winston Montague if I could go to his place. He said, "Yes, I will have to write home tho." You write as well.

```
                                    BUCKLAND HOUSE,
                                    BUCKLAND FILLEIGH,
                                    BEAWORTHY,
Telephone: Shebbear 222.            N. DEVON.
                                    EX21 5JA
```

The roaring cars fumes everywhere the drivers only care of winning! Oil on the road get onto the morse code a furious race was going to be told of they went. 1 cars wheels was bent at the start everyone thought he was fixed, every car spinned and turned all except one which groaned.

I made it up myself.

Rupert

Creative writing

22

Pretty Letters All In A Row

It was one of those dank, grey nothingness, winter mornings. Day four or five of being forced back to Buckland House School. Tuck that shirt in zombie walking.

Remembering how to tie a tie. We quietly processed down the back staircases to reach the flagstone corridor floor. Several boys, one after the other, others joking before joining the monastic lines, from the dormitories to the assembly room with the heavenly dome, taking in how automatic it had all become, along the way. Nothing noteworthy said. It was hardly talking, more well-wishers mourning the Morning light. Undertones of sickness and interruption from the kitchen wireless strains of Status Quo. A thin noise that seeped through the kitchen walls invaded the quiet of the flagstone corridor. Our footsteps in time to the beat of the school drum. The humdrum. As more boys appeared at the top of the stairs descending, down, down and down to our level.

Buckland House
January 18th 1975

Dear Mum
Thank you for your letter. The film on Sunday was Flipper I had seen it before. In chess, I was beaten by Thompson. On Wednesday we had a fire practice. In had work I am making a snake I have almost finished it in one lesson!! On Wednesday I tried to ring you up but you (where) must have been out. (Watching a film.) In Scoop I am getting Murder on the Orient Express!! The film you saw, I rang about 7.15? When I was going to ring you I was going to say that my raincoat had come and all the other stuff and could you send me my red pistol? The film on Sunday is about "the Three lives of Thomasina". It is about a cat.
Lots Of Love Rupert X

We sit, half asleep in an envelope of silence. I have a cold. I quickly scan an old letter and put it back in my pocket. Not let anyone else see. The winter has arrived and with it this cold. The wet mist and grey skies, the low fog and the silence of the countryside. It leaves room for our little boy thoughts to roll around our shell-like heads. Empty headed and as clear as a glass light bulb.

A white bowl slides under my nose. Three stewed slug prunes set in sticky brown juice look up at me. I think they have given up. They no longer try to swim around my plate. For all I care, they might as well be Raven's hearts and if I eat the plateful, I might well turn into something ghastlier than I already am. I am not hungry which is odd for me.

It is compulsory to eat. The younger boys pull faces. Breakfast, breakfast, breakfast... I can't taste anything. My nose is blocked. I want to go home. I want to go back to bed. I want to sleep and dream of being anywhere but here.

Buckland House
25th January 75

Dear Mum
How are you? I miss you very much. Thank you for ringing me up on Sunday.
Today we had a run I came 20= with Winston Montague. I have almost finished my snake. All I have to do is sew some eyes on. The film on Sunday is "Savage Sam". It is about a dog who rescues some children from Indians. In carpentry, I have started my coffee table. We have not played games at all this term. I had a letter from Brother Number Four, I have written to him as well.
My efforts: Latin 9th Good Maths 10th Average English 11th Good French 11th Good History 7th Good Geography 8th Good Scripture - Science Average Final – Good 21pts
Lots of Love Rupert x

Buckland House
31st January

Dear Mum
Thank you very much for sending my gun and sweets and peanuts and handkerchiefs. I got a letter from Brother Number Four. To-day we got scoop. I got the book "Murder on the Orient Express"! I have not started it yet, but I will probably read it in bed tonight. Also I tidied my desk!! (which was very messy!) The film on Sunday is called "Merry Andrew". It is about a clown in a circus. I am still keeping my diary. To day we had a new- mini-bus. On Wednesday there is a colts match against St Petroc's. Mr Blackwood is trying to keep us tidier! It is table change tomorrow.
Lots of Love Rupert x

Buckland House
8th Febrauuary 1975

Dear Mum
thank you for your letter. I am glad you were allowed to get the things from Brixham. The Headmaster let me make a camp in the school grounds and I have got Winston Montague and Rhys Jenkins in it. I am head of the camp. Half Term begins on Thursday. We had some games of kickball yesterday and Today also I am almost in the 1st XI. We have played some matches. The 1st XI lost 10-0 and the colts won 2-1. Both were against St Petroc's. On Sunday the film is called "Plymouth Adventure," it is about the ship the Mayflower, which voyages to America in 1620. I have got a plus for music.
Lots of Love Rupert x

Buckland House
21st Febraaury 1975

Dear Mum
Thank you very much for your parcel. To day in football I scored a goal. When Aunty Florrie and Aunty Ruth came, Aunty Ruth gave me a pound note! I bought some soldiers and I bought Aunty Ruth a scarf. On Thursday the Judo boys had grading. Hunt got a green belt. He is only the 4th boy to do this in in ten years. When the 1st XI played against Woloborough Hill they lost 7-0! Tomorrow the 1st XI and colts are playing against St. Michaels. On Thursday also we had a Badminton match. We lost. I played with Ellison we won most of our games. I have got a whole plus from Mr Blackwood this week for not getting any untidiness in the whole week I also got a ¼ for Geography and History and one whole and a ¼ for music. I am doing a duet with Thompson, I do the lower part. It is the Headmaster's birthday on Saturday. He will have a large cake (scrummy!)
Lots of love Rupert x

Buckland House
Saturday 1st march 1975

Dear Mum
Thank you for your letter. Yesterday I scored two goals in football. In hobbies I made a little carrot and a little maggot! Also a sleeping bag for them and a purple thing. I will write on Sunday to Brother Number One. The 1st XI and colts won their matches against St Michael's last Saturday. This Saturday they play against

St Petroc's at home. On last Friday evening the choir went to a "Music Workshop" in Okehampton Church. Please could you send my bracelet to me?

My efforts Latin 11th Good Maths 16th Good French 9th Excellent English 12th Good History 6th Good Geography 7th Good Scripture 11th Good Science 7th Good Final Good 33 points

Love Rupert x

Buckland House
14th March 75

Dear Mum

thank you for the letters. I sent the birthday card off to grandma. On the same day I got a letter from Brother Number Four and he sent me these. To-day we walked around our cross country run. (boo) for tomorrow's cross country run. On Tuesday it is the merit half holiday. So far I have got only ¾ minus this term! And tons of Pluses. On Wednesday the 1st XI + colts drew against Mount House. Hope to see you soon! In handwork, I made a mouse in one lesson.

my efforts•Latin 9th Good Maths 11th Good French 10th Excellent English 12th Good History 10th Average Geography 13th Good Scripture 5th Good Science 12th Good Final Good

Love Rupert x

Holiday-not-Holiday

12th April 1975 – Mother and I travel by overnight boat and then all day on the train to Hannover. Brother Number Four picks us up and drives us to Celle where he lives with his wife, Helena. They're both teachers in the Gymnasium school there. At least that is what I am led to believe they are. They could be secret agents. Unlikely.

13th April – We tour around Celle and are shown the hairy house.

14th April – Mother and I catch a bus into town. Brother Number Four writes down on a piece of paper, the destination and the return point. The joke was that he did this to save Mother the embarrassment of having to say in public the word Fahrt. Fahrt means to ride in German. At least that is what I am led to believe was the reason why. On the bus, I looked out the window and was somewhat shocked by an old war memorial. A statue of a soldier on one knee, head bowed, as if in the act of laying down his sword. The thought occurred to me, although obvious, the penny didn't drop until I saw it with my own eyes, that the enemy back then also had people who died in horrid ways and had unresolved anger and grief too.

15th April – I buy a dice tumbler and six white dice and a scoring pad so we can play endless rounds of Yahtzee! Brother Number Four falls ill.

16th April – Cricket Club Celle. Brother Number Four and I go to the gym at the school, where we play with the German teenager students that Brother Number Four has successfully taught to play indoor tennis ball cricket. I show off my skills. The girls practise speaking English. The boys swing hard but consistently miss the tennis ball.

17th April – Brother Number Four was told by Mother that I, Rupert would probably stay Buckland House, for fear I would be very lonely if I stayed with Mother in Hove.

Hirt Mit Schweinen. (Shepherd with pigs)

18th April 1975 – Brother Number Four drives us to Bremen from Celle. It takes ages. We wander about the city. I am encouraged to go into a bakery and buy something to eat. I am rehearsed on the necessary words to say. I am made to sit on a bronze pig whilst Helena takes my photo.

19th April 1975 – more cricket and mini golf, and Brother Number Four gave me in the evening, a shot of Ratzeputz, it is a schnapps made from root ginger in Celle, Germany. 58% alcohol. Needless to say, I spat it out, cried and have never forgiven him.

Before we left, Brother Number Four gives me a 50 pence piece and some chocolate for the long train ride back. At the borders, officials board the train and want to know who everybody is. I ate all the chocolate before they got to me.

We return by train, six and a half hours with two changes to Hook of Holland, then step onto a boat to Harwich, England, a six and a half hour crossing, then train to Brighton, Taxi with suitcases back to the basement flat in Hove to see out the rest of the holiday-not-holiday.

23

The Basement Flat Feelings

THE SLATTED FLOORBOARDS BEND apart and Brighton Pier creaks as if it were a sleeping dragon. Everything is alive. I give the vintage Mutoscope the once-over. Yeah, I'll give it a go. I press my face against the viewer and grip the handle. Inside, tiny wheels begin to turn. Small square images drop down, at first all blurred then sharp pictures reveal a ramshackle, make-do theatre stage.

I have never seen such a stuttering effect before, the individual photos slot into place, one after the other. The tall naked lady dances with ostrich feathers. Her magnificent headdress and high heels. She kicks her heels high into the midnight air, the imaginary air that is ever-changing the faded colours, they're washing away with every frame. Like waves running in and falling out, such eye-popping extravagance. I wind the handle on some more.

Just then the central circular room of the Brighton Pier fills up with distorted people. A grand-looking Wurlitzer barrel organ comes bursting through the wall and starts to jump up and down. The snare drum rattles, the high hats clatter and the bass drum pumps, nervous as a lover's heartbeat. I am being swept along, by mechanical emotion, the exaggerated noise. I spin like a top. This place is all over me. Ping-ping-ping goes the slot machines. Bom-bom-bom goes the drum.

Frantically, I separate myself from the octopus tentacles, pushing them away, manifesting out of the Mutoscope and tying me up in knots. I stand a safe distance back from a grabbing tentacle and watch them spiralling, coiling a revolting dissolve down through the floorboard slits of the pier. I gaze between the slits, feeling the cool sea air, the irregular waves, swell and slop. The oily black sea is stirred by the giant pillars, I can't help but feel a little bit giddy. My tongue slips across my lips and tastes salty bitterness. I wish I was home. The audio mixture of watery waves and mechanical music buzzes, whirrs, swoops, chinks, blips and beeps, it does not falter in its relentless entertainment. It never fails, never falls, only sometimes stalls to change gear, the cogs turn to catch up, raising a cantilevered clutch and grinding its teeth. It is an electronic cacophony that punctuates the pulsing red, blinking yellow and pumpkin orange lights. They're screwed onto the sodden wooden walls, the rotten wooden doors and the trodden wooden floors of this gigantic funfair ride.

Laughter cuts across the gloom in the room. I skip the slot machines to find the penny roll amusements. I wait, study the movement and find the moment to release the penny coin I have pressed against the thin slot with my thumb. The penny rolls along zebra lines. It glides across to the map "C'mon win, win, win!" The trick is to get the penny to land between the parallel lines.

The lines move away and the coin curves to the right and flops over onto the conveyor belt canvas. The coin has stepped over the edge of the black line. No win. The penny drops into the darkness through the hole at the end. No win. Ten seconds of pleasure, empty pockets, no more coins. No win. Empty pockets and no win.

Far beyond the arcade, there is an almighty crump, a loud thud. I stumble, as I rush to catch the outside air, stubbing my toe on the door sill, I overbalance and fall out of the room and onto the promenade decking, crashing into the ornately decorated Victorian rail. No blood, carry on.

In the sky, four rays of sunlight have ruptured a massive black cloud and beams of mirror-ball light radiate across the spinach-green sea. Whilst all choppy and in no way serene, the top edges of each oncoming wave are a gentle flap and they unfurl crinkled white lace. And pale horses race towards the shoreline to break apart, to disintegrate into a soothing rush against the rolling pebbles, wash, wash, wash them clean, retreat and breathe.

Mother lived alone in Hove and worked as an all hours telephonist at the Hotel Neanderthal Brighton, a monstrously large hotel with revolving doors for an entrance. It struggled to nestle along with the other hotels on the seafront because it was so big, like three million rooms big. Once or twice, I would push through revolving doors and smile at the receptionist. They waved as I made my way through a secret door to plunge myself into the hotel's innards. The hotel's telephone exchange. A place where you pulled plugs and wire and reconnected the wires into switchboard holes. Mother would go through the salutations and the guests would be linked up with their call. Many ladies within the exchange, all talking at the same time. But mostly I would wake up in the basement flat in Hove alone and find a written message on the pine table.

I'll return at 2 pm here is some money. You can have 10p. Make yourself some breakfast. Rose might drop in to see you later on, love Mum.

Here comes trouble, it didn't take long, I soon learnt that if you want to melt chocolate on a saucer on the gas cooker ring, that the saucer would split in two.

The chocolate didn't melt when it hit the flame. I picked up the shard of the broken saucer and burnt my finger and thumb for the trouble. It was a chocolate bunny, Easter chocolate. I wanted to make hot chocolate to drink. Willy Wonka style melted from my Easter egg. I ran cold water from the cold tap over my hand and ate the rest of the chocolate with the other. I didn't cry, felt nice, so quiet so sad. I'm used to it. Self-reliant pain.

The best holiday-not-holiday learning I got from living in Hove next to Brighton, as in Hove not Brighton, was that people are strangely caught up in their stupid rules and conditions. I took my 10p and in need of sweets only three streets away found a sweet shop. The old-fashioned kind where rows and rows of large confectionary jars brim full of multi-coloured sweets are just waiting, inviting me to choose.

Oh! The head swoon of floral scents, sugar coated sweets in a musty old confectionary shop. So many colours to grab your attention but I know what I want. Not sure how to ask for it so I'll have a stab at it.

"I would like please, half a pound of wine gums."

"Are you sure? Half a pound, that's… that's rather a lot!" The rancid old woman replied looking across at the oldest shopkeeper ever, equally bunged-up, I would say.

"Yes, I would like half a pound," I said. In my mind, I asked what was wrong with that, you rancid old woman, you stupid old goat. Give me the wine gums.

'No!' said the oldest shopkeeper ever in full support. "Give him a quarter of a pound. That is the correct amount."

The rancid old woman weighed out the wine gums. She was careful not to go over the four ounces but did because, at the last moment, her shaky hands shook a little bit too much. At first, she put a red one back into the wine gum jar and then because the scales showed the weight to be a teeny-weenie bit over four ounces, the rancid old woman repeated the same thing but this time with a black wine gum. I closed my eyes in disbelief. "We don't want you to get drunk!" She added with a smile. I didn't think, for one moment, you could get drunk on wine gums.

I hate old people, why don't they just die? I slammed the 10p coin onto the wooden counter, grabbed the bag, said thank you and pushed on through the door annoyed but at least with a small white bag of wine gums. I headed toward the beach. If I'd had any wits about me, I should have found another sweet shop and bought another bag. Sadly, I wasn't that bright. Besides they probably rang all the other wine gum-selling sweet shops in the Brighton area and told them not to sell that little boy with the wild man of Borneo hair, brown V-neck jumper and green eyes any more wine gums because obviously, he wanted to get drunk.

On the beach, I looked out to sea. I'm not interested in the silhouettes of ocean-going tankers that perch on the distant horizon like Swifts on a phone line. I am certainly not bothered by the tremendous cauliflower clouds blowing up from the South. Stood by the rocks, I flipped molluscs and plunged my penknife into their hearts, the way Nod showed me. I throw them at stupid old seagull birds. Stupid for getting too close to me. I don't need old birds or old people for that matter. I need things to keep far away from me. I pick up a grey stone and drop it into the sea. That feels better, I throw a stone at a herring gull. It lifted effortlessly out of the way of the stone.

I brush the sand off my fingers and greedily eat the last wine gums two or three at a time. Losing control as my mouth soaks up the overload of blended blackcurrant and orange tastes that I allow to invade my mouth. Everything is done to the extreme. I have worked myself up and the walk back to the basement flat is slow as the sugar rush tails off. I let myself back in and find something to do. I switch the TV on but then switch it off because I don't want to watch it. I look at the telephone, I want it to ring so I don't have to answer it. In the kitchen I look for a can of fizzy but I find the radio instead. I turn it on push the small dial away from me. White noise hisses out of the silver speaker blended with a distant voice, French, German or Dutch, I don't make any sense of it. I turn it off because now I'm bored.

What I would like to do is take my Mattel Winchester Buffalo Hunter rifle, a faithful toy replica out to the top step and shoot old people in the back as they walk past. When you pull the trigger to release the spring it makes a satisfying CLACK! Not exactly a gunshot sound but close enough, however with perhaps a roll of red caps loaded in it was closer to the truth of desired noise to satiate most levels of boyhood destructive energy. Toy guns were quite the fascination whilst on holiday-not-holiday. Caps and small boxes of exploding jacks when snapped off hard stone pavements or thrown against pebbledash seafront walls were quite the thing.

The reason I don't go out with the rifle is that last time I did I got a rollicking from some old man. With much wagging of finger, he ran towards me and took great exception to have to see old people getting their heads blown off.

Frightening old people.

The penultimate day arrived. The tide went out, the holiday-not-holiday ship was about to set sail. The need to do something nice before departure reared its ugly head and a visit to the Royal Pavilion was embarked upon and as I suspected the experience was beyond boring. I did not appreciate the gold and lush red carpets, the imagined fabulous wealth and fortune laid out before me.

Yeah? Well, it appeals for about thirty seconds then come on, move on... can't we do something else... I don't know... just not this... I don't know... We're sitting under a parasol in the outdoor bit of a seafront cafe. Watch out! I feel irascible and as angry as the wasps caught in a transparent prison, scaling the walls of an overturned glass on the next table. Mother scrapes butter over her charcoal brown toast with an oversized silver cutlery knife. "Why don't you talk?" She demanded rather than requested. She lifted the poached egg onto the toast and split it in two. The yellow ran down the sides of the toast and onto the plate. In my head I considered all the questions she'd asked in the previous weeks and thought – I dunno.

It was agreed after a telephone call, that we would meet my sister and her boyfriend after work. He walks the outer style. He's cool. For Christ's sake he has an acoustic guitar. And sometimes he's compassionate and maybe even understands. Rose's boyfriend is called Nod.

Mother doesn't like him. I am conflicted. Does that mean I shouldn't like him either? That's going to be difficult because I kind of like him. So far, he is different. I like different after the diet of school, home, being parcelled off to brothers' houses and having to fit in with their routines.

Suddenly life is not boring because together we step into twilight Brighton. We stroll through The Lanes soaking up twinkling bright coloured lights, strawberry red, banana yellow, glass bottle green and blue jeans blue. I am not hurting inside. I choose and pick a hot salty, vinegary chip out of Nod's newspaper wrapper and then, and then, and then, around the corner - amusement arcades. Whoa! The slot machines of Brighton, the first encounter with the miraculous mood-enhancing air hockey. Shove more money in quick, let's play again and again and again.

No, no, no I am not tired and I do not want to go home and I do not want to go back to school. Mmm... I ... I ... and I don't want to go back to Devon on the train.

"Why can't I go to school here?" I say putting my hands into my pockets.

I surprise myself. The lights in the amusement arcade sparkle. I frighten myself. The others look on, not saying anything. Nod rolls and lights a cigarette. He looks me up and down and sniggers. Then he chuckles a lot which earns him an elbow into his ribs. He is laughing because he sees the anguished look on Mother's face.

At last. I know what I want...

The talk of a change of school was knocked into some sort of shape. A fine, suitable, outstanding, Edwardian establishment was found on the outskirts of Brighton, on a hill. I was offered the chance to sit an entrance exam. I wore a blazer and tie.

No, no, no this isn't it.

And therefore, I could not have been happier for the devil I know than the devils I feel are lurking in the shadows of this Edwardian establishment. It's the same old, same old and so my revulsion and realisation of having to go to yet another possibly worse school of porridge guided my pencil to write wrong answers. I felt the need to reject the questions of the 11+ exam.

I knew it would and it did ultimately lead to a letter arriving, the contents being read out. It read, thank you, but no thank you. This was followed by an hour of embarrassment and a glow of guilt. A stroll along the sprayed edge of the tidal sea smashing against the rocks along the edge of the water by the seashore, streaks of realised failure, the conflict within that flicked and dripped like an abstract slap, like a Jackson Pollock. Complicated clusters and streams of primitive emotion, borne out through thought lines still make no sense. I considered no change to be good. I did, didn't and don't know what I want... Well, I do but I can't have it. Not since the divorce. Not since we don't talk about what's happened. Not since...

This is why I feel so sad. I miss my dad.

24

Tooth Spit Calamity

WE HAVE NOTHING TO say to each other. At the age of ten, I certainly don't want to be here. Mother insists that I am. As we wait for the front door to open, a moderate sea breeze pushes past us raising dust, flipping, dragging and tossing a discarded sweet wrapper along with it. The errant wind makes its way to the beach. I return my gaze to my sandals. I know at the end of the terrace, that a well-established wisteria is busily overhanging, looking gorgeous, and that it underlines its sheer beauty by the way it gently sways in the breeze. The delicate violet-white encapsulated flowers are shaken by the wind, they float down all fairy-dreamlike to the pavement below. But I don't want to look at it or engage with the sentiment. And as if to be even more annoying, I can pick up from the Wisteria, a faint trace of perfumed air.

The sun retreats behind an ever-growing build-up of an enormous bank of dark grey clouds. From the top of a telegraph pole, a herring gull drops its head before raising it to deliver one of those deafening speeches that really say nothing at all. Other herring gulls join in, sparking a chain reaction of sound-sculptured events. Police car sirens, blue lights, a light aircraft passing overhead and two dogs start aggressively barking at each other. And for several minutes, the background wash of city traffic noise returns like a high tide, before it once again recedes from my awareness. It's always been there but after a week or two of being on holiday-not-holiday, I am no longer conscious of it. It's a bit like my relationship with Mother. Because Mother works shift work, I never know if and when she is going to be around. And since the divorce and now since my father died, she takes whatever work she can. Her current job is working the telephone switchboards, inside one of the larger hotels, that do so dominate the long stretch, that masquerades as the Brighton seafront.

I give Mother a silent stare, questioning with practised prep-school insolence, *why are we here*?

"Oh c'mon!" Said Mother. She has been ignoring me for some while now. Her intention is to get through this front door. Again she prods the doorbell button, then presses it again and again, only this time with her thumb. She knocks on the door; in case they didn't hear the doorbell. I am used to her impatience. I am not saying I like it. I am just used to it, and I have come to expect it when things aren't instant or done right. I should probably say something but there really isn't any point. I was about to let out a sigh when a young lady with an abundance of personality ripped open the front door. It's a bit sudden and unexpected and we all stand hovering for a moment before her broad, enthusiastic toothy smile wins us over. She invites us in.

From the outside, it didn't look like a dental practice. More of a townhouse with its stuccoed façade and balcony. Once inside, the room is warm and after being outside, respectfully quiet, therefore I presume this must be the waiting room. Nice furnishings, wooden double doors between freestanding bookcases. Gold letters run down the spines of medical books behind glass. Some comfortable chairs crowd around glossy magazines on the glass coffee table. A nice straightforward waiting room. I sit down, fold my arms and wait. I think it's all a bit too perfect, too nice, too clean. The sun returns, streams through the front window and a bright rectangle of light glides across the waiting room's nice carpet. Before too long, the wooden double doors swing open. We acknowledge the presence in the room.

The dentist wears a pallid orange jumper over some casual dark trousers. He was dressed down and did all the talking. I am introduced. The dentist smiles at Mother and he gives me a lop-sided concerned look. I hold on tight to my poker face. So, you're the dentist.

He has day-old stubble and cold blue eyes. I get the feeling this guy is the sort of bloke who might at any moment, sprout horns from his head and whilst standing on one leg, rip out beguiling tunes on the devil's violin, forcing me to stand up and dance because he would know that nobody from my collective likes to dance. We are shown through the double doors into another room. A large metal-framed, modern-looking chair stands opposite a small open fireplace, the chair rather dominates the room. It strikes me as peculiar and I am not sure what it is for. I feel fearful.

Within a couple of minutes and after a lot of upbeat talk, I find once again that I am the patsy in the room. I am a bit slow today. The dentist asks that I sit very still. A large black rectangle thing moves slowly around my head. It makes a horrid clanking sound, not dissimilar to the noise, when I'm bored, that I can get by twanging a ruler on the edge of a table. The point was to capture a 360° X-ray of my teeth. It was all state of the art, so revolutionary and blindingly obvious when he explained what the machine did. Mother can't wait to see the results. I feel giddy with apprehension. I don't understand what is going on.

Days went by and I forgot about the visit to the dentist. Back inside our basement flat in Hove, I play with new toys, I eat wine gums and when I go out, I am on the beach skimming stones across the flat waves of the English Channel.

We drove back, back to the dentist's house. That's not good. My mother and I were shown the X-ray, and the dentist told us of the calamity of my mouth. Mother said because I was the last of six children, she believed she didn't have enough calcium to produce healthy teeth for me. I roll my eyes. That's what you always say. The X-ray is quite cool. It shows us the outline of my skull, a lot of teeth and a lot of empty space where a brain should be. Lots of tiny white teeth all jumbled together standing on tip-toe like a bagful of dried cannelloni beans.

"So, you see..." He said, already I feel irritated. "We have to take out the baby teeth for the adult teeth... that you can see here and here to..." He paused to smile at Mother then added confidently. "To come through. So, what I'd like to do is put Rupert under, to sleep, and pull these teeth here, here and here, leave that one and possibly this one too..."

Hang on. What was that last bit again?

"...And then over time these teeth, here, here, here and hopefully this one will grow through, to give Rupert a mouthful of healthy teeth." Mother smiled, she was in full agreement and signed the dotted line.

Why doesn't anyone ever listen to what I have to say? I don't want to be put to sleep. Pulling teeth? No!

"So." Said the dentist placing the X-ray onto his desk sitting back and rubbing his hands together. "We'll see you Rupert, early next Wednesday..."

No, you won't...

Several days came and went, and again I forgot about the visit to the dentist. I got on with other things like playing with new toys, eating wine gums, watching TV and being bored.

And so, when I awoke one morning, surprised to see Mother was home and breakfast already on the table, I did like she asked and got quickly dressed and went into the front room to find my shoes. It was then, had a feeling Mother might have slipped a powdered sedative in my morning milk or might it have been sprinkled over my Weetabix, or carefully poured and gently mixed into a lightly boiled egg. I don't know. I can't think straight or tie this shoelace without feeling dizzy.

At speed, Mother drives the car with comfortable leather seats through the back streets of Brighton. I must have been drowsy because Mother helped me out of the car. I have disengaged with my body because I see myself taken to a door and being reticent to proceed further. Mother coaxes me with a firm hand on my back, and into the dentist's house we go. All is calm and quiet. We are met by the dentist, and I am taken to a clean room with modern instruments and another odd-looking chair. Mother, like usual, disappears. I am invited to recline; a needle is quickly stuck into my right arm. I don't like needles. It felt like a cold day, the sort of day where you get back indoors to quickly find a favourite jumper to pull down over your head, soft and warm, and it all goes dark. The last thing I remember was my jaw open like it just went slack. Slack-jawed and fingers on my head. He pushes my head up to slot into the seat's head-grip-strap-restraint-rest. I consider I have fought against the sleep drug well. Have a medal Rupert, well done. We will take it from here.

I open one eye and it's all about the mouth. Drooling, sucking numbness, smiling like a dolphin, my mouth aches, feels like the dentist chucked a bag of barbed wire thorns into my mouth. So sleepy, so drowsy, slowly, slowly I shall make a return to the waiting room from these realms of ancient light. It has been so dark. I don't remember paying the bill or getting to the car, but I do remember being shoved into the back seat. The engine fires and looking up, I see the back of Mother's big fat head, looking this way and that, as the car rumbles along driving over every bump in the road.
"I've only got three teeth," I said talking out of my left ear. I close my eyes to help count my teeth. I put a finger into my mouth and feel around the numb bloody holes, firstly on my lower gums, secondly on my upper gums. "Three on the bottom, two at the top and... I've got five er... nine. I've only got nine teeth... I've only got nine teeth." The horror was absolute.
After Mother had said "Shut up!" several times, and "Don't be so stupid," she didn't speak. She got on with the driving, driving me around the bends of Brighton, and driving us back home. Sometime later, I am in bed, and I sleep. I awake as my mother kicks open the bedroom door. The bedroom we shared. I ease myself up onto my elbows, still feeling wiped out. I have a tight grip on my small transistor radio. It offers soothing medium-wave washes of white noise static.
The Mother *and I say this for dramatic effect, say it in a loud booming voice.* **The Mother** carries the tray over towards my bed and sets it down. On the tray, a

banana, and a bowl of tomato soup. It is all I can manage to eat. Not sure I want to eat. Not with face ache.

After a week, I am allowed to try jelly and ice cream. When the nerves stop jangling, I could even manage a plate of baked beans. Learning to eat with the front teeth. I am only able to chew on the right-hand side of my mouth. No teeth to chew with on the left. No apples, no sweets, no toast - just squelchy food. My head soft as a doughnut.

In the mornings, I lay in bed with my small radio, listening to the breakfast show. When Mother went to work at the Hotel Neanderthal, Rose and her boyfriend Nod would sometimes look in on me to take the piss, or as they would say cheer me up. I needed it after the constant banality of BBC Radio One. How many times do I need to hear *Seasons in the Sun?*

I know my mother was shocked, but she would not admit to the amount of damage that had been done to my mouth. Notwithstanding, it was all a bit late now. Unintentionally the dentist, *at least I hope it was*, had succeeded in one visit, to strip my mouth of its bite. I think this tooth-pulling business might have affected my confidence. I didn't smile much after that, and I spoke softly. I had to be careful not to open my mouth. I didn't want to show people that I'd got no teeth.

You know what, I think it did dent my confidence. From then on, I never smiled a big toothy smile for a photographer again.

Say Cheese!

Rupert smiling, still waiting for those adult teeth to grow through.

25

I've Got Some Troubles

Look, I was searching for the spirit of friendship and love in this monastic life. Reluctantly, I returned as a train boy to school from several homes whilst on summer holiday-not-holiday and in order to fit back in, I was asking for Hunt, Thompson, or Brian Pike?

Hunt was from overseas so he took a little longer to get back, but the other two should be here. I went looking. In the corridor on the way to the shower room, I met Wilson and Ralph Brompton who told me word had got out that there was a new master. Mr Lewis was his name. Built like a brick-out-house and wrote both left and right-handed. There was a pretty Mrs Lewis too. They lived in the bungalow way up the far end of the school playing fields. He was an imposing all-year-round sports-master with a medium rare anger. He liked shouting. He taught English mostly, to the brighter high-end boys. English and all the sports, including table-tennis, which he was really good at and enjoyed stuffing us boys, putting wicked spin and swerve on the ball and after he'd destroyed you, you were told to shove off, let someone else have a go.

I didn't like it when he was shouting. I told Mr Whitaker, who told the Headmaster, who told Mr Lewis, who told me that I should have told him about it rather than Mr Whitaker. But what he didn't seem to realise was that I couldn't have told him because I was fearful of him shouting. I was a fragile possum. He still picked me, a colt, for the 1st XI cricket team. So he could really shout at me. But he didn't, he just sighed and looked the other way. I did ok on the cricket field.

I brushed my teeth, pyjamas, and dressing gown, *walk, don't run*. Ok, so I will float back to Bryanston dormitory to end this ritual before lights out. Did the wind change direction? Has the Moon become full? I leap into the dormitory, charge over and jump onto Thompson's sagging bed. It's OK he's not inside it. He is across the way talking to Bradley Edwards. He chases me around the room. I am caught and pinned to a bed. He smiles, he's excited, the pupils in his deep brown eyes swell and he drops his head down, *Hold on! What's he doing?* Oh crap! He really wants to kiss me. I struggle. I do not want to be kissed. Jesus, I don't kiss anything or anybody. The last time I absolutely had to kiss somebody, was one of my moustachioed aunts. And that would've only been a *goodbye thanks for a lovely day* hen's peck on the cheek where no emotional connection was required. This was a different beast altogether. Resistance is the only option. My arms straighten, forcing a temporary stalemate, only he has gravity and determination.

Buckland House
3rd May 1975

Dear Mum

Thank you very much for my parcel and letters. I am very well. But I have got very sore lips, so I am going to surgery. I am reading a book called "Five Have Plenty of Fun!" Today I received a letter from Brother number four and his wife they sent this postcard. They also sent an octopus a very small and rubber one. Today there is a wedding in our church at 2.30 p.m. I hope you like the newsletter I wrote some of the "If I was a headmaster." I will show you when I get home.

Love Rupert x

"Alright lights out!" Snapped the headmaster someway off from the dormitory door. On hearing the Headmaster's voice, Thompson freaked and bailed like a WWII gunner. He kicked out, whilst untangling himself from the cramped conditions, struggling to put on his silk parachute to pull himself to the only available escape hatch at the back of the burning Lancaster bomber. I rolled off the bed, deployed my parachute, eyes fixed on the floor, hoping to float back to my bed without being noticed. I did. A noise way off, of an exploding Lancaster bomber distracted the headmaster enough for him to turn on his heels, without switching our dormitory light out. It must be a full moon. I didn't have the presence of mind to look out the window to see if I was right or not. If, however, I did change my mind and wanted to look, I now could not, because Thompson, with a hop, skip and a jump, was back on top of me, on top of my bed, giggling. And saying "No!"

I protested. "Get off!"

Ralph Brompton muffled an under-your-breath kind of KV*! warning. It swept halfway across the room before dissolving into nothingness.

*'KV' *Cavere* is Latin, it means Beware! Therefore 'KV' is the shortened version.

He shrugged his shoulders as if to say *Hey, I tried to warn you guys but hey, like he was already here*. Not much help at all. Thompson was blissfully unaware of the imminent catastrophic danger we were in, as the ME 109 spiralled round to bring it's guns to bear on our plane. Coming in fast, tracer bullets light up the night.

"What *are* you boys doing?"

We stopped struggling, I closed my eyes.

"Judo Sir...," said Bradley Edwards. *Nice save.*

Mr Whitaker shook his head and smiled switched the lights out and closed the door. Thompson leapt to his feet with all the assurance of a drunken tightrope walker. He stumbled his way back to his bed, punching the air in the semi-darkness. We laughed. For an encore, he kicked the metal bed leg and properly stubbed his toe. He howled and he yelped too dramatically for most of us, talking about how best to kill Mr Whitaker with a single karate chop to the neck. It was all about how hard you should hit him. Hunt demonstrated with a convincing blow to his pillow. Others thought it was too hard and preferred a lighter quicker sock, to the back of the neck. Also, it was less likely to be heard by anyone else. More James Bond. In the meantime, Thompson was holding his foot feigning he had busted it or at least broken three toes.

We ignored him until eventually we asked. *"Do you need Matron?"*

"No."

"Is there any blood?"

"No."

"Then shut up!"

"HEY!"

"Ssh! Shut up..." Said Bradley Edwards, "someone's coming."

"No, you should say KV when someone's coming..." Wilson does protest.

"I did. KV!" Hissed Ralph Brompton.

The light blinded anyone not pretending to be asleep and stupid enough to have his eyes open. If this was who I thought it was, then we were in trouble. Big trouble. Time to play dead. Very dead, like roadkill rabbit dead in our beds. Oozing maggot Rabbit dead. I tried not to laugh at that thought. I reminded myself that I was once given six of the best for laughing. Yeah, for laughing.

"Right..." Said the headmaster, "what is going on in here?"

Silence. *Actually, we were all asleep Sir! Switch the light off as you leave.*

Buckland House
10th May 75

Dear Mum

How are you? My trunk has not come at all? I am sorry to hear that Nod has got tonsillitis. I have had another letter from Brother Number Four sending me some photographs. For my project, I am doing paper mills the one Brother Number Three is at! There is a cricket match on Wednesday against Wolborough Hill School. WHS! I am in it. No, I would not like to go camping with Andrew and Peter. On Sunday I wrote a letter to Brother Number Three. I have found out the author's name of Charlie and the Chocolate Factory he is called "Roald Dahl." When I was batting in a game Thompson was the wicketkeeper and I tipped the ball and the ball hit Thompson on the head! (!@$%)

My effort marks are: Latin 8th Good Maths 10th Good French 7th Excellent English 11th Good History 4th Good Geography 4th Good Scripture 12th Good Science Good Final Good

Love Rupert x

Buckland House
Tuesday 20th May 1975

Dear Mum

Thank you very much for your letter. How are you? I had a good time with Brother Number Three and his family. All Amy ever says now is Ah! and Oh! We got back safely about 6 o'clock so I showed them around and Amy kept running away! Our swimming pool is almost filled, and we will be swimming on Wednesday, tomorrow. When we played Woloborough Hill last Wednesday we lost! I got 1 wicket and 7 runs, and I was caught out by their captain. I have put my name down for putting. It is sunny outside but not very warm.

Brother Number Three cannot make it on the 24th May because he is working all the time but that does not matter. I bought my Bazil [sic] Brush back to school for some company! My table should be finished by half-term so Rose and Nod might bring it back then? Brother number three bought me an early birthday present it was two racing cars a JPS and a MacLean [sic] the big sort of ones. My trunk has come, it came on Monday after I sent the last letter! I like the pictures of Brother Number One's son.

Lots of love from Rupert x

P.S I do not think it is a good idea, to sale the flat in Hove and move to Devon.

Mr Beaumont's red face turns scarlet with rage. He jumps up and down on the driveway. He shouts but can't be heard. He shakes both fists at four Royal Marines helicopters that hover three feet off the ground. Right in front of us, the whole school sat on the low-level bank in front of the main school building. A smattering of parents too.

The helicopters were so close, we could almost put out a hand and touch them. We cover our ears and yell. The noise is incredible. At any moment, they look like they might land on the cricket square. Ah! That's what's wrong with Mr Beaumont.

This must be one of the most exciting things we have seen all term. Apart from when P. J. Jackson split open his gastrocnemius calf muscle on his left leg falling out of a tree, nasty gash right to the bone. It didn't bleed much until he reached the cricket square. He came hobbling quietly across the square, arm over a mate's shoulder for support. You could tell from a distance he was proper hurt. "Action stations!" I yelled and directed people to do something. Later, all the wrong people got Headmaster praise and accolades for helping. Which was par for the course. I'm not bitter.

Gazelle helicopters are like noisy hair dryers but a lot bigger and today, they manoeuvre up, down and forwards. They fly out from behind trees, and we are unimpressed. They split off and show us attack manoeuvres. We shrug our shoulders. Two disappear around the back of the main house and then swing out from behind the rookery. We half-heartedly cheer, and add on a few claps but only because we are told to and don't want to get shot at. Ultimately however, helicopters after three minutes are boring. We felt it was rather disappointing that none of the Gazelles ran out of fuel and belly-flopped into the swimming pool, or collided, or out of control flew over our heads to **WHAM!** into the front of the main building. We all would have liked to see that. Hot splintered rotor blades twisted shards of shrapnel lacerating and decapitating the schoolmasters in the crowd. We are programmed always for the worst case scenarios. There's doom in the boom, brings a perpetual gloom. Alas, soon we'll all fall asleep watching films and TV.

Helicopters blow up and crash in James Bond movies. We did briefly get to see a couple of baked bean-type canisters roll across the cricket square as thick yellow smoke belched out from them. We did see soldiers run, soldiers shout, soldiers prostrate themselves, lift their heads and start shooting blanks, *Tak! Tak! Tak!* At imaginary bad guys. We yawned and picked at the grass and pulled the heads off daisies.

"We do that," I shout at Clifton Wentworth. Ralph Brompton waves at the helicopter. Wilson ran back into the house.

"What? I can't hear you." Clifton Wentworth shook his head. "What?"

Of course, the only reason they turned up was that some idiot's father was one of the helicopter pilots. This could be seen as a good opportunity, an early recruitment drive for an ignoramus, blockhead, nitwit, dullard, plank, birk, twit or pillock to join the circus. After all, the two public schools we were expected to feed into were merely breeding grounds for future officers and squaddies for the armed forces. And why not? Someone's gotta do it.

Over the centuries, private schools have been a part of the growth and decline, of the pink bits on the world map. All *nice* and English and drinking cups of tea. Singing *Onward Christian Soldiers*.

"So whatcha think of that Green?" Mr Whitaker shouted all stiff in the neck and a bit deaf from all that noise.

"Loved it, Sir."

"What are you going to be when you grow up?"

"Helicopter Sir!"

"Well done! Kelly College is Navy, Blundell's Army."

"Thank you, Sir. I'll remember that when I'm the last batsman walking out to bat for England against Australia in the Ashes Test at The Oval with a mere 387 runs needed to regain the Ashes, so help me God! Forward defence, Sir!" I demonstrated with left foot forward and a high elbow.

"I beg your pardon?" Said Mr Whitaker taking cotton wool out of his large ears.

"Nothing Sir, I'm going up the cricket nets."

About half an hour ago, the helicopters did a goodbye salute thing and quickly left. We waved and flicked V signs until they were no more than the size of mosquitos and a faint buzz over fir trees on the horizon.

Mr Beaumont stumbled out of the rhododendrons, brushed himself off and asked us to line up if we wanted to punch the boys whose father had just wasted the entire afternoon and ruined the cricket square. He's so dramatic. Those interested lined up, Hunt, Bradley Edwards, Winston Montague and Thomas Arnold among them and with Mr Beaumont's orders ran off to find the helicopter boys and drag them by the legs to the gym.

"And duff them up!" He shouted after them. His words, not mine.

As the bright orange sun sunk below distant woods, a cool shadow sprang out across the front of the house. Time to put a cardigan on. The stragglers, most notably the more local families with boys attending the school, stood by open car doors holding off the moment before they started to say a final farewell. I see parents laugh, hug and warmly kiss on the cheek. They smother offspring with love and affection, for it must last until the end of term. All that warm heartbeat love spread over their lovely bright children. Sweetly, gently the mother closed the car door and mouthed "I love you" with a hand pressed against the window glass simulating a wave au revoir, not goodbye.

Moved and trembling, I remembered that my mother was a no-show. I was all bottom lip, find me a blue bottle to pull the off the wings. I sniffed and slunk into the cold shadows in search of something sweet to steal and eat. I hate to see parents showing love to their sons and I don't like helicopters for making me feel this way.

Buckland House
Friday 20th June 1975

Dear Mum

I hope you are well. When the 1st played against Mount House we won, I scored 55 runs and I got 4 wickets and I have got my colours!! But when we played them again, I scored 2 runs and was then caught then our total was only 51 and I dismissed 2 people I ran out one person and got a boy called Drum L.B.W. We lost the match. The weather has been good. In Carpentry I have only to put the top on the table and I have finished. Today I was the server on our table. I am going to write to Brother number three for some information on Paper Mills.

Love Rupert x

One sunny carefree lunchtime, my mind elsewhere, being a server, holding dinner plates, loaded up with pink spam, mash potato and corrugated beetroot. You know, going to and fro, sharing a joke with the other servers, keeping our minds on the job in hand, when holding the dinner plates. Delivering the plates to our tables, walking calmly back. Joining the end of the server's line as it went outside the dinning hall and around the corner.

I didn't see where the headmaster came from but he appeared and he wanted to talk to me. He fixed me in a stare and held my arms above the elbows. The server line halted. A ghastly moment.

"Now, Green I would like it if when you return from half term holiday that you do not cry when you are dropped off. It isn't a good for the other younger boys and you shouldn't be crying now at your age. So do you think you could do that for me?"

I swallowed and blindly agreed, the Headmaster went off to get some lunch in the staff room. I looked down at the tears splashing on my shoes.

Buckland House
12 July 1975 Saturday

Dear Mum

The match against St Peter's was cancelled. In exams, I came 8th! The weather has not been very good. I have become a paddler! Also, I have swam 5 strokes underwater and jumped in off the side. On Monday it is a merit half-holiday! Last Thursday we had a choir half holiday we went to Bideford to see the Four Musketeers; it was good and exciting.

My exam percentages are: Latin 6th 67% Geography 11th 57% Maths 11th 27% Scripture 12th 40% French 3rd = 48% Science 10th 45% English 4th = 40% Points 357 History 10th 33% final 8th

love Rupert x

The best advice my Mother ever gave me was that sex was the backbone of a marriage.

The worst advice my Mother ever gave me was to tuck my vest into my pants.

26

Rules Of Rugger

NOT EVERYBODY GETS IT. I didn't, which was why I was chewing my little finger, sat next to Thompson, behind an old wooden desk. There were twenty-seven of us dotted about the four rows of desks, all pointing towards Mr Lewis. His voice is helped to feel important, aided by the barn-sized reverberation the room affords. Aromas of paint, new term white paint, a rushed job judging by the drips and splashes on the caged storage heaters.

"Don't sit on the radiators, you'll get piles."
"What's piles sir?"
"Shut up!"
"Do you mean piles of laundry?"
"No. Shut up. I mean you'll know what piles are when you get to my age. If you keep sitting on radiators."
"How old are you sir?"
"Shut up!"
"Sir!"
"Go and stand outside."

A dank radiation from non-use pours out, in waves of warmth, for the benefit of our hungry bones.

Buckland House
Saturday 8th November 1975

Dear Mum
I hope you are well? I have finished my spice box all I have to do is sand-paper it. I had my music exam this morning and we also had a rugger match against Woloborough Hill we lost about 30-0 I was not in the team. There are three films tomorrow about Wild-fif life starting at 6 o'clock. On Thursdays I am going to do lettering. *Last Thursday Matron took me to the dentist he said come in a fortnight and give me 2 fillings is that alright if not ring the Headmaster. And find out. **Is

Sheila alright? I have not been doing much this week. There are no effort's this week. An we have been doing practice C.E papers!
Love from Rupert xxxx

Last Thursday Matron took me to the dentist he said come in a fortnight and give me 2 fillings is that alright if not ring the Headmaster. As promised by the Brighton Dentist, not all the second teeth had appeared, leaving me with an empty mouth, difficulty chewing and feeling somewhat adrift. Like a small fishing boat out on the English Channel, blown off course by an ill wind and now heading out into the Atlantic Ocean.

**Is Sheila alright?* Sheila had a collision with a milk lorry that skidded on wet gateway mud down a steep valley lane near Beaford. She broke her right leg. She survived. She was convalesced by Mother in The Porridge Cottage in Beaford. The cottage where the visiting, travelling, interesting actors, directors, producers had a temporary room. We had one bedroom, shared bathroom and the run of the house. The Beaford Art Centre house, where Mother had a job being their head cook, confidant, housekeeper, drinking companion and somebodies lover. Beaford is only nine miles from Buckland House School.

Mother, Rupert, Brother Number Four smiling. August 1975.

The Christmas term sport is rugby. What is rugby? Mr Lewis will tell us. He swipes clean a large blackboard and chucks the duster to land with a slam on the desktop. That woke me up. A puff of chalk dust billows out and before he shows us his forthright manner, a respectful silence. Then, like the starting up of a chain saw, he grinds out the rules of rugger. Cutting trees down to build H posts at the beginning and end of his lesson.

When Mr Lewis paused for breath, boys punted their paper-thin knowledge towards him, with a hope to gain a little more knowledge. To maybe gain themselves that inch of something more, a little nudging, begrudging inch in front of someone else. So that they might become more than a spectator on the touchline, to become a rugby player.

I remember cold windswept soggy Saturdays holding the odd shaped ball on the far away touchlines, wiping the mud and rain from my eyes, alert to a whistle blast to throw the ball into play and onward to battle. Getting flattened and stamped on. Run over by a steam roller. Squashed necks, twisted fingers and tufts of hair pulled as we wrenched, elbowed and pushed players out of the way. If quick enough, we dodged, hopped, skipped, jumped past grabbing hands to run down the touchline, only to be bundled into touch by a huge lump of a full back.

The 1st XV maul, where a mass of bodies pull in tight and push in different directions, the younger brothers let out their aggressions without intention of winning the ball. Hitting mouths, burst lips and bloody noses with cold knuckles, stamping on feet, and scratching fingers to gain another inch as the mass falters before the whistle hails stop and its eventual collapse. Then the post mortem. The ticking off and the respect of how to behave in a ruck.

Lots of crosses, like kisses tapped onto the blackboard, each denoting a player, followed by a long arc of blistering speed from which an arrowhead would be placed, indicating direction. Thus punctuated with a jaw jutting twitch of Mr Lewis's chiselled chin. His dark brown eyes flash out across the room to see who is with, or against him.

Sporadic spurts of conversation would erupt from desktops only to be extinguished under the flare of his withering sarcasm. Thomas Arnold, sat atop a desk, good at rugby and he knew it. He was strong and tough, large for his age and was one of those younger brothers. Learned his trade as he traded punches with his elder brother. Why else was he sat on top the desk with such a relaxed demeanour. Whilst Thomas Arnold is given the floor, he imparts pearls of wish-wash. I chewed, not taking the slightest bit of interest. After all, he was a shoo-in for captain. On this occasion, my purpose was to be part of the background, back of the room boys. Shadow creatures with cloaked invisibility.

I was only interested in the summer sunshine sport. And I don't mean catching butterflies, falling in love, swimming or tennis.

You see moments come and hang around for a bit and some moments come and go; my moment at this point has departed to the astral plane of existence. I stood up and followed with curiosity as it took me upon a silver cloud across our galaxy to the black-hole at the centre of unknown universes... Without warning and with all the pomp of an exploding light bulb, ushered by celestial beings back into my real self.

Clunk! I am back in the room.

Mr Lewis's room, Mr Lewis's moment. Medium rare, that's Mr Lewis. The brick-out-house.

"Thank you. Hmm..." Mr Lewis freezes his eyebrows in the up position. Did everybody just stop breathing? Seconds before, we had all seen him demonstrate a studied tap, kiss, kiss and an arrowhead shot past a try line and concluded with a most emphatic tap.

"Green, what is it when you take the ball over the opposition try line," and this is where he growled, "and put the ball down?"

Fright! Flight! Fight... no, I can't...

I felt the top of my head had been kicked off. I watched it sail between the uprights. Three points.

"And the answer is..." He circled the kiss and punctuated it with impatient tapping. I took my finger out of my mouth. Mr Lewis swelled his brick-out-house frame and looked as if he was about to square up to a sailor who'd asked him for a dance... Thompson spoke telepathically to me. It didn't work. Clifton Wentworth looked across the room at me and rolled his eyes. Hunt started laughing. The answer was that easy. Mr Lewis counted to ten. Thomas Arnold hand pumping the air was whimpering, pleading "Sir!" – cocked and ready to give the correct answer. Thompson sensing I was about to step on a landmine whispered, "It's a try!"

"It's a try." I gurgled. Mr Lewis smiled and rubbed all the arrows and kisses off the board.

"Thank you gentlemen." Concluded Mr Lewis, "Now shove off!"

◻

27

I Was Hurting, He Was Hurting

DEEP INSIDE MY SHELL-LIKE head are walls of brittle bone. Curved walls polished by timeless creation, pearl smooth and anytime, anytime I want, I can be sat there watching and waiting as carnivorous creatures roam, the fragile light pours sense and meaning onto the Skull Cinema screen. A variable screen cut from the cloth of humdrum boarding school life. I watch with interest...

I am in Australia, it is hot. I am standing on a high red mountain place, and Brother Number Two is there, and we exchange a smile and a laugh in a brotherly way. An imposing kangaroo confronts me. It swivels round, its tail brings an all-consuming fire. I fall as the earth around me crumbles.

Half awake, half asleep. Half in bed, half out. Half a sixpence, half a mo... I am a lot more places than I used to be. But I am still a bit of a shambles. Wait where am I?

The Blood Moon holds back the daylight, it is looking in through the windows of the big house, not quite time to invade. An eclipse is imminent.

The covers are over my nose. I look about the room from behind this bedclothes mask. Bunk beds on the left with pale blue blankets, boys turning in sleep. The single iron beds follow the edge of the room leaving a space for the doorway. The door is closed.

Buckland House
6th December 1975

Dear Mum
How are you? I have just had a letter from Grandma. Here it is! It is merit half holiday on Monday and on Tuesday it is the Christmas dinner and on Wednesday it is half day and on Thursday we go home.(After the service. At 2:15pm it starts) Are you busy? I have asked Mrs Stirling for the photos of the choir and she has changed the money so we should have the photo by Thursday. When we played our inter house Brownes won (I'm in Brownes) I was full back. I have had a chill blane

start on my left foot big toe. Has the mouse been in and out? Have you got a cat or some traps or has the poison killed it?
Love from Rupert xxxx

Mr Beaumont was mad. He taught English and French and in the summer term, looked after the 1st XI cricket square that was situated on the front lawn. English was his subject and he was pretty annoyed about it. During one fateful English lesson, Mr Beaumont read out a story from an intensely dull leather-bound book, written by someone who despised children so much, that the author wished when his book was read out loud, in the school classroom, the effect would be to drain the children, of their very life force. So much so, that all that would remain of the children would be small, desiccated husks, hunched over wooden desks.

And the reader, the reader of this book, would be rewarded handsomely. The reader would be invigorated by the energy transference of the children's energy into the book and by the very act of holding the book, the prose would ensure an energy transaction.

Therefore, what other possible reason would you need to multitask on listening to the story and bring a sardonic concentration of disrespect to a mad Master of English?

All was going well and our dull merriment was palpable. Three of us play acting with the words of the story, our excitement growing as others in the class noticed, becoming complicit. Mr Beaumont wasn't as mad as we thought he was. He was also clever and mad and brutal.

The words dried up. We continued to smile and smirk restless at our desks scratching the nits in our hair and wondering when break was. Remember, it was an awfully dull story. Mr Beaumont continued, stopped and hurriedly took his reading glasses off and rubbed an ever-reddening face. His complexion was a continuous five o'clock shadow. Brown bloodshot eyes now wide open stared out through black strands of hair and his hearing now obviously as acute as a vampire bat. He knew what to do. He snapped shut the book, allowing his rage to drop down a few more levels, low enough to calmly explain what was about to happen.

"Uh-Oh!" I said, inside my head.

Mr Beaumont wrongly identified Brian Pike as the ringleader. It was me all along. I wasn't going to own up. No way. Mr Beaumont delivered a succinct monologue on the merits of not paying full attention in his class. And then to our surprise, he invited everyone in the class to get up and punch the ringleader. I didn't but nearly everybody else did. They were obliged to. With each sickening blow, Mr Beaumont, with a detached sense of calm and tranquility said, "Hit harder."

Brian Pike's arms up for protection, glared at me through moist eyes of hatred and through gritted teeth and I could see him, imagined him saying "Yeah mate, I am taking all this for you." I was hurting, he was hurting, everybody was hurting.

"That's enough boys, return to your desks." Mr Beaumont said in a calm, hushed tone. He returned the reading glasses to his nose, opened the book up, found the exact word where he left off and continued reading. After that, the general dynamic within the class changed. No more mucking about when this guy was running the class. Oh no! And I tell you, I can't wait for our next English lesson to demonstrate this. I experienced guilt and shame but best of all, I experienced getting away with it physically. Slow to realize just how much I was being beaten up. Mentally. Constantly.

Might this have something to do with my standing in the bathroom or stood at my dormitory window, cold, numb, not being able to move.

The imagination hung like rotten apples, waiting to fall from the tree and each year another crop.

28

Laughter In All The Wrong Places

THERE IS NOTHING LIKE finding a good stick in the hedge and destroying a few dozen stinging nettles. The cane is a stick. A bamboo stick. Bamboo is a lot more rigid than any sticks we find. Bamboo doesn't grow on trees or in our hedges. I don't know where it comes from. Of course I know where bamboo comes from.

The cane as long as your arm and as thick as a packet of fruit pastilles. Several canes lived at one time in a deep drawer in the headmaster's study. A wooden drawer at the bottom of a wall of cupboards and drawers in the headmaster's small study come office, although I have to say the study come office was larger than a fridge freezer and a walk-in larder put together.

In the dark flagstone corridor, mounted on the Headmaster's study door architrave, are a stubby red light and green light. One to denote your presence was required within, when lit, not before. The other suggested not to enter at all. Because inside the study come office, someone was probably getting their ear bashed and their tail thrashed.

Green light. I pushed hard to open the yellow door because the red carpet offered some resistance. I walked in. The headmaster pointed to where the telephone was. I changed direction and picked up the receiver.

The study come office was more square shaped than rectangle but then again it felt more like a rectangle with half a century's worth of clutter about the surfaces. On the desk to the right, behind the door, a lamp and the telephone.

I wanted to call *home* (Beaford) to see if Mother could or would come get me, pick me up for the next day, Sunday. So I could get some time off the reservation, as it were. Please...

I was in the study come office with the headmaster who appeared calm. I was shown the phone again and I got on with dialling the telephone numbers needed to make a connection with my Mother. Beaford 573.

There was a knock at the study door, a small boy entered, I was not small at 12 years old and a few months. I was growing up fast.

"Oh look how Rupert's all grown up and how. He never says a word, has his voice broken?" Said Mother's elder sister's Aunty Florrie and Aunty Ruth.

"Yes, I expect it has." Replied Mother pouring them a cup of tea and offering slices of homemade sponge cake. Meanwhile in the hallway under the stairs a telephone continued to ring... ring... ring.

I read the file names on folders, cluttered and collapsed on wooden shelves. Old Accounts from 1967, boiler-room and other manuals, a thin alumni folder. Loose sun bleached envelope folders, stained coffee cup rings like crescent moons and illegible Milky Way words, scrawled lines of blue biro to navigate the contents within. All of a sudden I feel numb. Cold legs. Next to reference books, a well loved, thick Oxford English Dictionary. The ring tone sang out from the tiny earpiece speaker.

Bring! Bring!

The study door opens and is firmly shut. I hear the distinctive rattle of the bamboo canes.

Bring! Bring!

I turn around to see another small boy, as in a different small boy already bent over. A shiver of fear washes over his shaking body.

Bring! Bring!

His fear magnetises all the living things in the room. The three of us. Five of us if you include a dried up Aloe Vera cactus with obligatory cobweb. On the floor by the french window, a flaming dragon's tongue plant, its leaves held together by a medium sized terra-cotta pot. Six of us if you count the cane in a raised hand.

I thought, couldn't this whipping wait?

Bring! Bring!

But now I am attracted to it. I could have snapped like a breadstick. I don't want this but here it is, I have no immediate defence.

Bring! Bring!

And I think, surely he's not going to do that now, not now, not with me being stood here,

Bring! Bring!

I don't want to see this. What is the headmaster playing at? I should say something. But I don't. I think Er... hello I am stood right here. Do you want me to see this? Don't you think I wont tell everyone? Little old me...

Bring! Bring!

...stood here holding the telephone receiver to my ear watching you, you spanner!

Bring! Bring!

The Headmaster gripped the cane firmly, he drank in the reassurance, the parameters it gave him within this Victorian regime of discipline.

He lined up the first shot. It is all about the timing. A deliciously difficult moment. And I suggest, one to savour when practised enough. Pure debauchery delivered on a plate of sadomasochism.

Bring! Bring!

For the culprit of said punishment. The barn doors open, letting in expectation, fear, worry, guilt and the seconds turn into hours of waiting, waiting...

Bring! Bring!

THWACK! Stroke one! *OOH! That stung!* Waiting...

THWACK! Stroke two. *OOH! That might've hit the same place as the first. Ouch!* The boy makes an adjustment. Half a step forward to steady himself. Head down little cries and gasps, the pain is dribbling from his lips. The headmaster perceives the boy is trying to get away. His quick reflexes grip the boy's shirt collar. A colder voice you will not hear. Think Komodo dragon rasping as it swallows a live mouse. "Keep still!" Waiting... waiting...

THWACK! Stroke Three. It is pitiful to watch. That last one hit real hard.

Bring! Bring!

One more stroke for luck... another long awkward pause... No that's it.

I thought to ask the headmaster, *"Just going to be three strikes today is it? Well played Sir! Well done!"*

Each stroke delivered with rising and falling mixtures of control, fear and dominance. The mark of a true brute.

The boy bangs into the door, fumbles with the handle and is told to stand aside as the Headmaster leans over the boy to pull open the door. The boy disappears as a gust of corridor air gets sucked into the room.

There's me, the innocent bystander. Headmaster drops the cane back into the draw and slams it shuts. He closed the door behind him without saying a word.

"Hello, Beaford 573. Who is it?"

At last, Mother and she is talking!

Mother who used to beat me for being really naughty with a wooden spoon. Naughty like burning next door's garage down. Naughty like letting an arrow fly in the general direction of my niece's head, who went and told on me. "But it missed!"

Whack! Whack, Wackity! Whack!

"H-Hello..." My shaky voice. "Can you come take me out like now... er... tomorrow on Sunday?" Thinking, please say yes. Please say yes.

"Not this weekend."

"Oh…" I wished I could simply evaporate or pass through the wall or maybe click my fingers and vanish.

The headmaster has returned. I put the phone receiver down. Disconnected from the call. I turn but am careful not to make eye contact. Must not reveal my hand. I look past the headmaster.

I don't want to join in with his daydream.

Mouth half open, his tongue licks the soft bottom lip, moves over the cracks in his teeth, the soft wet insides of the nicotine loaded mouth and with the tip of his tongue revealed the red of his bottom lip, he is lost somewhere, he looks delirious, he is out of his mind. I don't think he knows I am still in the room. He stuffs his hand into his trouser pocket. Alarmed, I lower my gaze even lower and quietly slip past him to escape the room. I everso gently close the door behind me.

And breathe. At high speed with wings on my heels, I fly up to the classroom block, I dare not look back.

A week or three goes by and with better communication, I am allowed to bring a friend home to Torridge Cottage, Beaford.

Brian Pike and I laugh at anything and everything. He had jet black hair. I'd been to his house. We laughed all day there too. Apart from the moment I saw and remarked on the framed photograph alone on the mantelpiece.

"Was that your elder sister?" I asked without thinking.

Maybe that's why we laughed all the time. Laughed at everything because it's all so absurd, bloody absurd when you're carrying these things around with you. His mother put it on the mantelpiece for all to see. Therefore I was allowed to make a remark. But after I had done, I didn't feel like laughing anymore. And I guess I felt closer to Brian in that moment but was unable to go beyond recognition. At least they had a photo, it was more than I had.

We arrived at Beaford for a Sunday day out, 11 am to 4 pm.

You were allowed three Sundays or a weekend and a Sunday per term.

Mother on her knees, builds up the fire with old newspaper and kindling sticks, she picks up a box of matches and strikes a match and broke wind. It is difficult not to split our sides laughing. We escape to the kitchen.

Back at school, on the Monday, after assembly, after breakfast and heading to class, Brian wanted to pick up a book from Wellington dormitory. Veering away from the crowd we snuck into Wellington. No sooner than we are through the doorway, we see two cleaning ladies in traditional orange tabard uniforms stood over Brian's bed with the blue blanket in their hands. They continued to talk and generally ignore us, stretching the blanket down over the top of the bed frame. We took in what we saw and it wasn't until we looked at each other did the laughing start. I can't be sure but it was probably me who went first. For a start, it was unexpected to see cleaners, well ever. They normally operated when we were in class. Then they were stood over Brian's bed and remaking it. Like he didn't make it properly himself. So I guess they were hiding until it was coffee time, making things to do. And they had such sour puss looks on their faces. We are talking Coronation Street levels of disillusionment. And the problem we now had, was how was Brian going to interact with these strange creatures, he still wanted his book.

I laugh, he smirks. I laugh even more. He laughs, we burst out laughing. We gone full tilt laughing. The cleaning ladies don't find it funny at all. And issue a threat. Brian dodges around one of them to collect his book and we run out the room in fits. To get to class on time. Didn't think anymore about it.

On first break, we are all told to line up in the Assembly Room, the general bonhomie is good that is until like a Medusa, the Headmaster's wife, slithers in and out of the space in one movement. "Malcolm McGregor and Brian Pike. You are to go and see the Headmaster." And then for dramatic effect she achieves a slight return and announces. "You *know* what it's about..."

The assembly room fell into a void of blindfolded impartiality. I am crestfallen. "You *know* what it's about, you *know* what it's about..." **I know**.

But why Malcolm McGregor? I stand, set ready, on the starting blocks waiting for the starting pistol to shout my name. I prefer non-interference. Head down, I made my way out and got back to class. Within ten minutes, I was found and sent to the headmaster's office. I passed a relieved Malcolm MacGregor along the way. I stood like a fish out of water, outside the yellow door with a red light on. Brian next to me. That long dark corridor. Both hot and cold at the same time. My emotions being ratcheted up and up.

Out of the kitchen steps the Headmaster's wife, holding several teacups and saucers in both hands. She is on the boil. She is doing the hokey-pokey. Her lips move but we don't hear anything she is saying. Our indifference to the power she perceives she wields, only makes matters worse. A cup slips from her grasp. And in the time it takes to drop, Brian and I connect and share the confusion as to what all the hullabaloo is about. We return to watch the teacup shatter on the flagstone floor. Inside with nowhere to go, we are churning. Holding back the convulsions of laughter shuddering through our bodies. I am fit to be blown to kingdom come. The headmaster's wife returns with a dustpan and brush. She stoops. We make like we are stone monoliths with our backs to the wall, eyes front.

Laughing as a weapon. Nowhere to go when someone's laughing. Laugh it off, having a laugh. Laugh your head off. Laughing all the way to the bank or in this case the headmaster's study. All this for laughing. Laughing. Having a laugh! The right of any small boy is to laugh.

I dare you to breathe.
The light switched to green. The yellow door swung open. Behind it stood an irate grizzly bear, rolled up sleeves, fangs out, red eyes burning, Brian is told to get in. The door firmly closed behind him. A breeze whistles along the corridor. The front door must have been opened. I turn, cast my stare down the passageway. All I can see is the misery ghost, come to collect his dues. It brushes past the dinner gong. Walking stick taps along the flagstone floor, coming ever closer.

THWACK! Behind the yellow door after words, punishment meted out.
THWACK! Behind the yellow door, lashed turbulence.
THWACK! Behind the yellow door, the justified shouts.
THWACK! Behind the yellow door, impermanence.

The yellow door opened. Brian, red faced, jet black hair, brown jumper, white shirt, gasps and rushes out. With the door still open, I am hauled in. My turn.

It is regrettable. I am twisted around and around like ivy wrapped around a wind blown tree, amid a raging tempest, grey rolling clouds deliver hot bolts of high lightning.

The rod hits my backside and it splits as it shatters into my shins, I jerk and spasm as if dangling from a rope. I drink in each bite, but only one bite at a time. Scratch lines scar warm buttocks. Now tainted, stained with the bamboo blade. A marker for all to see. Worn as a trophy, four deep parallel red lines, strike lines, distinguished the wearer as rogue, warrior, sinner, perpetrator of darkness, he did not play nice and now he wears the badge of forgery. Like the mockery of a cheap tattoo.

I am alone and I am responsible for myself. I have to survive this suffering, solitude, solace, solidarity, no solution, revolution or rage required, only despair because it is just not fair. I told him why and he did not listen. What am I to become, what is there that is beyond this point in time. The pointlessness of time. I am fed up with school.

The same merry go round of large darkened masterpieces of purple. Poorly lit, regret where in shadows, we are all forgotten. I want no more to speak of this darkness, I want to go somewhere I can call home.

Brian Pike and I rock up to the cricket nets to tell the tale. Ralph Brompton, Fin, Thomas Arnold and Bradley Edwards stand and listen but that's all. We watch Clifton Wentworth block a few cricket balls. I don't feel like bowling and decline the offer. Fin tosses a ball over. I catch it and throw it back to him. Hunt arrives and leaves. He is looking for Thompson. Bradley Edwards runs in and delivers an express train, Clifton Wentworth does everything right but with his eyes shut. That is why we cheered when he got bowled. Although he swears he was watching the ball. He must have blinked.

With the outside bell now calling us in for lunch, Brian Pike and I begin to walk slowly back to the main house.

"Do you think when we are all done, dead and gone something of us will return here. Will our souls return to this place, to take a look?" I asked.

"What, to haunt it?" Grinned Brian. We laughed like we had just eaten a hearty plate of roast beef and Yorkshire puddings.

"I believe, I am going to." I said in all honesty. Brian smirked, stopped and looked at me for a moment then returned his gaze to the ground.

"Why would you want to come back here?" Brian asked adding, "what about the Masters, wouldn't they be here still?" I let that thought settle. I regarded the wind bending the tops of the trees. We walked on a bit further, stopped again.

"I dunno. I hope not. I want to see what it was like. To catch up with old friends. See if anything's changed, return and measure how well, we have, might have, done..."

"Sounds like to measure how well you have done. I'm happy with who I am. Are we friends then?" I let out a nervous laugh before answering.

"Yes, I dunno, I expect so. I've been to your house. Haven't I..."

"And I to yours. But does that make us friends? What do *you* think a friend is?"

"We laugh all the time... I dunno, seriously you want me to answer that?"

"Nope, not really. Not sure I would want my soul to live out the rest of my life here. My death I mean. You know what I mean. With them here too. Watching over us."

"Telling us what not to do all the time." I added. "Have you made any plans, about what's going to happen tomorrow?"

"Do you mean what's going to become of us?" Said Brian avoiding the raised cobble stones.

"Yes, I suppose I do. You're good at explaining it. Much better than I am."

We turned the corner past the sheds and headed back indoors in silence.

29

When It Comes To Football

Mr Hatt was among the last to arrive off the late 1960s desk-bound teacher training conveyor belt for low to mid-range English and Scottish preparatory schools. Our Headmaster lured Mr Hatt to our little school, nestled in the Devonian backwaters, promising fresh air and mental prosperity. And so it was, Mr Hatt arrived one bright clear day, clutching a suitcase full of Old English books and a squint. We were never sure who he was looking at. And although he appeared confident, Mr Hatt took a little while to settle in.

Masters came and Masters went. Mr Hatt intended to teach English and nothing else. "And that," he would often shout as he fastidiously bookmarked and closed one of those dreadful books, "And that boys, is real English, the old-fashioned English which you no longer speak. But I do." Mr Hatt brought institutional wisdom to the party and believed he could shed light on the finer aspects of Anglo-Saxon poetry.

The Christmas term of his first year arrived and he was ordered by the headmaster to get some fresh air. Promoted to the position of 1st XI Football coach, Mr Hatt was at best reluctant to take on extra but being the youngest at fifty, and the newest arrival, the duty fell on him.

Whilst taking a moment in the common room during morning break, Mr Whitaker was overheard by the room saying to Mr Hatt, "Congratulations old man!" Mr Whitaker leant against the staffroom radiator, which was neatly housed under the shelf beneath a tall single-pane window. Mr Whitaker took a gulp of hot, milky sweet, instant coffee and bit into a second custard cream.

"At least you'll be able to keep up with the little buggers."

What he didn't spit across the room, tumbled as crumbs from the edge of his mouth. The crumbs clung onto his V neck burgundy pullover. He tried but failed to brush them all away, however, he only managed to make things worse. Mr Hatt dived out of the way and avoided being drenched, however the coffee splashed onto the windowsill, dripped and slid down the radiator. Mr Whitaker swallowed down the dregs from the cup and placed it in its saucer on the carpet. A call went out across the room for Mrs Lancaster to go to the kitchens for a cloth and clean up. Mr Hatt wandered over to the sideboard to make Mr Whitaker another coffee.

Weeks later, alone in the staff room, with pen in hand, Mr Hatt reflected on Mr Whitaker's comments as the heat from the staff room radiator departed like the coffee, biscuits and Masters. Mr Whitaker's white cup had been knocked over but remained on its saucer. Overlooked on the wooden floor that edged the well-worn carpet under the radiator.

Mr Hatt continued adding comments in the last ten reports, having completed thirty-four in this sitting. Every child had to have at least one sentence about their progress in either English or Football. Each name conjured a tiny face that boomeranged away and back in his mind's eye as his pen scratched out a line of encouragement followed by his initials.

He loathed football as much as he loathed washing dishes...

"Pointless game, running end to end kicking a bladder..."

Mr Hatt rubbed his face and clapped his hands twice.

"Come on Hatt. Pull yourself together."

Mr Hatt found himself somewhat uncomfortable sitting alone in the staff room. Cramp attacked his leg and as if bitten by a dog, he leapt up and swung his leg over the armchair to straighten it. He bent over forwards, bent over backwards, and did a little dance before once again, sinking like a thick sock wrapped around a foot into the Wellington boot-like leather armchair. Now settled, his Montblanc fountain pen could be heard in the corridor notching up a few sentences on specially printed and watermarked sheets of chalk-white report card paper. The scratching stopped and for a moment Mr Hatt sat still, feelings of being flustered and confounded washed over him like detergent soap suds withering his hands from the after-dinner dishes...

He stared at nothing. An echo of the past began to sting his memory. The black ink dried. With a weary hesitancy, he discarded, rather launched the penultimate school report to land amongst the others in what now appeared in his mind's eye to be an acreage of winter snow reminiscent of Bruegel's The Return of the Hunters. A painting that had so stunned him into silence housed in the colossal Kunsthistorisches museum whilst on Winter vacation in Vienna, Austria. What started as organised, now resembled at best, haphazard. Snow drifts of paper covered every wooden table, chair and floor in the staff room.

Mr Hatt sat back and lightly tapped the end of the pen against his teeth. A shot of pain travelled up his back and across his right shoulder. He stretched out cold fingers and rubbed his thumb because it felt numb. The wall clock chimed 1565.

Mr Hatt didn't realise how late it was, his throat dry, he swallowed, eyes world weary. He hid a frowned expression of guilt behind the palm of his hand before he vigorously rubbed his calf muscle, still stiff with the cramp.

He picked up the last report. A resigned chuckle escaped with his breath as he scanned the name, age and form. Green R. J. 11 years old, Form 5.

In life, the penultimate day before the weekend, using a candle to light the last cigarette in the packet because you've used the last match in the box, the last minutes of a game, the end of the last lesson on the last Friday of the month and the last boy that talks out of turn. These are the things you need to be most wary of, because invariably, these are the times disasters happen.

With the back of his hand Mr Hatt brushed cigarette ash from the knee of his Walnut brown corduroy trousers, as if they were all those memories. He took another drag on the cigarette and the memories came flooding back.

He picked up and hovered the fountain pen over the last blank box on the page. He put down the pen, took off his reading glasses and checked the lenses against the solitary light bulb hanging from the Rococo plasterwork. He wiped the moisture from his eye. Carefully placed the glasses back onto his nose, straightened them, and let out an anguished breath. Steadying the piece of hardboard, he had rested on his knees, he picked up his pen and scrawled twelve words within the box. Twelve words that summed up the last football match of the term and not the whole season.

All winter during games, I did my best along with my classmates to keep warm as we ran all about the football pitch in different directions, avoiding being nominated as goalkeeper.

Not listening to Mr Hatt berate us on the off-side rule, we carried on kicking the football. I would invariably find myself tip-toeing up and down the touchline before rushing infield, shouting at deaf ears, whilst chasing after the boy with the football, probably Wilson, "Here, here, pass it, pass it, pass it here, pass the ball, pass the ball here, over here. Pass it! PASS IT!!"

Then someone on purpose kicked the football over the hedge, probably Smit, into the road because a look out, probably Thompson, had seen and signalled the milk lorry was coming. We all knew the ball would be run over in such a narrow lane. It made a delightful pop! We would cheer and again run in different directions until a frustrated Mr Hatt told us in Anglo-Saxon to "Go jump in the Serpentine Lake!" Which meant games was over and it was time to get our hair washed in a warm shower.

The weeks went by in a blur. Then the last football match of the term arrived, against Mount House School from Tavistock. Their beaten-up van pulled up outside the front of the house. And as the van doors opened, an intense bunch of boys fell out, holding kit bags and studded boots. And when the whistle blew at the start of the game, they tackled hard, kicked our shins instead of the ball, they barged into Ellison and elbowed Smit out of the way before they fly hacked Clifton Wentworth who tripped over his own boots and landed face down in the mud. I stood and watched, then traipsed after the ball.

Late in the game, we were going end to end, the score was still nil, nil. We had energy in our legs, but they were as good as us. In the last minutes of the game, Ellison broke down the wing, we rushed forward in support, Ellison still on the ball, crossed it in from wide on the touchline on the right wing. I stood waiting with both feet planted on the edge of the six-yard box and I watched as the ball lifted off the ground and travelled at speed, curving in towards me. The ball landed at my feet, a perfect cross. I didn't panic. To give the kick some oomph! I started swinging my arms like a windmill. I stretched my right leg back as far as it would go and hacked at the ball. I made contact. Their goalkeeper looked surprised, then amused and then he ducked out of the way as the projectile whistled over his head and into the back of the net. I scored a goal! Oh! Hang on... Scratch that. My football boot did.

It turns out, I missed the ball by a couple of minutes because an opposition defender had snuck in and cleared it. The Mount House defender passed the ball to their hotshot centre forward who unmarked, was quite alone. Why? Well, because all our players were bunched together holding the Mount House boys in an Agincourt-like crush in the Mount House goalmouth.

The hotshot centre-forward was serious about football. He swivelled and began to dribble the ball towards our goal. The headmaster started shouting waving his arms. His face turned beetroot red. "No! No! No!" Came the cry. We stood miles away and watched in horror. As did the whole school. A roar went up.

Mr Beaumont, having lit a cigarette, howled, "Kill him!" On hearing this, our rotund goalkeeper Bradley Edwards, misguidedly ran out of his area and launched himself, studs first at the centre forward's chest. The Mount House centre forward merely sidestepped and let our goalkeeper Bradley Edwards and his blood-curdling war cry fly past. Bradley Edwards our rotund goalkeeper landed, rather bounced before he collapsed into a heap on the penalty spot. The poor fellow could only watch and writhe in agony as the Mount House centre forward stopped and looked around. He did this to see if we were all looking.

Which we were. He tapped the ball over the goal line, threw his arms into the air and yelled, "Goal!"

Mr Hatt the match referee, arrived at our goalmouth. He caught up, having run the length of the pitch, a minute or two after the main event, gasping for air. He looked at his wristwatch and not seeing an offside flag, allowed the goal. Three loud blasts on his whistle signalled the end of the game. Mount House had won. Ellison shouted a string of expletives. The latest Matron, young, pretty, fragrant and fey, fainted with the back of her hand to her brow. Luckily for her, Mr Harrington was on hand as she fell into his arms. But not before he barged Mr Beaumont out of the way. "Oh you poor thing." Said Mr Harrington, lifting the dainty Matron off her feet. Rumour had it he carried her all the way back to the surgery and that she didn't mind.

Head down, I sloped off to the changing rooms. The whole school panicked and ran this way and that. Mr Hatt, his left eye twitching, tried to bring some order to the proceedings with multiple blasts on his whistle. It was pandemonium.

When winning is everything, Toulouse is the fourth largest city in France. It is not an option. Win at all costs. Win or don't come home. It was bad that we lost because a few hours earlier over lunch, the Headmaster had unwittingly reminded the entire school how proud he was. He revealed through choked-up emotion, a little-known fact that the school football team hadn't lost a home game in fifteen years. Talk about jinxing it!

That is why I sloped off to the changing rooms. I knew ten tonnes of blame would crash down onto my shoulders. Fifteen years for crying out loud. Besides it wasn't my fault, I wasn't the one who let the goal in. And a draw would have been as good as a win. Ugh! I don't do football, give me cricket any day.

And what of those twelve words Mr Hatt used to sum up my sporting achievement for the winter term?

"When it comes to football, Rupert lacks finesse in the goal area."

30

Kiss Chase

MOTHER OPENED THE BROWN envelope containing the school report. She read it out loud, so Rose and her boyfriend, now husband, Nod could be in the loop. They were here for some reason. Oh yeah, that's right, Happy-not-Happy Christmas-not-Christmas everyone.

Not finding any toys in the removal boxes. Wondering what happened to the cat. At home-not-home on holiday-not-holiday, bored, bored, bored, bored. Again, Happy-not-Happy Christmas-not-Christmas everyone.

I crunched on cornflakes, declined a piece of toast, drank several cups of tea. I listened and waited. And there it is... the moment, it arrived and everybody else found it so amusing. That moment, above all the other wonderful comments, accolades and praise. The moment the put-down arrived. That bolt of light that splits through the monotony of beige curtains, kedgeree, custard creams and would you like a cup of tea or coffee? Tea or coffee, Tea or coffee or you could have coffee and tea, you decide. Which one, Rupert?

"I honestly don't mind, whatever you are making."

Again and again, it was read out from the school report, taken with much mirth and to keep me in my place, it was frequently read out at subsequent Christmas-not-Christmas Dinners around the country, when I stood up to stroll across the room to switch the television off last thing before going to bed, and in the morning getting down late to breakfast. The words travelled well and adapted to any given situation. Even whilst opening the fridge door.

"When it comes to taking milk out of the fridge, Rupert lacks finesse in the kitchen."

They would laugh and tell me they didn't mean it. I wanted them to shut up because right now I can't take a joke. Everything's still too raw. I feel jangly, even in the quiet moments. How come we don't talk about it? Not the school report. It's just that sometimes, you know. I still miss him, terribly.

Easter Term begins. A new year, 1976 and it is bedtime again. And again on Mr. Whitaker's instruction, we kneel beside our beds, clasp our hands together and through screwed-up eyes, wish for something impossible. Mr. Whitaker called it prayer. I didn't. I called it Bible-gum. I wished to be anywhere but here...

One last thing Lord, one last thing, please. Hear me out Jaheeezus... no sorry I didn't mean it like that. Well, actually I did. Hold on don't go. Dear Lord, when I go home, next time I go back on holiday-not-holiday, please can it be the same place as last time. I liked Suffering in Suffolk. And I liked my toys and stuff. I'd like to hold on to some of them, all of them. And my cricket books. Can't you tell my mother to be happy and stop moving jobs all the time? She is always on about you. I liked living in Brighton and Hove too. South Molton sucks. Dunkeswell was the worst. And Kentisbeare what happened, why did it all fall apart? Where are you?

I opened my eyes and felt the need to glare at someone. "Why am I still here?" I said all frothed up and angry. Ralph Brompton shrugged his shoulders and got off the floor and jumped into his bed.

Buckland House
Tuesday 13th January 1976

Dear Mum
Thank you for the letter. In the choir I am a Dark Blue which is second head! In football our team won 5-0 I did not score any goals! I am in the same dormitory as last term and form. I hope the rats or mice go away quickly after the poisonous poison is put down!
Brian Pike who I took out one Sunday has not come back to school! Because he is having Maths! At home! Today in Hobbies we are playing Chess. I am keeping my diary up to date. I have been using my maths book. I can not think of anything else to say but please can you send me my slippers and radio out of my pound note + earphones.
Love Rupert x

God-awful maths, I hate maths.

Buckland House

Saturday 31st January 1976

Dear Mum

How are you? We beat St Petroc's 2-1 on Wednesday and today we were going to play Mount House but their pitches were much too hard. We have now got a head boy called Armstrong. Yesterday I wrote a letter to Brother Number Three. Also yesterday we had a run and I took my radio! There was not much on! The film on Sunday is called 'Spy With My Face.' It is a man from UNCLE! With David McCallum.

I do not understand formulas and formulae in Maths. Please can you help me?

I will not be going to the dentist for a long time Matron says! Thank you for your letter. I do not like the cold weather either. I have got a running nose as well. Yes, it is very cold playing football.

Love from Rupert X

Maths is now a mystery to me. I am now so bad at it that I recently got two marks out of a hundred in an exam test thing. The joke went around that I only got those two marks for writing my name on top of the paper.

This term to our astonishment and for some bewilderment, the assembly room was full of girls…

I count five. Well, that's a lot! By the word girl, I mean not a boy. Incredulously we find the girls to be wearing the same school uniform as us boys, even the school tie. They skip happily about, waving their arms and laughing. But not like us boys. Girls are a mystery. Like maths. I count again. This time out loud, now there are seven… no six. They run over. Some of the girls talk to their brothers. The rest of us boys look on and listen. They smell different, have long hair that they put in a ponytail and when they smile and make eye contact, I feel discombobulated. I find it was curious that all the girl's names begin with the letter V and W.

The girls arrived through nefarious means, by their older or younger brothers. It must have been an entry requirement. One boy had two younger sisters Veronica and Vera who caught everyone's eye. Then there was Violet, Valerie, Victoria and Wendy. I asked some boys some important questions but to this day nobody has any answers.

"What are they doing here?"

"They won't be allowed to play cricket with us, will they?"

"Can we count on the girls?"

"Can they help me with formulas in maths?"

Now the girls are here at school. I don't suppose they'll ever go away. They all have brothers too. They are a distraction in a good and a bad way. Because I believe they have special powers and I feel things, different things, feelings. Not like anything I have felt before. The sudden attention they bring. Happy, I'm excited, wanting to see a girl, just to watch her walk past or have them dance up to you and talk, smile, laugh. Girls are light and bright. And yet they bring a competitive edge like when two or more boys like the same girl. I don't understand maths and I don't understand girls! Neither do those boys. And the fights that ensue are all shouting taunts, baring of teeth and full on headbutts.

I am not saying it's their fault. However, everything was easier before they arrived. The boys never settle their differences and the girls seem to like that.

But I suppose you could say it was a good thing, after several weeks of rubbing shoulders, a girl or two would find me interesting. One of them liked me enough to chase me three times around the entire school. I didn't know why. There is no rule book or any mentors to explain what was going on. However, it was rather exciting to be persistently sought after on wet Saturday afternoons, running with a handful of toffees from the tuck shop.

And how was I to know you were supposed to let them catch you.

31

Private

At prep school, every Saturday morning after morning assembly, we were obliged to trudge single file in silence to the classroom block. Once behind our desks, we are told to take our headed letter-writing pads out. This month, before we were allowed to start writing our weekly letter home, the master would show us again how to spell February. Putting particular emphasis on the silent R. Feb-oo-ferry, I even think he wrote it up on the blackboard like fifteen times, before throwing the blackboard duster at whoever it was who was laughing. Now we all were laughing. The trick is not to be when the master twists around. Hence the well-directed blackboard duster is being planted at considerable speed into someone's face.

Buckland House
Saturday 7th February 1976

Dear Mum
Thank you very much for the gloves you knitted me I am wearing them nearly all the time! Today the match against St Michael's home is on! I am not in it. The film last week was very good! The film this week is called 'The Absent-Minded Professor' One day in the week I scored a goal and on Friday I did as well! It is not long until half term. In Biology we are planting beans to see if they grow in the dark and things like that. Have you seen Tinker? Have you got a course in over half term? I almost finished my lampshade in Hobbies on Thursday. I do not know when I shall be going to the dentist.
Love Rupert x

PRIVATE

Telephone: Shebbear 222

BUCKLAND HOUSE,
BUCKLAND FILLEIGH,
BEAWORTHY,
N. DEVON.
EX21 5JA

<u>Monday 23rd February</u>

Dear Mum,

I hate school. I wish I could leave straight away. I am fed up with the boys and Masters. I cannot do maths. I want to get away and talk to you quietly. This morning a boy wanted some marmalade and breakfast was over and ███████████ says that you can't have any more after breakfast and he punched me in the front of the mouth straight away for no reason at all, and he did it again.

Please come and take

me away from the stupid school as soon as you get this letter. the film was quiet good yesterday. it bit boaring.

from

Rupert

PS if he crosses my path again I will kill him.

An extra prep school letter

I stuffed the 'PRIVATE' letter into the envelope and marched quite angrily to the headmaster's study where opposite, by the stairs, was a box high up on a cupboard into which one could deposit a sneaky letter to be posted. I reached up onto my tippy toe to slam-dunk the bad news letter. Boiling over with anger, I wondered what to do next. It felt better writing the letter. It felt like I was a bit too emotional. An unexpected turn of events sent me out to Jupiter and now I was spiralling back to Earth.

"That should do it!" I said to Hunt.

Needless to say, I did not get taken out of the school. Nobody even talked about it. Not sure if my mother rang up or not.

Also, I did not kill, the boy from earlier, who punched me in the face, when later that day in the changing room, after games, he crossed my path. I couldn't help notice a tension evolve as Hunt pointed him out saying, "There you go..." For a moment there the boy looked anxious.

I looked at the boy and felt nothing. "Nah!" I replied. "It's not worth it."

However, I like to think that maybe one moonless night I would have woken around 03:33 AM in an impotent rage, pyjamas saturated in sweat and whilst looking for cold revenge. I would slide out of bed, slink through the door, disappear into the darkness, and escape one dormitory for another, the one where that boy slept. And with a soft gentle pillow, I might forcefully smother every last living drop of life out of his body. Push his face through to the back of his head, such was the tornado gathering within me. Notwithstanding I could have followed him, at a distance, around the school for a week or two noting where he liked to play, and his good and bad habits. I could make notes as to when the boy was descending the back staircase. I could hide and step out as he passed, to raise my leg, kick him headfirst into the abyss. A snap of bones, twisted cartilage, broken bloody teeth, and a fat distended tongue, you know the sort of death thing. Quite a crumpled heap on the flagstone floor. You only have to watch twenty minutes of television to see all this and worse. It is a constant drip. Nothing should be left to the imagination. Television is my instructor on how to be cruel in life. Switch it on so I may hear life's lessons. Nevertheless, I conclude that I could have simply poisoned his mid-morning milk with drops of mercury delivered daily from pipettes stolen from the science laboratory. "Here mate, have this one..." I would say thrusting the glass under his nose. *"Hmm... delicious milk, it is so good for you!"*

32

Pancakes

IT'S COMING. PANCAKE DAY, Shrove Tuesday, Fat Tuesday, Mardis Gras. Everything winds up before the fast. No more sweets before Lent starts. Two fingers to Lent, we don't do that. Yes we do. No we don't...

Tuesday 2nd March 1976. Shrove Tuesday, a waxing crescent Moon rises before noon in the east, faintly visible.

Mr Sinclair, the school cook, let out a low growl as he snapped open the plastic lid from the big food box container and emptied the sultanas and dust from the lid into the pancake mix. He looked across to the love of his life, coughed and smiled. His cough caused a bit of ash to fall from his cigarette. It crumbled onto the corner of the worktop and failed to land in the mix so Mr Sinclair, ever considerate, carefully cradled it up in the palm of his hand and sprinkled it into the pancake mix.

"Won't do 'em any harm." He chuckled, as he winked to Mrs Sinclair, also a school cook.

"Roughage." Came an echo from across the kitchen. He turned and looked at his precious, his love and he pulled a face that you'd only pull if you were in the pub and were very annoyed about something someone had said and you were gearing up to forcefully push a pint glass through to the back of that someone's face. "Exactly!" Mrs Sinclair said. "To hell with 'em." She picked up another tray of brown eggs and began emptying the insides out into a gigantic bowl.

"Believe it or not." Said Thomas Arnold, passing an empty dinner plate down the table. "Today's dessert is pancake! Yes Wilson, I did say pancake. Listen, my brother told me, in all his time here, never before, in his time at Buckland House, did we ever have pancakes. Imagine that!" We opened our eyes wide. Smit, Ralph Brompton and Wilson licked their lips and rubbed their tummies.

"Pannenkoek!" Said Smit, he gestured excitedly. Clifton Wentworth started a whisper that quickly went around, it turned into a froth of excitement that ballooned around the room, only to bounce aimlessly off the refectory wall and pop when the headmaster glanced up from his newspaper. He sensed a change in the mood of the room. He looked around. We all had our heads down as if in silent prayer. He returned to the world news section before turning the page to read the obituaries.

The babble of conversation left the dining hall as expectation and illusion entered. We could hardly have known, we should have known. We should have read the Master's faces, knowing that the pancakes we were about to receive would be a pale imitation of the delicate, light and crispy crêpes our dear mothers this day would conjure from thin air in warm sun-lit kitchens across this our green and pleasant land. *Oh, what are the chances?*

Excitement returns, all eyes are on the servers, who like a line of worker ants, carry plate after plate with great efficiency and speed from kitchen hatchway to table. Our noses were quick to detect white flour, egg, fine white sugar, milk, a sneeze of nutmeg, and a hundred or so wrinkled, old sultanas. We imagined all the ingredients knocked together without an air bubble in sight. We are delirious and full of unrealistic expectations. A procession of plates were passed down the line until everybody had a white plate and on it. Finally, a pancake. It was like a dozen hefty bricks being thrown through the large refectory windows such was the shattering of the Pancake illusion. However, few let their disappointment and sudden unsteady pangs of homesickness show. Thomas Arnold, the warrior that he was, broke the stunned silence.

"Three cheers for the Cook! Hip, hip..."

The room erupts with a jubilant "HOORAY!"

Under the noise, Hunt confides to Thomas Arnold. "That's not a real pancake!" He said then he whispered to Winston Montague the closest boy on the next table "More like what you find underwater swaying in the gentle current of some tropical reef." He did the actions to great effect. He should know, he lives on a remote island overseas.

A nervous laugh rattled along the tables. Eyes kept low for fear of being singled out for dissent. Winston Montague turned a little pale and asked to be excused. We sat on table four with a high status, aloof sometimes nice, but mostly detached Matron. Matron's came and went like the school Masters. This Matron was a little bit harsh to the level of spinster. She sat po-faced at the head of the table. Didn't like to make eye contact. She could pass for a limestone statue with its nose knocked off in the British Museum. A lonely sister.

Two places away meant in two days time, I would be sitting next to her and her halitosis. She sat like all the Masters at the head of the table. With a broom for a spine. Each day we moved around one place. It meant we all got a go at serving, clearing and getting some manners knocked into us by our elders and betters. No matter how weird or monstrous the manners were.

Sometimes, if you were lucky or caught the moment right, one could elicit a conversation of sorts, cut through to the human inside, so to speak. The human that cowered behind the persona that got a wage, rather than as some saw it as a wager to educate the young middle to upper-middle-class minds of this, our great slowly deflating nation.

"Would you look at the news, just now, Sir?" Said Malcolm McGregor prompting a master into conversation.

"I'd rather not. Er... Elbows."

"Sir, what's happening in the outside world? Please tell us..." Asked Ralph Brompton.

"Elbows off the table or go and stand outside." Quipped Mr Fairfax before saying, "I'm watching you, boy!"

Mr Harrington trotted into the dining hall holding a plate like he was some fancy French waiter. The room fell like dominos into a significant silence.

The Headmaster smiled, approving Mr Harrington's tactic. The whole school sat bolt upright, alert, waiting. You could hear your own breath. I concentrated on how I was going to pick up my fork because my hands were trembling. No sooner had the order to eat been given, did we hit the white plates before us, devouring the sweet treat pudding like wolves tearing at a stumbling reindeer.

We sat up straight, eyes and cheeks bulging, others struggled to swallow the coagulated sultana slime. Regurgitation was not an option. That would only lead to hours of being teased and a furry tongue. Some wiped their plates with a forefinger to snap up errant grains of sugar. Others beamed as their tongues rolled over their lips. The fat, the thin, the tall and the short boys belched. Matron looked disapprovingly at her charges.

"Er... Manners." She demanded banging a clenched fist on the tabletop.

So why, in heaven's name, did I thrust my hand, arm, and overly excited face into the air when Mr Harrington announced, "Would anyone like seconds?"

It must have been the sugar rush because all of a sudden, just about everyone started screeching like herring gulls fighting over discarded bits of fish, at the tail end of a trawler. I bounced along with the others sat on the wooden bench. It was very bouncy. We got louder and louder. Matron shot a withering look at the headmaster.

"SILENCE!" Shouted the headmaster and nodded to Mr Harrington to continue. A process of elimination began as to who was worthy enough to receive the last pancake. Only one pancake left over.

The last pancake looking like a wrapped chamois leather cloth, soft-boiled sponge sea creature, plonked on a side plate and now in Mr Harrington's hand. He wafted the dish around the dining room air. There wasn't any chance the pancake would fly off. It was stuck on with coagulated fat and it was beginning to smell. And as was Mr Harrington's want, he stretched the elimination process out to another one of his fifteen minutes of cruelty...

"Now," said Mr Harrington, curling his top lip. "Hands down anyone with bright orange hair."

"But sir! That's not fair, Sir!"

"Sir! Not fair, Sir!" Echoed Ralph Brompton, Smit and Wilson, who clearly all had dark brown to black hair and just needed to let off some steam.

"Shut up, be quiet, put your hand down, Campbell. I don't like you, boy." Continued Mr Harrington.

"But Sir! Not fair..."

"CAMPBELL!" Bellowed the Headmaster his eyes as piercing as helicopter searchlights. Duncan Campbell went bright red, he always did. He smiled showing his white teeth, and his blue eyes twinkled. This angered the Headmaster even more, who incidentally also had an orange head of hair, not as bright and youthful, more greying around the edges, more the colour of ginger cake than say, tangerine. "Get out!" Said the Headmaster. "Go and wait outside my study, Campbell. I simply will not have it."

The perceived flare-up by Duncan Campbell probably just earned him a stroke or three from the cane. I looked at Mandrake for some confirmation of this notion. Mandrake and Hunt both nodded in the affirmative. I nodded back without moving my head. Mandrake scowled at my arm still being raised. Hunt smiled and put his thumb up. It irked Mandrake that I had not learnt anything, what with him being my guardian. He had tried to teach me about getting by, but I just shrugged my shoulders and carried on in my own sweet way. I was going along for the ride. Besides, there was no way I was going to win. I took a deep breath in and slowly let it out.

My arm was beginning to ache. Mr Harrington looked around the room and fired out "Hands down if you've got a double-barrelled name." Followed by the customary, now accepted, "I don't like you."

I was beginning to get worried. I began to suspect something was amiss. I perceived the humiliation level was rising. I couldn't now legitimately drop my arm down; it would be noticed for sure by my enemies, whose eyes were sweeping the room. I thought of the pancake. The last pancake. The pancake everybody but nobody wanted. I wanted. Hang on... Scratch that, I like the idea of pancake.

The last pancake what does it mean? It means I want to win. I looked at the faces attached to the remaining hands in the air and an upsurge of brain juice flooded my mind. It wired me up to make every effort to win.

A crow flew past the dining room window. Caught my eye. *Oh, look a crow...* That was a mistake, you should never disengage with the room, another thing Mandrake had tried to teach me. I missed what Mr Harrington had said when I returned to the room, I heard, "I don't like you, boy."

I could feel all the eyes in the room. A cold draught of air hit me, I felt like a fraud, an imposter, pretender to the throne. I no longer wanted the pancake. However, Mr Harrington smiled and personally handed the now stone-cold pancake on a white plate, plonked it down right in front of me. He stepped back and did one of his famous blank, oddly strange, disengaged stares. He would have made a good robot. I took the plate in my left hand, such was the shock of winning, the groans from the other boys, the envy simmering at the table, the jealousy percolating from enemy to enemy. Mr Harrington snapped back to reality, his top lip snarled, and he smirked as if he had spat on the pancake as he brought it from the kitchen hatchway.

"Here you are everybody, Green is the winner." He said and stepped away. I smiled at the conquest that I perceived I had won. Mandrake looked at me and raised an eyebrow. "Ah!" I said and slowly I lowered my right arm which had been locked upright in the air all this time.

The room was eerily silent as slowly I picked up my fork, expecting the pancake to deflate when punctured. Matron leaned forward fixed my eyes in a stare and said. "Aren't you going to offer your pancake to the young lady sat opposite you? Where are your manners Green?" For a moment, I had a sense of humour failure. The second hand on the clock on the wall stopped, the cogs and springs in my mind sprang loose. I went through some mental gymnastics as synapses fizzled to near extinction then slowly recovered.

My good boy kicked in and with my best English accent said, "Err... Would you like pancake... my pancake. Try my pancake. Would you like my pancake?" I said without looking at her. Victoria, the young girl, equally horrified at being singled out by our bombastic matron somehow smiled graciously and said, "No thank you." She shook her head, smiled again, and pulled her long hair over her face. I looked at Matron, who nodded, and I was able to proceed with the first mouthful of cold pancake.

"Taste good?" Asked Matron. "The whole school's waiting for you."

"Mmm..." I replied, careful not to speak with my mouthful. How I would like the floor to open up now and swallow me, like I swallowed the last spoonful, of what has now become in my eyes, a sweet pulsing lump of congealed nasty. I open my mouth and insert the spoon, bite down and take the spoon from my mouth, holding it up to show everyone. I swallow the pancake down and thump my fist against my chest to stop the gag reflex throwing up all the pancake, lunch, breakfast and first break milk, from yesterday.

I smiled half a smile at the envious ones. And I smile the other half at the jealous ones. Their thoughts bounce off my head and seep into the dining room walls for later, another time.

I tried not to belch but belch I did. My plate and spoon were cleared away and in a soporific silence we filed out of the room to play outdoors until the bell tolled for us to return to the classroom for afternoon lessons.

Buckland House
Sunday 14th March 1976

Dear Mum

How are you? Thank you for your letters. You are probably wondering why my writing is so scribbly! Because I am in bed with the flu! Brian Pike has also. Not long till the end of the term [is it] I am looking forward to seeing you again. I am making two mats, one for you it looks like this: I got you a postcard as well. I hope you are still dieting?! You should have lost pounds! [lbs.] Term ends on 18th Thursday and at 12 o'clock morning not before. That's what Matron said! I should be getting up quite soon. Perhaps Monday.

Not much to write.

Love from Rupert x

33

Life On The Front Lawn

I LOVE THE FRAGRANCES cut grass offers, its infectious, and each year, on, on and on, the first cut fills me with expectation for the cricket season yet to come. Already this year it is hot and dry, very dry. Somewhere a lawn mower starts up. Somewhere, a rag rubs linseed oil into the surface cracks of an old cricket bat. Somewhere cricket pads get a second coat of whitener. And somewhere another term brings a boarding school back to life.

Buckland House
1st May 1976

Dear Mum
How are you? Thank you for your letter. Last Thursday some of forms 8 and 7 went to Dartington Glass factory in Torrington. It was or seemed a very boring job to do!
I have at last been made cricket captain of the 1st XI! Our first cricket match against another school is on the 12th May.
It has not been very sunny hear although our history master Whitaker says that Summer is already over! (what a pessimist)! Not long till my birthday is it? Maths is getting on alright. When you look at the blue bit of paper with all the things, we do this term you will see no 2nd long Sunday. But it says that it can be arranged for one.
Love from Rupert John! x

A car turns into the drive. We watch it speed up to the grand old house covered in mid green Virginia Creeper leaves. At first, we think it is the advance party of the opposition team. It is not. It is Mr Whitmore, who returns in his light blue futuristic Citroën DS and parks by the four pillars at the front of the main schoolhouse. He clambers out of the car, he's always so smartly dressed, very sauvre and with it and totally out of place in this setting. He gives a wave, hand above his head as he skips round the long sleek bonnet, dances up the steps into the house through the main entrance double doors. We wait for the director to shout "Cut!", such was the smooth entrance.

Not sure who he was waving to but knowing him, it was probably a wave for everybody, along with a chuckle and a little sidestep mannerism that he had. Rugger was his passion and cricket, as far as he was concerned, could go to hell. He taught French. And when he wrote numbers, he wrote them with bends and flourishes that attracted my eye. Very continental.

The opposition is a little late. I don't mind but then I do, late is late if it is all the same. I am not helping with anything because everything is done. I am out of my body somewhere else. I am in the zone ready to play. I feel in my pocket for the coin I will be using at the toss. I am reassured; I still have it.

I walk on air back to my team. They sit on the bench in the warmth of the afternoon. The kit bag overturned, Clifton Wentworth pulling pads and gloves out and matching them into pairs. Then the shout goes out that they are here.

Within minutes of their arrival, I am intercepted by two boys from the opposition, I recognise one of them as the captain, because over the years he has always been the captain. The other, I guess, because he held a book and a large zipped bag is the scorer. The scorer is desperate to know what's going on. I suggest we walk to the middle, as is tradition for the toss but without the scorer. My thoughts are elsewhere as the scorer followed and talks nonstop. I laugh at his description of their journey over. Tales of cooking inside a hotter-than-hot car, bendy roads, hill climbs stuck behind slow-moving haystacks and a tractor belching thick black smoke. "Did you know, diesel fumes suffocate people?" He concluded a little scared. An idea popped into my head.

"No, I didn't," I said. I began to think that after that journey, the last thing they would want to do would be to bat first. I stop, their captain motions for the scorer to back off. I snap the coin. It flies high up into the air. A silence of expectation crept across the field as onlookers around the ground held their breath. Looking to be first to call what the decision is and who will bat first.

"Heads!" Spits their Captain. The coin lands, rolls and flops on the grass, tail up.

"We're going to have a bowl," I said picking up the coin. I try not to laugh as the opposition captain berates his scorer sending him off towards the desks positioned nicely next to our large black homemade scoreboard.

A small responsible boy has been appointed scoreboard operator for the match. To do the dance with the numbers. Payment is a cricket tea where he will get the chance to once again taste the most cherished of cricket tea sustenance, namely a

Victoria sponge. The boy stands to attention beneath the gargantuan scoreboard, he is at the ready.

"Made several centuries ago by a former pupil with nothing better to do." Says Rhys Jenkins, Buckland House's cricket scorer, in answer to the opposition scorer's barrage of questions. He gave the monolithic structure a cursory glance and continues. "A magnum opus that is also practical, it is the envy of all the prep schools this side of Exeter, all eight of them. Yours included. Don't shake your head, I know I am right."

On closer inspection, the scoreboard boy appears to be having a little trouble as he practises which numbers to turn. A little nervous, he does eventually manage it with instruction from Rhys Jenkins.

The scorers settle themselves down to exchange their respective team sheets, to remark on spellings and with sharp HB pencils, they make good with polite conversation and anecdotes of the season thus far. From deep within handbag-sized pencil cases, the scorers hunt for, and find, favoured lucky charms. They synchronise their movements to place on the desktop their respective custard cream-sized Indian rubbers for the unforeseen 'adding up' mistakes before they, like the bright sun, sink into the sludge to waste a pleasant afternoon, to feign interest with a constant flow of diatribes and hand-signals back and forth to the schoolmaster umpires, who are way beyond shouting distance. They witness and diligently record every detail and delivery. The small boy juggles the numbers on the scoreboard.

Mr. Hatt lobs the blood-red cherry over to me. I catch it and throw it to Bradley Edwards, who turns and marks out his run-up. The small boy steps back to lift his head up and folds his arms a broad smile on his face. The scoreboard gives him plenty to do, what with the individual batsman scores to rack up. Hands-on his hips, the job is done, all the numbers read nought, nought, nothing, nothing for none. He turns in time to see Bradley Edwards, a tall rotund boy, wheel around and charge at great speed towards the crease.

Arms and legs in beautiful rhythm to bowl the first ball of the match. He grips the brand-new red rambler seam up, with a light finger tip touch in his right hand. The gold lacquer of the maker's name sparkles pure tiny splinters of mirror ball light out across the field invisible to the naked eye.

Bowling over the wicket, Bradley Edwards reaches the crease. In slow motion and side on, he leaps majestically into his delivery stride and for a second, is mid-air motionless. Perfection. His back foot lands. This exquisite moment brings silence and serenity. The fielders already walking in. The wicket-keeper crouches ready to pounce.

His front leg slams halfway across the white popping crease line. In a blur, the bowling arm turns over, and the new ball releases with a flick, seam up. Now airborne, the line is about an inch outside the off stump. It hits the hard dry pitch followed by a loud crack. The sound rang out across the field like a shotgun. Made everybody jump.

The batsman stands for a moment, holding his bat up in the air behind him. Not a high back lift, he was going forward, what he did, all he did wrong, was miss the ball. The ball swung in and hit the top of the off stump. The two bails lift off the stumps fizzing like fireworks. They traced a high arching trajectory. The sort of thing mathematicians would have conversations about, to conjure formula around a blackboard for hours.

The bowler and wicket-keeper spontaneously throw their arms into the air yelling HOWZAT! The black rookery birds take to the wing. The batsman stiffens, looks awkward, drops his head and trudges off. In the distance, the next batsman picks up his bat and gloves and takes a faltering step towards the boundary line and onto the gallows that is the cricket square.

"New batsman." Shouts the boy standing at mid-wicket. We clap the batsman in. He takes guard.

"Middle stump please, Sir." Mr. Hatt the umpire directs the opposition batsman towards middle. "A little towards you, a bit more. That is... Right arm over, five balls to come."

The boy adjusts his pads and looks nervously around at the excitable fielders who grin, their wolf eyes raging as they bay for his blood. "Play." The Umpire, Mr. Hatt says, with aplomb. He takes his left arm from a position behind his back and brings it through, past his torso and on forward out in front of his now slightly bent left knee. His hand leads but his index finger points. There is a hush on the field. The game continues. Bradley Edwards sets off on his long run up.

Within a very short time, we were batting with a meagre 39 runs needed to win. We reached our target with a few good hits. At the fall of our first wicket, I strode out to bat. I managed to hit the first ball I faced for four runs. I stroked the ball, it fizzed along the ground, beat the fielder at square leg and disappeared down the slope, out of sight, bounced on the concrete and splashed into the swimming pool. Now try and bowl with that I thought. We won the match with the loss of only one wicket. All wrapped up, finished with hours and hours to go before tea.

Over by the entrance to the house, the Headmaster appeared, motioned for Mr Hatt to join him. After a few words the Headmaster went back into the house.

"Now then boys." Said Hatt jogging over to us. "Are we... are we all good and happy with your win?"

"Yes Sir. Can we have tea now?"

"Yes, I am quite happy too." He said. He wasn't, I could tell. "In fact, well done. Er... The Headmaster. Not too impressed." Mr Hatt scratched his temple and screwed up his face. "Never mind. So now we shall have to have another game. Nothing serious, just some fun. A fun game. Yes, that's what we shall have. I suggest this time, we bat first."

"Sir?" I said. Everyone else groaned. "We thought you would be pleased with us. After all, we did stuff them. Sir."

"Quite..."

34

Ralph Brompton

"Has anyone seen Ralph Brompton?" Asks the Headmaster at the beginning of morning assembly and way before breakfast. He held up a big handful of first post letters, gesturing with his eyes, *you're not getting any letters until I get an answer.*

We didn't know anything about it, but must have given the impression we might know something of his whereabouts. The Headmaster stood in silence, hardly moving, looking straight ahead. After a minute, he let out a long sigh and unfolded his arms and said, "Ok, does anyone know where Ralph Brompton likes to go? Which trees he climbs?" No one said anything. Even Malcolm MacGregor did not appear to be any the wiser.

"Where's he gone, Sir?" Asked Kingsley the head boy, but before the Headmaster could answer, Mr Whitaker put his head into the room.

"Er... Headmaster." Said Mr Whitaker waving a finger in the air.

The Headmaster left with Mr Whitaker and we speculate. After five minutes alone time, Mr Harrington arrives, looks scruffy, his hair needs a brush, he ties a Windsor knot on his necktie stuffs it under his V neck jumper. He suggests, as he fastens his top button and straightens his tie, that members of Ralph Brompton's form scoot around the grounds and have a little look for him. Just to make sure. Those boys leave and Mr Harrington invites the first line to walk single file, in silence, into breakfast. Mr Harrington yawns. The other lines follow suit.

Once we are all in the dining hall, Mr Harrington says grace and we continue to speculate as benches slide and tables shudder, as we all sit down. Servers lineup and Mr Harrington walks behind the serving table, smiles and nudges the young, pretty, fragrant and fey, Matron who blushes, smiles at Mr Harrington with her eyes and picks up the milk ladle and absentmindedly stirs the doorstep cold milk. Mr Harrington steadies himself before he dives into the colossal Cornflakes box. The servers move along the line. The human mechanisation begins.

I am quite disappointed. The letters didn't get handed out and wonder when they will be.

"He might...," said Wilson.

"Might what?" Inquired Thompson.

"He might've fallen out of a tree."

"When did he do that?" Asked Thomas Arnold. "At midnight? So you're saying he was stuck up a tree, yelling... and nobody heard him?"

"Something's changed in him and he wouldn't let it out. He was missing last night in our dormitory." Said Thompson.

"It looked strange this morning, to see an empty bed." Said Bradley Edwards plonking two bowls onto our table before walking off.

"Happy birthday Rupert." Whispered Violet. "It is the 24th isn't it?"

"Ssh! Don't tell everyone." I said, I did not wish to be chased around the school just to be given a dead leg and the bumps. I returned Violet's smile. But she was no longer smiling at me. She took a deep breath in and spoke.

"So, if anyone's interested. I know what's happened to Ralph Brompton." She Chirps. Then Violet smiles at me. I felt fuzzy and knocked two bowls of cornflakes together.

"Hey, steady..." Snarls Thomas Arnold, "That one's yours, stupid!"

"I overheard the Headmaster talking to Mr Whitaker." Violet said absentmindedly sliding a plate of cornflakes down her side of the table.

"What?"

The table is incredulous. We do not believe her.

"What did you hear? Tell me." Said Bradley Edwards with two more bowls. "Quick, tell me." He urged as he hovered at the tables edge before walking back to the serving table.

"He ran away in the night, took a bike with the intention to ride back to his home in Launceston. I hope the bike had lights." Violet spoke eloquently.

"Whose bike was it?" Asked Thomas Arnold. He stared at Wilson. "I hope it wasn't yours Wilson. It would have taken him forever to peddle home."

"Forty-three miles..." Figured Bradley Edwards sitting down with the last of the cereal bowls. "That's a lot of peddling."

"Police found him half hour ago, five miles from school." Violet smiled.

"No lights then." Said Thomas Arnold. "He must've waited until first light." We agree with Thomas Arnold.

"Is he coming back?" Asks Wilson picking up a spoon. That was a good question. Not a question we could easily answer at this point in time. We will have to wait and see.

"Violet, how did you manage to hear all that without being seen, Violet?" Said Wilson. I tapped Wilson on the shoulder, he turned. "What did I tell you, Wilson... strange powers!"

After breakfast, the Headmaster held another assembly where he told the school Ralph Brompton had been found, was alright, had been taken back home and that he would return in a few days, probably on Thursday. And we should give him some space.

The rules state, no running inside the house and you couldn't go to the right of the pillar by the main stairs. If you did and were caught you would get a minus point. Get four minus points and you get the cane.

No talking in the changing rooms or you'll get the cane.

No laughing in the wrong places or you'll get the cane.

No hitting girls or you'll get the cane.

If you are caught talking and not in your bed after lights out, you'll get the cane.

If three of you are caught trying to feed a tadpole to a smaller boy, you'll get the cane.

And if you're on a Sunday Walk, throwing stones at each other in the disused quarry, and a stone draws blood because it gashed as it bounced off your friend's head, you'll get the cane.

And yet, if you take a bike without lights and you run away, you don't get the cane. You get space.

What's that about?

35

The Last One

AND NOW, I AM the boy who stood shivering at the cold hard concrete edge of the school's outdoor blue water swimming pool. The warm breeze turned cool because the cloud covered, not only the entire sky, but the Sun too. And because it was a compulsory swim, it meant everybody had to get wet.

I am all prickles and bumps, sensitive to touch, clenching my fists over my heart, shivering like a snow monkey wearing snazzy orange, lime green swimming trunks. I pick up my towel and turn to go.

"Get in." Said the Headmaster. He had a habit of appearing at the worst possible time.

I had to at least get in. Half an hour ago, I was minding my own business. Then I was found. I was not hiding, merely avoiding, in the billiard room looking for woodlice under the floorboards. I was dragged out and given orders from above. The Headmaster requested I changed, in order to swim, or in my case paddle. And to hurry up because I was the last one.

Down at the swimming pool, on the top step, I grabbed hold of the silver handrail, turned round, waited for the grim reaper to drown me. Shouts of encouragement ricocheted off the cold water.

Everybody knew this was, for me, an insurmountable challenge.

"Get in." Said the Headmaster with a little more insistence.

"He can't Sir." Said Thomas Arnold. I swallowed. A bead of fear rolls down the side of my face. I don't see any reason why I can't walk down four steps and bob about in the water. Irrational fear grips at the sinews in my right hand. My legs aren't interested in moving either. Getting all this unwanted attention wasn't helping.

"Come on Green. Get into the water. I've got other things to do."

"He can't Sir. He's afraid." Winston Montague said, partisan to the cause and now we had ourselves a little scene. Inquisitive boys wrapped in towels following their noses, scenting fear, turn and move towards the water's edge. There is an expectation as to how the drama might play out. I began to cry.

"Very well, go and get changed. Next time Green you will be going in."

"Oh! Sir that's not fair." Sung the chorus of boys shivering in their towels. "It's a compulsory swim."

The Headmaster checked his wristwatch and growled. Everybody shut up. I picked up my towel and headed at speed to get away from the horrible water. The Headmaster still managed to walk past me as I stepped onto the tarmac drive. He was pretty red-faced, he looked daggers at me and stormed off in the direction to go through the main double doors of Buckland House. I scuttled around the side of the building to get back in and drop down into the changing rooms, all the time singing the match of the day theme tune.

And a score just come in… Rupert 1 – Headmaster 0.

Buckland House
Saturday 12 June 1976

Dear Mum

How are you? It was nice ringing you. The weather is dull hear and not much Sun. There have been some Compulsory Swims lately the water was rather cold.

A boy called Bradley Edwards and I have been asked to play in the team of prep schools in Devon to play Swallowfield's School at Mount House Tavistock on June 27th I was thinking Brother Number Three might be able to take me as well as you if you are free then and see me play? Common Entrance starts Monday coming not for me tho, other boys take it after half term.

Love from RupertJ xxx

P.S. See you soon.

The letter said Bradley Edwards and I were invited to play against a youth-touring cricket team from Swallowfield's School, a traditional all boy boarding school from deepest Hampshire. They were to visit Mount House School and a team of the best of the best would be picked from the private schools around the area to pitch up and play them. Two of us from Buckland House were selected. Which was all rather jolly.

We were dropped off at the school, the sun shone. The collective schools team batted first. I was to bat number three. A wicket fell quite early and I walked out to bat. Just like any other time. Only it wasn't. I wasn't used to this. And I got out first ball. Which is a pretty dumb thing to do because it brings with it a range of feelings. Embarrassment being the main one. Disappointment – yeah that is high on the list too. I made a mistake. And you only get one chance in cricket and I made a mistake on my first delivery. Instead of playing a forward defence,

I leaned into it and hit the ball with too much right hand. Popped it up for an easy return catch for the bowler as he followed through, he adjusted and took the catch. Gratefully accepted it. The fielders mobbed him. Of course they did. It was a jolly moment for their team. And the bowler's individual achievement.

I stood in total disbelief. What have I done? A few seconds of anguish, realisation, disappointment and a long dark walk back to an empty pavilion and obscurity. Boy! I was mad with myself. Caught and bowled first ball. What a donkey. That's going to go down well with the Headmaster. I thought. He didn't like cricket.

There has been another goal, Rupert 1 – Headmaster 1.

My mother was due to attend the match, was late and got lost trying to find the ground at the school and this infuriated me. After all, I could not blame myself. Maybe my ego got the better of me and I thought I was better than I was. I could hardly show my face at tea. Not a great day. The game went on and on. Fielding was a chore and I didn't get to bowl. We lost.

It was a super idea and wonderful to be asked along. Cricket - The great leveller. Today I hate cricket. Hate myself and I hate prep school. But tomorrow I will love cricket.

Buckland House
26th June 1976

Dear Mum

How are you? There has been a lot of swimming this week and it has been lovely and warm about 70°F! We have been practising for sports day this week as well.

I hope we shall start camping soon and please could you send a sleeping bag with someone on Sports Day. Early morning swims will start soon.

We have all put all our tents up and it looks quite funny with all the different sizes of Tents. On Wednesday the Colts played St Michaels and won by 9 wickets!

The first XI are playing them on July 10th last Saturday of the term! Not long until Sports Day. Next Saturday. Some or lots of bees have been making a hive outside our classroom window and swarms of them are all over the windows

Lots of love from RupertJ x

Buckland House
10th July Saturday 1976

Dear Mum

How are you? I have been sleeping out some of the time and doing other new things like we went to Bude on Thursday! Thank you for your letter. It was a great coincidence when I saw Phyllida Sewell on Crossroads! [I saw her a few minutes!] So turn on the box and see her! We are having our team photos today. Not long until the end of term on Thursday 15th and also not long until your Birthday on Monday.

I open my eyes underwater now and collect stones and pennies from the bottom.

We also have our cricket match against St Michaels today. We had swimming not long ago I was head holder. England isn't doing very well in the Test Match we were rather beaten in the first innings.

Love from Rupert x

P.S. Will we go back to South Molton first before we go over to Brother Number Three's and shall I take my tent and sleeping bag?

To forget the last innings, I bat big in the nets. It's a sunny afternoon in July. I am always the last one in the nets. Fin slings the ball down; I dance and connect. I am happiest here. A sweet crack! Lifts the ball over the end of the net, watch it land in the next field. It's all about timing. In that split second moment of bat to ball connection, that can feel like an eternity. An eternity in a second.

Rupert in cricket nets July 1976. Photo: Ralph Lynch

36

General Synopsis

New Low Expected, High Becoming Rough Later

LADY WORTHINGTON-WINTHROP WANTED MOTHER to up her cookery skills. Quite right too. She, my mother is to spend time in London on an all paid for Cordon Bleu cookery course and when she's not doing that, then she can jolly well help out Lord and Lady Worthington-Winthrop and their umpteen children. Winter in London but no space for me, not invited. I wonder where I'll be?

Buckland House
18th September 1976

Dear Mum
How are you? What is your address in London? I am in Marlborough dormitory. In hobbies I am doing shooting and Chess and piano. I will do grade 2 theory this term. I am in the same form as last time and head of a table. We have played some games of rugger so far this term. I am captain of our house called Brownes.
The weather has been nice so far but has rained in games. It is the Harvest feasterful on Sunday so we will not have a film (BOO, HOO!) I should be shouting today so I shall see how it goes. On some nights I have decided to do some star gazing!! You can look at the calendar and see when you could take me out for a weekend, before you go up to Lord Worthington-Winthrop in London.
Lots of Love Rupert x

Buckland House
16th October 1976

Dear Mum
There is a match today against Mount House at home. When we played St Petroc's we lost 22-10, I was Hooker. There is a Doctor Barnardo's Homes lecture this Sunday instead of a film. There have been a lot of new paperback books at school now and I found the book 'Animal Farm!' So I have decided to read it. I finally got a letter from Brother Number Three please could you tell them the half

term arrangements. There is also another match this Wednesday coming against St Michaels at home. It has been very cold in the mornings.

When you open the shutters in the morning do you see thousands of Pheasants crawling all over the garden? [I hope not]

Lots of Love Rupert x

Buckland House
23rd October 1976

Dear Mum

I hope you are well? Thank you very much for sending the bible book to me. Mr Cavendish is reading it now! It is not long before you go up to Lady and Lord Worthington-Winthrop's in London. This week the film is about the "Royal Navy". We have seen it before.

When we played Shebbear College, last Wednesday, we won 22-3! And afterwards they did not have a shower and put mud down all of Wellington Dormitory's beds! And also ripped someone's pajamas and the Headmaster says that, that would be the last time they played us at home. We were meant to play St Michaels but they had got a bug, and did not have enough players. The "Doctor Barnardo's" lecture was boring put it was something to watch I suppose.

It is not very long before C.E exam about 16 more days! And not long to Christmas! Thank you very much for the Snoopies also! [Ha!Har!]

The weather has not been very nice. Our camp which we have got down the woods, is coming along nicely and also the trees are hard to cut down. Shooting is getting on alright. Altho I have only had a few targets! I am going to ask Miss Duncan if I could write the names for the people in the Christmas dinner in lettering like usual. I have lost the address of yours in London so please could you send it to me!!

love from Rupert x

Buckland House
6th November 76

Dear Mum

Thank you for the letter and the £1 which I got today. I am glad you like it there in London, and also the Cordon Bleu course and all the different people from all over the world! Are they young? The Headmaster said that you would have to come and cook for our school because the cook's are retiring at the end off this term!

When you get this letter you will probably be doing C.E! Last Monday we had 'flu jabs! Or swine fever jabs! Maths is getting on alright. Instead of games we are having stupid runs and Exercises! We went around the cross country twice which is

about 6 miles! And the master said he would go around twice but he didn't the silly coward!! Not much been done this week.
lots Of love Rupert x
P.S. I hope Brother Number Three and Jo come to the fireworks!?

No fireworks for me to watch as I was coerced into leaving early.

"Fireworks aren't cool at your age... are they?" Said Brother Number Three. He is persuasive. Always has been. If he didn't want to do something then that was that, nobody did it. Nothing changes.

"No, I suppose they aren't." I follow the script. Something about your elders and betters. The usual Blah! Blah! Is this mind control, like from that *Man from UNCLE* film? I feel so angry.

I wanted to see some fireworks, lose myself for a while. But I couldn't tell them, I couldn't speak up. I have no choice, no voice. I do have silence. The roar of silence in my ears. That's why I like to stand on the pebble beach in Hove, listen to the silence, the waves of silence.

I can't express myself without getting like, really annoyed. I can't control these feelings, but I must. It is what is expected of me. Once again, my eyes look out onto the world. I don't I am somewhere else.

Instead of fireworks and perceived fun and jollity, we sloped off like thieves in the night, I crawl into the depths of the darkened backseat to watch a few rockets go off as the car indicates to turn out onto the minor road and dissolve into the night.

Once again, I endure the twisty Devonian roadways. In the darkness, the headlights illuminate the odd white line before a stop sign, usually tangled up in a beech hedge. The exhaust fumes mix with cigarette smoke. I scratch an itchy nose. I sneeze, I cough, and I splutter. Much like Brother Number Three's old rover car. It's alright, I get my own back.

"You haven't got a cold, have you?" Asked Brother Number Three with an audible TCH! And a look to the heavens. Like I just infected everyone. He lights a cigarette with the cars glow red, element thing.

"No." I said.

I like staying with Brother Number Three and family but this time I am not so sure I shouldn't have gone somewhere else. I don't think there is anywhere else. I am prickly, easily bored, feel restless, everything is too slow. Uffculme sucks! So boring with nothing to do. I want music to have more . . . BOOOOOM! TAH! BOOOOOM! TAH! Screaming guitars, lots of yelling... I want to scream and I want to shout. I want to be left alone. I want to meet some people my own age. I don't want to get up in the morning. Don't tell me to go to bed early.

The next day, sat on the floor in the front room of Brother Number Three's council house. Still annoyed, I wanted to scratch up my brother's record collection with an old sixpence found earlier, in a tobacco tin of bits in the tall corner cupboard that smelt of happier days when it stood in the living room with the inglenook fireplace at the long-gone post office in Kentisbeare.

The '45 singles he owned, all these years, no longer did it for me. The needle landed and the screams come out of the small speaker.

I curbed a curse, ripping the needle off the record, I slam another vinyl down onto the turntable. I am raging internally. Outwardly, I am fine, a normal and polite well-mannered little boy. Hearing only the frustrated noises coming from the front room, my sister-in-law Jo figured she should intervene. She shouts from the kitchen.

"Rooopert! Would you like a cup o'tea?"

"Yes!" I squeak like a mouse, then growl like a bear. "Please."

Spontaneous giggles overflow from the kitchen. My voice has just started to do this. I have no idea what's going on. Then, Brother Number Three choking with laughter yells...

"Your balls have dropped."

37

The Last Letter

With twelve days to go.... I write my last letter home.

Buckland House
28th November 1976

Dear Mum
Thank you very much for the Guinness book of records which you sent me. We had a match yesterday against St Michaels, we lost! But Mr Whitmore said that I hooked very well. In church today a man we do not know red out the sermon about Gideon and they have given us all a little New Testament and Psalms book! It is very nice.

Not long until end of term and away for this school for good. I am glad that I am leaving know because I have had enough of everything!

I would like to stay to the tenth of December instead of the 9th when we are meant to go.

Lots of love Rupert x

The end of term. The last morning. The end of Buckland House.
"Or so you thought." Said **Blue Monster**.
One last look around, Kingsley, Malcolm McGregor, and I are down by the swimming pool. A sheet of ice covers the surface. They wrestle a shoe off me and throw it across the ice. And there it stays.
Somebody is coming with a telephone message written on a piece of paper. Kingsley and Malcolm McGregor get a stick and push the shoe to the other side of the pool. They reach across and pick it up, give it back, but they didn't want to. I get the feeling they wanted to test me, knowing my fear of the swimming pool, I don't think they would have wanted to drown me. Kingsley takes the message and we leave the pool side.
We didn't have much of a connection. We walked separately back to the main house. Their people turned up.

"Yes, they did." Said **Blue Monster**. "And you were a nincompoop, a complete wazzock, a dunderhead, dullard, fat-head about it!"

"Shut up!" I said, swishing at the air above my head.

"Mind you, it was interesting to see the gene pool they heralded from." Concluded **Blue Monster** with a chuckle.

I detached, watched them load up their belongings into their cars and leave. No smile, no wave, no emotion, nothing registering on our faces. We shall never see each other again. That's a full stop. The good, the bad and the indifferent. The place feels deserted. A cold blast of wind. A solitary crow lands on the tarmac. It struts about, stops, looks up at me, cocks its head to one side and then flaps its wings as it picks up its claws and flies off.

Mother was late.

"Uh-huh! Typical…" Said **Blue Monster**.

I sit alone on my trunk out front, everyone else is gone. I look out across the front lawn to see if I am out there with a bat, hitting fours, scoring 50 runs on a sunny day. That is something to think about.

This is a fitting end to five years of growing up backwards, playing the sideways game, fitting into everything inside-out. Growing, not necessarily up. Stood behind me, I am sat on the trunk, a large ephemeral blue figure. I know he's there. He knows, I know he is there. He holds, with both hands, onto a black cloth.

"A lot happened on and off the field. In five years." Smiles **Blue Monster**. "I should go now?"

"No stay a while longer, I don't want to be left alone."

"You do know I'm not much company. It's not why I am here."

"I know. But now you're all I've got."

Blue Monster scratched his head, chuckled and calculated its next move.

"If I stay, can have your anger?"

"Sure."

"And all your grief?"

"Sure, why not, I don't care."

"And you can have this black treacle to smear on yourself whenever you feel you can't cope." And with that he throws the cloth over my head. Metaphorically of course.

In the distance, a car turns into the drive. Spots of rain hit the trunk. I stand up and take a deep breath. I wonder where I am going to be living. As the car pulls up, Mother opens the door, jumps out. She leaves the car engine running. The car doesn't mind. As long as the engine is running it is alive.

I turn and take one last look at the place I never called home or a holiday camp. Porridge, maybe. I now must detach myself from it.

"So now where do we live?" I asked breathing heavily.

"Get in." Said Mother lifting the trunk into the boot of the car. "Cornwall. You'll like it. It is nice." We climbed in, I grabbed at a seatbelt. Mother rattled the gear stick, stamped on the clutch. Handbrake, foot down. I closed my eyes. I sure was churning up inside. The wheels screeched as the car took off.

From the back seat I heard **Blue Monster's** mocking laugh, "I wonder if you've still got toys…"

38

Words, New Found Wisdom

Thomas Harold Spencer Green (1915-1974)

Exeter
23rd December 2024

My Dear Dad
How are you?
No really, how are you?
From time to time, I think about you.
And where you might have gone since you passed. Since you died.
I need to write this letter to you, to help myself heal. I hope this comes across because it is difficult to write.

Dad, since the day you died, Blue Monster has been trying to outgrow me, to become me. I feel like it wants to swallow me, to devour me. Some days it does. And I become something I am not. It is like I am covered in a thin coat of varnish that, if I can be bothered, I have to crack through, like the top of a crème brûlée. I feel like I am eating my brains from the inside, I can't hide my disappointment at the way you and Mother treated me.

Anger, grief, and sadness have helped it to grow. It gets longer and more stretched out, always after me, stepping over me. Stopping me from feeling anything.

Dad, I've got to do something about it.

So, I am going to try and thaw this compacted snow and ice that I have wrapped around my bottle-green heart. Help me mend my broken heart. I want to crack the ice. See if I can't feel better about some things.

Not feel so rejected and betrayed... See if I can't get some kind of peace of mind and cast out Blue Monster.

Dad, come with me now as I reach back into the long-forgotten tunnels of shadow time. I want to tell you and younger me that we have so little time, that we should speak a lifetime's worth of everything when we are together. We shouldn't leave each other's side. Talk about it all. I want to know everything about you... And everything I meant to you.

I want to accept love. Allow myself to heal. So, I'm gonna tell a story to let you go or rather to be released from your intertwined cobwebs and currents – so that we can encourage each other to fly... Continue to live, love and fly.

Because that is what love is.

Love Rupert x
P.S. When I grow up... I want to write; I am going to write. I am writing. I want to write books... and sell them. And I want to get what I want.

I want to be a writer.

39

Prospectus

I just wanted to share with you these words. They are from the prospectus of the time I was there...

Buckland House Prospectus

The aim of the school is to develop, in a free and friendly, though firm, atmosphere, the physical, mental and moral qualities of each boy. Understanding help and guidance from all members of the staff encourages his initiative and enterprise; at the same time he gradually comes to realise what is meant by responsibility as a member of a community, in the sharing of things, the care of property, and in learning to be tolerant and considerate of those about him. He should find that he, in co-operation with everyone else, has something useful to contribute towards the successful running of the School.

Prayers are said daily and the boys attend a School Service in St Mary's Church each Sunday. The scripture-teaching is designed as an introduction to the study of the Bible, and it is felt that religion, to be of real value, should not be confined to Scripture lessons and services but that the principles laid down in the New Testament should be taken as a basis for everyday life.

All are encouraged to make full use of the library, both for recreational purposes and for finding out things for themselves. A boy needs to learn to think logically and independently and to express himself clearly. By the time he leaves Preparatory School he should be able to work and think, a good deal on his own.

Besides other times, two afternoons a week are set aside for hobbies, among which are carpentry, shooting, the learning of musical instruments, pottery, art, gardening, leather-work, photography, riding, bicycling, judo, badminton, tennis, fishing – any other suggestions are welcome!

The health and welfare of the boys are cared for by the headmaster's wife, in conjunction with Matron and her staff. The School Doctor lives only two miles from the school. He pays regular visits and keeps in very close touch with the health of the boys. He and his partner are "on call" at all times. Being a country school, the boys are encouraged to spend as much time as possible in the open air, which undoubtedly contributes to our reputation for turning out robust and healthy young people.

We are not a co-educational school as such, but we have provided special accommodations and facilities so that boys' sisters may also be considered for entry.

The fees are £720 per term, payable in advance. The only necessary extras are in respect of laboratory fees, swimming, textbooks (as needed), £2.50 for stationery, etc; any special medical supplies or nursing: cleaning, and laundry. Total fees at this time average £750. In the event of removal of a boy, a terms notice must be given, in lieu of which a term's fees are required. The headmaster reserves the right to request the removal of a boy at any time if, in his opinion, such a course is in the best interests either of the School or the boy himself. The decision of parents to send their children to Buckland House is regarded as an earnest of their willingness to abide by the rules and regulations in force at the School.

The School Outfitters are Messrs, PINDER & TUCKWELL, of Exeter, and in order to preserve as much uniformity as possible, parents are requested to make use of their services whenever practicable. Certain articles are only obtainable through this firm. For the convenience of parents, a representative of the firm will normally be at the School on the day the boys return. In an emergency, therefore, any replacements may be made on the spot.

Only the briefest outline of the boys' lives here can be given in this short prospectus, and, in making one's choice of school, there is, of course, no substitute for a visit. The headmaster and his wife (who have two young sons of their own) are always pleased to meet prospective parents, to show them the School in action, and to tell them more about its aims and objects.

23rd December 2024. Return to Buckland House.
Photo: Nicola Green

We had acres of space to ramble about. Diving in and out of the rhododendrons, rolling around on the grass, throwing, kicking, hitting balls.

We went climbing trees, disappearing off into the woods, playing it, throwing, kicking, hitting each other with sticks, using sticks for guns, kicking each other in the balls.

On the lawn next to the church we played British Bulldog...

And now it has all gone.

Time to leave and somehow I'll find my way home.

Printed in Great Britain
by Amazon